Welcome to the *EVERYTHING*® series!

These handy, accessible books give you all you need to tackle a difficult project, gain a new hobby, comprehend a fascinating topic, prepare for an exam, or even brush up on something you learned back in school but have since forgotten.

You can read an *EVERYTHING*® book from cover-to-cover or just pick out the information you want from our four useful boxes: e-facts, e-ssentials, e-alerts, and e-questions. We literally give you everything you need to know on the subject, but throw in a lot of fun stuff along the way, too.

We now have well over 100 *EVERYTHING*® books in print, spanning such wide-ranging topics as weddings, pregnancy, wine, learning guitar, one-pot cooking, managing people, and so much more. When you're done reading them all, you can finally say you know *EVERYTHING*®!

FACTS

Important sound bytes of information

SSENTIALS

Quick handy tips

ALERT

Urgent warnings

QUESTIONS?

Solutions to common problems

THE
EVERYTHING
Series

Dear Reader,

Learning French is a journey. Why not get a guided tour along the way? French is much more than a language—it's a culture and even a way of being. It carries with it its own idiosyncrasies, its own strange expressions, its own logic, and its own style. In the chapters of this book, you'll find an insider's guide to the basics of the French language, giving you knowledge you can use wherever you find yourself in the French-speaking world.

You'll learn about French grammar, too, but it won't be hammered in. Instead, it will be introduced in short, easy-to-understand lessons. Whether you're learning French for travel or to impress your friends, this book will help you achieve your goal. Learning the French language can also help your English skills, too. Because each grammar lesson is also illustrated using the common English counterpart, you may find that you understand English grammar a little better after you work your way through some of the basic French constructions.

As you begin your French-speaking journey, don't be critical of yourself if it takes you some time to learn. Just take it slow and don't lose faith. Before you know it, everything will fall into place. You will learn the French language, and you'll learn it just like you learned English: one word at a time.

Vive le français!

Bruce Sallee   David L.

THE EVERYTHING®
LEARNING FRENCH BOOK

Speak, write, and understand basic French in no time

Bruce Sallee and David Hebert

Adams Media Corporation
Avon, Massachusetts

EDITORIAL
Publishing Director: Gary M. Krebs
Managing Editor: Kate McBride
Copy Chief: Laura MacLaughlin
Acquisitions Editor: Bethany Brown
Development Editors: Tere Drenth
                    Michael Paydos

PRODUCTION
Production Director: Susan Beale
Production Manager: Michelle Roy Kelly
Series Designer: Daria Perreault
Layout and Graphics: Paul Beatrice
Brooke Camfield, Colleen Cunningham,
Michelle Roy Kelly, Daria Perreault,
and Frank Rivera

An Everything® Series Book.
Everything® is a registered trademark of Adams Media Corporation.

Published by Adams Media Corporation
57 Littlefield Street, Avon, MA 02322 U.S.A.
www.adamsmedia.com

ISBN: 1-58062-649-1
Printed in the United States of America.

J I H G F E D C B A

Library of Congress Cataloging-in-Publication Data
Sallee, Bruce.
The everything learning French book / by Bruce Sallee and DavidHebert.
p.   cm. — (The everything series)
Includes index.
ISBN 1-58062-649-1
1. French language—Textbooks for foreign speakers—English.
I.Hebert, David. II. Title. III. Series.
PC2129.E5 S25   2002
448.2'421—dc2   2002006458

Illustrations by Barry Littmann.

This book is available at quantity discounts for bulk purchases.
For information, call 1-800-872-5627.

Visit the entire Everything® series at everything.com

Contents

Introduction

French is a part of the language family known as romance languages, so called because they came from Latin (which was spoken by Romans—get it?). Included in this family are Italian, Spanish, Portuguese, and Romanian; these languages share many similarities, because they all come from a common source. Despite the similarities, however, each are distinct and different, and many agree that French is one of the most "romantic" languages of all, even if they are referring to romance in a different sense.

French, naturally, originated in France, but you can now find it spoken around the world. In North America, you may run across French speakers in Canada or Louisiana. It is widely spoken in Europe and Africa, and even some Asian countries use French as a major language. In short, you'll never know where it may come in handy to know a little bit of French.

In this book, we concentrate on standard French, which is sometimes referred to as Parisian French. As the term "standard" implies, it should be understood wherever you find yourself, even if you have a bit of trouble understanding what other people are saying.

In a sense, the French language has its own governing body. The French Academy, or *l'Académie française*, was originally established in 1635 and oversees the development of the language. It registers all official French words; until the Academy approves it, a word isn't technically a part of the language. Despite their efforts to preserve the French language, some expressions still slip in: you'll inevitably be understood if you order *un hamburger* or *un hot-dog* in French, even if the Academy doesn't acknowledge these words.

CHAPTER 1
Pronouncing and Writing French

This chapter lets you dive into French, with a little speaking and a little writing. Here, you discover how to pronounce basic French letters, letter combinations, and words. You begin writing by focusing on punctuation marks and accents. You'll be pronouncing and writing like a French pro in no time!

The Alphabet

While French and English use the same alphabet, in French, the letters are pronounced a little differently. If you ever have to spell your name out at a hotel, for example, you want to make sure that you're understood.

TABLE 1-1

LETTER	SOUND	LETTER	SOUND
a	ahh	*n*	ehnn
b	bay	*o*	ohh
c	say	*p*	pay
d	day	*q*	koo
e	ehh	*r*	aihr
f	eff	*s*	ess
g	jhay	*t*	tay
h	ahsh	*u*	ooh
i	ee	*v*	vay
j	jhee	*w*	doo-bluh-vay
k	kahh	*x*	eex
l	ehll	*y*	ee-grek
m	ehmm	*z*	zed

THE FRENCH ALPHABET

Keep the following points in mind when pronouncing letters in French:

- The sound of the letter "e" in French is very similar to the beginning of the pronunciation of the English word "earl."
- The letter "g" is pronounced *jhay*, with a soft "j" sound, like in "Asia."
- The pronunciation of the letter "j" uses the same soft "j," but with an "ee" sound at the end.
- The letter "n," especially when appearing at the end of words, is pronounced very softly, with a nasal quality.
- "Q" in English has a distinct "ooh" sound in it; it is pronounced similar in French, but without the "y" sound.

- When two letter l's appear together, it creates a "yeh" sound. The letters are not pronounced the same as one letter; it sounds like the beginning of the English word "yearn."
- The French "r" is more guttural than the English one, made at the back of the throat instead of at the front.

Sounds

Most of the consonants in French are pronounced the same as in English, but many of the vowel sounds differ. It is almost impossible to describe the true sound of French using text. For best results, try to listen to actual French being spoken; only then can you appreciate the sound of the language. The following, however, is a list of sounds used in the French language. Practice making the sounds a few times, and say the example words out loud.

- *on*: Sounds much like "oh" in English, with just a hint of a soft "n" at the end. You will find it in words such as *maison* (*meh-zohn,* meaning "house") and *garçon* (*gar-sohn,* meaning "boy").
- *ou*: An "ooh" sound that you'll encounter in words such as *tout* (*tooh,* meaning "all").
- *oi*: A "wha" sound, much like the beginning of the English word "waddle." A French example is *soir* (*swahr,* meaning "evening").
- *oin*: Sounds much like the beginning of "when" in English, with only a hint of the "n" coming through, very softly. *Coin* (*kwheh,* meaning "corner") and *moins* (*mwheh,* meaning "less") are examples.
- *ai*: Sounds like "ehh." You'll find it in a great many words, including *maison* and *vrai* (*vreh,* meaning "true").
- *en*: Sounds similar to "on" in English, but with a much softer "n" sound. You'll find it in words like *encore* (*ahnk-ohr,* meaning "again") and *parent* (*pahr-ahn,* meaning "parent").
- *an*: Is pronounced the same way as *en.*
- *eu*: To make this sound, hold your mouth like you're going to make an "eee" sound, but say "oooh" instead; it sounds much like the

beginning of the English word "earl." *Heure* (*ehhr,* meaning "hour") is an example.

- *in:* Pronounced like the beginning of the English word "enter," but again with a much softer "n" sound. *Magasin* (*may-guh-zehn,* meaning "store") and *pain* (*pehn,* meaning "bread") are examples.
- *er:* Sounds like "ayy." You will find this at the end of many verbs, such as *parler* (*parl-ay,* meaning "to speak") and *entrer* (*ahn-tray,* meaning "to enter").

Sometimes, letters are silent and are not pronounced; this often occurs with letters at the end of words. The letters are still required in written French, of course, but you don't hear them. Here are the letters to watch:

- Words ending in -*d: chaud* (*show*), meaning "hot."
- Words starting with *h*-: *heureux* (*er-rooh*), meaning "happy."
- Words ending in -*s: compris* (*com-pree*), meaning "included."
- Words ending in -*t: achat* (*ah-sha*), meaning "purchase."
- Words ending in -*x: choix* (*shwa*), meaning "choice."

In French, the letter "h" is usually silent; words that begin with it are usually pronounced as if the "h" wasn't there at all. In French, a silent letter is known as *muet* (*moo-eh*), and the silent "h" as *h muet* (*ahsh-moo-eh*). There are a few cases where the "h" will be pronounced; it is then known as an aspirated h, or *h aspiré* (*ahsh-as-pee-ray*). The majority of French words that begin with "h" are pronounced with an *h muet*, so, when pronounced, they'll sound as if they begin with a vowel. Words that begin with an *h aspiré* are the exception.

Often, in spoken French, words are run together. This occurs when using words that begin with vowels after words that end in a hard consonant sound. When learning the language, this can cause consternation for new speakers, as it can be difficult to understand what other people are saying. In addition, words can be shortened, and contractions can be formed, adding to the confusion. Other times, the syllables are just pushed together, so two or three words can sound like one long word instead.

French is known for the rolling "r" sound. You can learn to roll your r's, too, with just a little bit of practice. Start to make a "k" sound and hold it. Close your throat a little bit, breathe out slowly, and start to say "raw." Don't worry if it starts to come out as "graw"—keep doing it. Practice this a couple of times a day, and you'll soon sound just like Maurice Chevalier.

In French, this is known as *enchaînement,* or linking the sounds together. Not all linked sounds are due to *enchaînement,* however. Liaison and elision are grammatical concepts that also result in sounds getting pushed together (see the following section).

Don't be afraid to try speaking French: French speakers are usually very patient when speaking with people who are new to the language. As a rule, native French speakers are pleased that someone is taking the time to try to communicate using their language, and they're usually happy and eager to help you understand. This is a European approach, quite different from North American expectations, which assume that everyone should speak English—and speak it well. You'll find the French to be very accommodating with your budding linguistic abilities; don't be afraid to express yourself.

Liaison, Elision, and *Enchaînement*

Some pronunciation areas are governed by the grammatical concepts elision and liaison, and *enchaînement* also affects pronunciation of certain words. Keep the following pronunciation points in mind.

Liaison

Liaison occurs when one word ends in a consonant and the following word begins with a vowel. It is only a concern in spoken French, of course, but it is still a part of the formal language rules. Its proper usage must be observed at all times.

Using Liaison with Nouns

Whenever an article or number that ends in a consonant is used with a noun that begins with a vowel, the final letter joins with the next vowel sound.

TABLE 1-2

LIAISON AND NOUNS		
FRENCH WORD	PRONUNCIATION	ENGLISH
un enfant	ooh-nahn-fahn	child
les abricots	lay-zab-ree-ko	apricots
deux hommes	doo-zom	two men

Using Liaison with Verbs

When a pronoun that ends in a consonant is used with a verb that begins with a vowel, liaison occurs. *Nous avons,* for example, which means "we have," is pronounced *noo-za-vohn. Ils ont,* which means "they have," is pronounced *eel-zohn.*

Using Liaison with Verbs in Sentences Using Inversion

When a verb that ends in a consonant is used in a question constructed with inversion (see Chapter 7), and the subject pronoun starts with a vowel, liaison occurs. *Ont-elles?,* for example, which means "Have they?" is pronounced *ohn-tell.*

Using Liaison with Certain Adverbs, Conjunctions, Prepositions, and other Expressions

Certain adverbs, conjunctions, prepositions, and other expressions use liaison. Here are some examples:

- *Chez il* (*shay-zeel*)
- *Vingt et un* (*vehn-tay-uhn*)
- *Comment allez-vous?* (*commahn-tallay-voo*)

Knowing When Liaison Must Not Be Used

There are some times when liaison must not be used under any circumstances, even though it may appear that liaison is appropriate or even expected. The use of liaison in these situations may cause comprehension problems, because native speakers definitely won't be expecting it. The resulting phrase may sound like some other phrase, causing your listeners to wonder what on earth you're talking about.

- After a noun used in the singular: For example, *l'étudiant a un livre* (*lay-tchoo-dee-ahn ah uhn leevr*).
- After *et*, the word for "and": For example, *vingt et un* (*vehn-tay-uhn*).
- In front of an *h aspiré*: For example, *des héros* (*day ay-ro*).

Elision

Elision occurs when two vowels appear together—one at the end of a word, and the other at the beginning of the word immediately following it. One of the vowels is dropped, and the remaining letter is joined to the following word with an apostrophe.

- *l'eau*, pronounced *low*, is an elision of *la + eau* (water)
- *l'été*, pronounced *lay-tay*, is an elision of *le + été* (summer)

Elision is a frequent occurrence with articles and nouns, but can also occur with verbs and subject pronouns, and even prepositions (see Chapter 9). This affects both written and spoken French, so it is an important concept to remember.

QUESTIONS?

When does elision, or dropping a vowel, occur?
Elision can occur with any of the following words when followed by another word that begins with a vowel: *ce, de, je, la, le, me, ne, que, se, si,* and *te.*

Enchaînement

Enchaînement, unlike liaison and elision, is a matter of pronunciation only; it does not affect written French. It does, however, operate in a similar fashion, pushing the sounds of words together. Instead of being governed by vowels and consonants, though, *enchaînement* is governed by phonetic sounds. And instead of affecting the last letter of a word, *enchaînement* affects the last sound.

- *il a* (*ee-la*)
- *elle est* (*el-lay*)

- *une école* (*ooh-nay-kohl*)

Capitalization

For the most part, French follows the same rules regarding capitalization as English, with a few exceptions. In French, a capital letter is known as a *majuscule*. Capitalized words are said to be *en majuscules*. The following shows the types of words that are capitalized in French:

- The first word in a sentence is capitalized.
- Both first and last names are capitalized.
- Names of cities, countries and continents are capitalized.
- Directions are capitalized to indicate a specific place, like *l'Amérique du Nord* (f) (North America). When used to indicate a general direction, like *le nord* (north) no *majuscule* is used.
- When words are used as nouns to indicate the nationality of a person, for example, *un Français* (a Frenchman), the word is capitalized.

Punctuation Marks

Written French looks very similar to English, so reading books in French should seem almost familiar. For the most part, French uses the same punctuation marks, and they function in much the same way as in English. Included in this section are the French terms for many punctuation marks; they are handy words to know, and you never can tell when you may be called upon to use them.

Brackets ⎡⎤

Brackets, called *les crochets* (*lay crow-shay*), are often used to show words inserted into quoted text to help explain the original. In English, they are sometimes referred to as "square brackets." They function the same in both languages.

Colon

The colon, called *les deux-points (lay doo-pwehn)*, is used to introduce another phrase that is related to the previous one. Usually, the following phrase will be an elaboration on a point or something that explains the sentence more clearly. The colon functions the same in both languages.

Comma

The comma, called *la virgule (la vehr-gool),* is used in the same way as English uses them, but remember that French also uses *une virgule* when indicating an amount of money. For example, 1.25 in English would be 1,25 in French, exchange rates notwithstanding.

Exclamation Point

An exclamation point, called *le point d'exclamation (le pwehn dex-kla-mass-yohn)*, can be used at the end of a sentence to indicate an element of surprise, excitement, or other intense emotion. The usage between French and English is, for the most part, interchangeable.

Ellipsis

An ellipsis, a series of three periods that's called *les points de suspension (lay pwehn de soos-pehnss-yohn)* in French, is often used to indicate sections of quoted text that have been omitted for whatever reason. In dialogue, it can also be used to indicate trailing speech. A way to remember the French term is to think that something is left unsaid when the marks are used, creating an aura of suspense.

Parentheses

Parentheses, called *les parenthèses (lay pahr-ent-ez)*, are used in the same way as in English, usually to refer to an aside statement without interrupting the flow of the sentence. Wrapping a phrase in parentheses indicates that the phrase is meant to elaborate but at the same time be self-sustaining, separate from the phrase that appears around it.

Period

The period, called *le point* (*le pwehn*), is used at the end of a sentence; anytime you use a period in English, you can do the same in French, except when indicating amounts of money.

Question Mark

A question mark, called *le point d'interrogation* (*le pwehn dint-hehr-oh-gass-yohn*), is used to indicate a question. In written French, you will most often see *est-ce que* used to indicate a sentence; in dialogue, however, you may encounter inversion or even plain sentences that use a question mark (see Chapter 7). In the latter case, the dialogue is intended to be read with *intonation*; the question mark is your clue.

FACTS

After the Norman invasion of 1066, French became the official language of England. The phrase "Pardon my French" gained notoriety in the nineteenth century as an apology for using off-color words in an ironic twist, presumably because French had been the language of the aristocracy for centuries (where such language would normally be highly inappropriate).

Quotation Marks

French quotation marks, called *les guillemets* (*lay gee-meht*), appear slightly different from English ones. Instead of using symbols that look like commas like we do in English, French uses small double arrows that wrap around the quotation, as follows:

Il dit: «*je ne sais pas.*» He said, "I don't know."

Semicolon

A semicolon, called *le point-virgule* (*le pwehn-vehr-gool*), is used to attach a phrase that is loosely related to the previous phrase in the sentence. Like the comma and period, its usage is primarily interchangeable with the English usage.

Accents

In order to provide guides to pronunciation, French uses accents, which are pronunciation marks that appear with some letters. There are three accents commonly used with vowels; the *grave*, the *aigu*, and the *circonflexe*.

The *Aigu* Accent

The *aigu* (*ay-gooh*) points upwards and toward the right, as in *é*. In English, it is known as the acute accent. Although it only appears over the letter "e," it can become an integral part of a word, substantially changing its meaning. The *aigu* accent also provides important clues about where the word fits in a sentence. Whenever it appears, it changes the pronunciation of the "e" from an "ehh" sound (like the middle "e" sounds in "treble") to an "ay" sound.

- *réveil* (*ray-vay*): alarm clock
- *épicé* (*ay-pee-say*): spicy
- *médecin* (*may-dehh-sehn*): doctor

The *Grave* Accent

The *grave* accent (pronounced like the beginning "grav" in "gravel") falls to the left, as in *è*. The *grave* accent can appear over the letter *a*, *e*, *i*, *o*, or *u*; however, it changes the pronunciation only when it appears above *e*. It's not so important in spoken French, so it can be easy to forget about. The *grave* accent must be used in written French, however, so pay close attention to the words that use it.

- *très* (*treh*): very
- *troisième* (*twa-zee-emm*): third
- *où* (*ooh*): where

ou = or (no grave accent)

The *Circonflexe*

The *circonflexe* (*sir-kohn-flex*) accent appears over vowels, like a little hat over the letter, as in *ô*. It doesn't modify the pronunciation at all, but the French Academy has opted to keep it, so it remains with the language.

- *forêt* (*fohh-ray*): forest
- *hôpital* (*owe-pee-tal*): hospital
- *hôtel* (*owe-tel*): hotel

The *Cédille*

The cedilla (in English ~~word~~, pronounced *se-dill-ah;* in French, the word is *cédille*, pronounced *say-dee*) appears underneath the letter "c" to make it appear like it has a tail: ç. It indicates a soft "s" sound instead of the hard "k" sound the letter "c" would normally have if it appeared before the letter "a." For example, the French language is referred to as *français*— pronounced *frahn-say*. The "c" becomes soft, turning into an "s." (If the cedilla were not present, the word would be pronounced *frahn-kay*.)

- *garçon (gahr-sohn)*: boy
- *façon (fass-ohn)*: manner
- *leçon (leh-sohn)*: lesson

The *Tréma*

The *tréma (tray-ma)* is the French word for the two dots that appear above the second vowel when two vowels are situated together. In English, it is known as an umlaut, and is used in some foreign words, including words borrowed from French. The accent tells you that the second vowel is to be pronounced on its own, distinct from the vowel preceding it. *Noël* and *naïve* are examples of French words that are commonly used in English; Noël is pronounced *no-well*, and *naïve* is pronounced *nigh-eve*; in French, the sound is softer and pronounced more to the front of the mouth.

- *coïncidence (ko-ehn-see-dahnss)*: coincidence
- *Noël (no-ell)*: Christmas
- *jamaïque (jam-eh-eek)*: Jamaica

Chapter 2

Using Everyday Expressions

This chapter gets you ready to speak French like a native! Here, you'll discover a wide range of expressions that don't necessarily make sense when you translate them word for word, but make a whole lot of sense to the French speaker you're communicating with. To aid in that communication, this chapter also helps you understand hand gestures, greetings, and basic numbers.

Colloquial, Idiomatic, and Other Useful Expressions

Almost all languages have some peculiarities that defy literal translation. English is rife with expressions that cannot be taken literally. Consider the phrase: How is it going?

How is *what* going? Wouldn't it be much easier simply to say, "How are you?" These types of phrases often cause problems for a new language student, no matter which language. You can probably think of other examples that would be difficult to translate into another language.

ALERT

Some expressions are widely understood by native speakers of a language, but attempts at literal translation will only confuse others. When learning a new language, in addition to memorizing the words and grammar, you also have to remember some unique expressions that only work in that particular language.

These nonliteral phrases are known as idiomatic expressions, which simply means that the expression is unique to that language. Whenever you come across idiomatic expressions, you cannot translate them literally. You must go to the heart of the phrase and instead translate its sentiment so that the proper meaning is conveyed. Idiomatic expressions usually follow a certain pattern of construction, and they are very much a part of the grammar of each language.

Closely related to idiomatic expressions are colloquial expressions. Often, colloquial expressions are also unique to the language, but the meaning of the term is slightly different. Colloquial expressions usually bend the rules of grammar a little bit, but are so widely recognized within the spoken language that it's acceptable to use them in everyday speech.

To remember the difference, idiomatic expressions are idiosyncratic to the language; they are unique to the language, and are also a part of the official rules. Colloquial expressions, however, are not part of the official language; despite this, they are still widely used. Colloquial expressions can take time to work their way into dictionaries, so don't be afraid to ask someone what something means when you don't understand.

This section shows the French language in action, with complete explanations. You'll learn how each phrase is constructed and what each word means, but don't worry about memorizing the explanations. Feel free to memorize the phrases, however, because you'll be happy to know them wherever you are in the French-speaking world. Don't expect to understand everything right away. As you learn more of the language, you'll be able to use these sentences as a point of reference, exchanging words for others to make your own sentences. French will seem easy. It's simply a matter of substituting the right word.

Comment allez-vous?

Pronounced *commahn-tallay-voo,* this term means, "How are you?" *Comment* means "how." It is often used to begin questions in French. *Allez* is a verb that means "to go;" *vous* is a subject pronoun meaning "you." Literally, the phrase means "How are you going?" As an idiomatic expression, however, it is basically equivalent to "How are you?" or "How is it going?" in English.

Normally, the subject pronoun *vous* appears before the verb, but this sentence uses inversion to form a question. When inversion is used, the verb and subject pronoun switch positions; you can find out more about inversion in Chapter 7.

Because this is a question, when pronouncing this phrase, your voice should raise slightly on the final *vous* sound, the same way your voice rises when asking "How are you?" in English. This is known as intonation.

Notice that the "t" sound at the end of *comment,* when pronounced, is attached to the beginning of *allez,* making it sound like "tallay." This is an example of *enchaînement,* the French name for stringing the sounds together (see Chapter 1).

Comment vous appelez-vous?

Pronounced *commahn-voo-zap-lay-voo,* this term means, "What is your name?" Literally, this expression means "How do you call yourself?"

Appelez means "call;" you'll notice that *vous*, however, appears twice. It's a versatile word that can pull double duty. The last *vous* is the subject pronoun, and means "you." The first *vous*, however, is used as a reflexive pronoun, and means "yourself." Jump to Chapter 13 to find out more about reflexive pronouns.

Je ne parle pas français.

Pronounced *jhun-parl-pah-frahn-say*, this term means, "I don't speak French." Using this phrase, you can let someone know that you don't speak French; often, the person will try to get by in another language or help you find someone who speaks English. You can even use it in combination with the next phrase.

Je is the French word for "I." You use it whenever you are talking about yourself individually. It only appears as the subject of the sentence.

Ne and *pas* are the French equivalent to "not;" they always appear together in written form, but the *ne* is sometimes dropped in conversational French. The *ne* is just a language pointer to let you know that the subject is going to be in the negative, while *pas* means "not." There are other negative expressions in French, but *ne ... pas* is by far the most common you'll encounter. *Français*, as you may have guessed, means French.

Parlez-vous anglais?

Pronounced *parlay-voo-ahng-lay,* this term means "Do you speak English?" This is a polite way of asking if another person knows English; it can also be used to address more than one person. *Parlez* is the verb, meaning "speak." *Vous* means "you," and *anglais* is the French term for English.

Note that there's no *enchaînement* between *vous* and *anglais;* because this is a question that inverts the subject and verb, the "s" sound in *vous* does not get carried to the beginning of *anglais.* Of course, if you slip up and accidentally tie them together, people should still understand you; be prepared, however, for a correction before receiving the answer.

Je m'appelle Frank.

Pronounced *jhe-ma-pell-Frank*, this term means "My name is Frank." This one will work only if your name is Frank, but feel free to use your own name and give it a try. It's the colloquial French way of saying your name; its literal interpretation takes a more circuitous route, translating as "I call myself Frank."

FACTS

Remember that with colloquial and idiomatic expressions, literal translations don't work. *Je m'appelle* is one of them. As you encounter these expressions, you'll get to understand the idiosyncrasies and be able to recognize when a literal translation isn't appropriate. Before you know it, you'll recognize these phrases and will be able to speak French like a natural.

Je is the subject, meaning "I," and *appelle* is the verb, meaning "call." *Me* is a reflexive pronoun; it works with the verb to show that it's an action that goes back to the subject, just like "himself" or "myself" in English. You'll find out more about reflexive pronouns in Chapter 13.

Où est la salle de bain?

Pronounced *ooh-ay-la-sell-de-behn*, this term means "Where is the washroom?" *Où* means "where," and *est* means "is." *La salle de bain,* if you were to translate it literally, means "the room of bath," with *salle* meaning "room" and *bain* meaning "bath."

Sometimes, words carry a unique connotation in a language that doesn't exist in another language. An example of this is the English word toilet—it's hardly acceptable for most polite conversations. However, in French, it's completely acceptable to ask: *Où est la toilette?* (*ooh-ay-la-twa-lett*), which means "Where is the toilet?"

When you think about it, it makes sense; in most situations, you're not asking for a room with a bath in it. You're looking for something else entirely. In French, they get right to the point, so don't feel bashful asking for the toilet. In fact, sometimes if you ask, "*Où est la salle de bain,*" you may even receive the response, "*La toilette?*"

Simply say *oui* (pronounced like *whee,* means "yes") and follow the directions; you can reflect on the differences between French and English while you're otherwise occupied.

Je ne comprends pas.

Pronounced *je-ne-com-prahn-pah,* this term means "I don't understand." Because you've just learned about *je* and *ne . . . pas,* you should have a fairly easy time translating this one. *Comprends* means "understand"—you'll notice that it's very similar to the English word "comprehend."

This phrase works only for you as an individual, though. If you were with another person and referring to the two of you, you would say it slightly differently: *Nous ne comprenons pas* (*noo-ne-com-prin-own-pah*), which means "We do not understand."

Nous is the French word for "we;" it is another subject pronoun. *Comprenons* is the same verb, with a different ending to match *nous.* In French, the verb endings change to reflect the subject of the sentence, just like some words do in English, even if only slightly, such as "I understand" versus "he understands."

French speakers worldwide will recognize this statement. They will either repeat the question or will try to state things a different way. If you find yourself stuck, the statements in the following sections can also help to get you out of just about any situation.

Répétez, s'il vous plaît.

Pronounced *rep-a-tay seel-voo-play,* this term means "Please repeat." *S'il vous plaît* is the French way of saying "please." Literally translated, it means "if it pleases you." *Répétez* is the verb, meaning "repeat;" because it doesn't have the word *vous* with it, though, it's an instruction. In linguistic circles, that's known as an imperative; you'll discover more about that verb form in Chapter 7. In a sense, it's an order to repeat; the *s'il vous plaît* softens it into a very polite way to ask someone to repeat something.

Plus lent, s'il vous plaît.

Pronounced *ploo lahn, seel-voo-play*, this term means "slower, please." Literally it means "more slow, please" but in French, this is an acceptable way to ask someone to slow down while speaking so that you can understand. French is an expressive language, and sometimes its speakers tend to move pretty fast; if you find that the person with whom you're conversing is speaking too fast for you to comprehend, simply say this phrase.

> *Plus lent* is a valuable phrase to know, but use it wisely—it's like a secret formula. People will slow down to accommodate you. Use it too often, however, and you may find people growing impatient with you.

You can also use *plus lent* in conjunction with both *je ne comprends pas* and *répétez, s'il vous plaît*. For example, faced with someone you don't quite understand, you could say: *Je ne comprends pas. Répétez, s'il vous plaît, plus lent?* Now, the person knows that you don't understand, and you have asked nicely if he or she would repeat it a little more slowly. Now you're speaking French!

French Gestures

Not all French is spoken. Gestures are used widely to complement the speaker's message. French speakers tend to be very expressive, and some of these nonverbal expressions carry meaning, too. English also has a few widely-used gestures. Saying "Shush!" while holding your finger to your lips is almost universally understood as a command to be quiet. Without the sound, most people will still understand what it means.

This unspoken component adds a great deal of character to the language. Watch French speakers as they talk, and look at their gestures and facial expressions. If you're exposed to it long enough, you will probably start to pick up these actions on your own.

But what does all this waving of the hands actually mean? Here are some gestures you may encounter while talking to French speakers.

- **Both hands covering the mouth:** This usually indicates an apology for something the speaker has said, especially when accompanied with an utterance of *pardon!* or *excusez-moi!*
- **Finger tapping the side of the nose:** This is very similar to the English gesture of tapping the head; it indicates that the person knows or understands something.
- **Arms crossed over chest, palms facing out, with arms dropping down to side:** This gesture, often accompanied by a phrase such as *j'ai fini* (meaning "I am finished") or *c'est fini* (meaning "it's finished"), is a symbolic swearing off of whatever the speaker wants to dismiss.
- **Raised eyebrows, with hands held up and palms facing forward:** This expression carries the meaning of "I don't know!" or "Don't ask me!" It's much more emphatic than the English shrug, almost reminiscent of the expected response to a command of "stick 'em up."
- **Fingers interlocked, with thumbs twiddling:** This one means exactly what it looks like. In English, we say that a person is "twiddling his thumbs"—the French sometimes even make the gesture.

The French use fingers to indicate numbers just like the English do, but there is a subtle difference. The English world begins counting on the index finger, indicating "one." In French, however, the counting starts with the thumb, and the index finger becomes "two." If you want one drink and hold up your index finger to indicate that, you may just end up with two.

- **Hand held out, palm facing down, tilting side to side:** This indicates an approximation. It can also be used with the phrase *comme ci comme ça,* which means "so-so," in response to a question as to how someone is doing. This expression may seem familiar; it is also used periodically in English.
- **Hand held out, index finger pointing up:** This is an indication to be quiet; it's similar to the English gesture, but you don't hold your finger

to your lips. Pointing the finger straight up in the air is sufficient. If the finger is waving, the gesture is even more emphatic, indicating perhaps a touch of impatience or even anger.

Salutations and Greetings

The following vocabulary list includes words and expressions that you can use as simple greetings or responses to address friends and family. Memorize these expressions; they are relatively easy to remember, and they go a long way toward making you sound like a natural.

TABLE 2-1

SALUTATIONS AND GREETINGS		
FRENCH	**PRONUNCIATION**	**ENGLISH**
à bientôt	ah bee-ehn-toe	see you soon
à demain	ah deh-mehn	see you tomorrow
à toute à l'heure	ah toot ah loohr	see you later
à vos souhaits	ah vo soo-eht	bless you (after someone sneezes)
adieu	ah-dyuh	farewell
au revoir	oh rhe-vwahr	good bye
bienvenue	bee-ehn-veh-noo	welcome
bonne chance!	buhnn shahnce	good luck!
bonne nuit	buhnn nwee	good night, sleep well
bonjour	bohn-jhoor	hello, good morning, good afternoon
bonsoir	bohn-swahr	good evening
bravo	brah-vo	well done
de rien	de ree-en	you're welcome
enchanté	ahn-shahn-tay	pleased to meet you (male speaker)
enchantée	ahn-shahn-tay	pleased to meet you (female speaker)
merci	mehr-see	thank you

TABLE 2-1	SALUTATIONS AND GREETINGS *(CONTINUED)*		
FRENCH	**PRONUNCIATION**	**ENGLISH**
merci beaucoup	mehr-see bo-koo	thank you very much
salut	sah-loo	Hi! Bye!
santé	sahn-tay	Cheers!
tant pis	tahn pee	never mind

Numbers and Dates

In addition to using the same alphabet (see Chapter 1), French also uses the same numerical symbols. In English, these are known as arabic numbers; in French, they are called *chiffres arabes*. Math, at least, looks the same in French. When the numbers are pronounced, however, there are striking differences.

The bad news is that you'll need to do a little bit of memorization work to become familiar with the numbers, as you'll have to learn new names for them. Fortunately, there aren't very many of them; they get combined to form larger numbers, just like English does with "thirty-seven" and "seventy-two." Unfortunately, the French rules are a little bit different, so you may also have to spend some time memorizing the way larger numbers are constructed. You may want to visit this section periodically to brush up.

There are actually two kinds of names for numbers. There are cardinal numbers, which the regular numbers "one," "two," three," and so on. But there are also ordinal numbers, which define the relationship of the number to others, such as "first," "second," and "third."

Cardinal Numbers

Numbers from zero to nineteen are fairly straightforward:

TABLE 2-2	NUMBERS FROM ZERO TO NINETEEN		
FRENCH	**PRONUNCIATION**	**ENGLISH**
zéro	zay-ro	zero
un(e)	uhn	one

FRENCH	PRONUNCIATION	ENGLISH
deux	doo	two
trois	twah	three
quatre	kat-ruh	four
cinq	sank	five
six	sees	six
sept	set	seven
huit	wheat	eight
neuf	noof	nine
dix	dees	ten
onze	ohnz	eleven
douze	dooze	twelve
treize	trayze	thirteen
quatorze	ka-torz	fourteen
quinze	kayhnz	fifteen
seize	sayze	sixteen
dix-sept	dees-set	seventeen
dix-huit	dee-zweet	eighteen
dix-neuf	dees-noof	nineteen

The numbers twenty through sixty-nine follow a consistent pattern, very similar to the English way of naming a group of tens—like "twenty"—and following it with another word, such as "one," to form "twenty-one." In written French, the numbers are combined with a hyphen, with the exception of *et un,* which contains two words and translates as "and one."

TABLE 2-3

NUMBERS FROM TWENTY TO TWENTY-NINE		
FRENCH	PRONUNCIATION	ENGLISH
vingt	vehn	twenty
vingt et un	vehn-ay-uhn	twenty-one
vingt-deux	vehn-doo	twenty-two
vingt-trois	vehn-twah	twenty-three
vingt-quatre	vehn-kat	twenty-four

TABLE 2-3

NUMBERS FROM TWENTY TO TWENTY-NINE (CONTINUED)		
FRENCH	PRONUNCIATION	ENGLISH
vingt-cinq	vehn-sank	twenty-five
vingt-six	vehn-sees	twenty-six
vingt-sept	vehn-set	twenty-seven
vingt-huit	vehn-wheat	twenty-eight
vingt-neuf	vehn-noof	twenty-nine

To form numbers between thirty and sixty-nine, simply add the appropriate number after the end of the word for the group of tens.

TABLE 2-4

NUMBERS FROM THIRTY TO SIXTY-NINE		
FRENCH	PRONUNCIATION	ENGLISH
trente	trahnt	thirty
trente et un	trahnt-ay-uhn	thirty-one
trente-deux	trahnt-doo	thirty-two
quarante	karant	forty
quarante et un	karant-ay-un	forty-one
quarante-deux	karant-doo	forty-two
cinquante	sank-ahnt	fifty
cinquante-quatre	sank-ahnt-katr	fifty-four
soixante	swahz-ahnt	sixty
soixante-neuf	swahz-ahnt-noof	sixty-nine

At seventy, a new pattern emerges. Instead of having a separate word for "seventy," "sixty," and "ten" are combined, to form *soixante-dix*. The numbers eleven through nineteen are used to designate numbers up to seventy-nine. Eighty doesn't have a separate word, either. Instead, it is designated as *quatre-vingt*—in other words, four twenties, which does indeed add up to eighty. Note that in written French, eighty-one becomes *quatre-vingt-un*, and does not use the *et* found in the earlier numbers. Ninety is very similar to seventy, combining the *quatre-vingt* of eighty with *dix* to form *quatre-vingt-dix*. The numbers then follow the same progression, up to ninety-nine.

TABLE 2-5

NUMBERS FROM SEVENTY TO NINETY-NINE		
FRENCH	**PRONUNCIATION**	**ENGLISH**
soixante-dix	swahz-ahnt-dees	seventy
soixante et onze	swahz-ahnt-ay-ohnz	seventy-one
soixante-douze	swahz-ahnt-dooz	seventy-two
quatre-vingt	katr-vehn	eighty
quatre-vingt-un	katr-vehn-un	eighty-one
quatre-vingt-deux	katr-vehn-doo	eighty-two
quatre-vingt-dix	katr-vehn-dees	ninety
quatre-vingt-onze	katr-vehn-ohnz	ninety-one
quatre-vingt-douze	katr-vehn-dooz	ninety-two
quatre-vingt-treize	katr-vehn-trayz	ninety-three
quatre-vingt-quatorze	katr-vehn-katorz	ninety-four
quatre-vingt-quinze	katr-vehn-kaynz	ninety-five
quatre-vingt-seize	katr-vehn-sayze	ninety-six
quatre-vingt-dix-sept	katr-vehn-dees-set	ninety-seven
quatre-vingt-dix-huit	katr-vehn-dees-wheat	ninety-eight
quatre-vingt-dix-neuf	katr-vehn-dees-noof	ninety-nine

At 100, everything starts all over again. The French word for hundred is *cent*; the other numbers are used after it to indicate the numbers between 101 and 199.

TABLE 2-6

NUMBERS FROM 100 TO 199		
FRENCH	**PRONUNCIATION**	**ENGLISH**
cent	sahn	one hundred
cent un	sahn-un	one hundred and one
cent deux	sahn-doo	one hundred and two
cent vingt	sahn-vehn	one hundred and twenty
cent trente-deux	sahn-trahnt-doo	one hundred and thirty-two
cent quatre-vingt-dix-neuf	sahn-katr-vehn-dees-noof	one hundred and ninety-nine

To indicate more than one hundred, the appropriate word is inserted before *cent.* English does the same thing; the only difference between "one hundred" and "two hundred" is the number at the beginning of it. When the number is an even hundred, *cent* is used in the plural—it has an "s" on the end to show that more than one is being indicated. The "s" is not pronounced, but it is important to remember for written French. (You'll find out more about uses of the plural in Chapter 5.)

TABLE 2-7

NUMBERS FROM 200 TO 1,000		
FRENCH	PRONUNCIATION	ENGLISH
deux cents	doo-sahn	two hundred
deux cent deux	doo-sahn-doo	two hundred and two
quatre cents	katr-sahn	four hundred
quatre cent quarante	katr-sahn-karant	four hundred and forty
neuf cent soixante	noof-sahn-swahz-ahnt	nine hundred and sixty

One thousand follows the same pattern as one hundred, using the word *mille.* Dates also fall into this category, when referring to a year.

TABLE 2-8

NUMBERS FROM 1,000 TO 2 MILLION		
FRENCH	PRONUNCIATION	ENGLISH
mille	mee-yh	one thousand
mille neuf cent quatre-vingt-dix	mee-yh noof sahn katr vehn dees	nineteen ninety
deux mille	doo mee-yh	two thousand
deux mille un	doo mee-yh uhn	two thousand and one
deux mille deux	doo mee-yh doo	two thousand and two
dix mille	dees mee-yh	ten thousand
cent mille	sahn mee-yh	one hundred thousand

FRENCH	PRONUNCIATION	ENGLISH
cent mille cent soixante dix	sahn mee-yh sahn dees	one hundred thousand one hundred and ~~ten~~ *seventy*
cinq cent mille	sank sahn mee-yh	five hundred thousand
un million	uhn mee-yohn	one million
deux million	doo mee-yohn	two million

ESSENTIALS

When talking about the year in spoken French, the numbers can be a mouthful. Consider:

- 1972: *mille neuf cent soixant-douze* (mee-yh noof sahn swahz-ahn-dooze)
- 1984: *mille neuf cent quatre-vingt-quatre* (mee-yh noof sahn katr vehn katr)
- 1998: *mille neuf cent quatre-vingt-dix-huit* (mee-yh noof sahn katr vehn dee-zwheat)

Fortunately, future dates will be much easier, starting only with *deux mille*, which is much easier—both to remember and to pronounce.

Ordinal Numbers

Related to cardinal numbers are ordinal numbers, which are used show a relationship between things or to indicate where a word happens to fit in a series. English examples are "first," "second," and "third."

In French, the word for "first" is the only ordinal number that must agree in gender and number with the noun it modifies.

TABLE 2-9

THE ORDINAL "FIRST"			
GENDER	**SINGULAR**	**PLURAL**	**PRONUNCIATION**
Masculine	*premier*	*premiers*	pruh-mee-yay
Feminine	*première*	*premières*	pruh-mee-aihr

The rest of the ordinal numbers don't change to agree with gender, but will still add an "s" to agree with a plural noun.

TABLE 2-10

ORDINAL NUMBERS		
FRENCH	**PRONUNCIATION**	**ENGLISH**
deuxième	doo-zee-ehmm	second
troisième	twah-zee-ehmm	third
quatrième	ka-tree-ehmm	fourth
cinquième	sank-ee-ehmm	fifth
sixième	see-zee-ehmm	sixth
septième	set-ee-ehmm	seventh
huitième	whee-tee-ehmm	eighth
neuvième	noo-vee-ehmm	ninth
dixième	dee-zee-ehmm	tenth
la troisième fois	la twah-zee-ehmm fwa	the third time

You don't have to memorize all of these numbers; you can learn to form them on your own. Ordinal numbers in French are formed using the cardinal number; this is very similar to the way English modifies numbers by adding "th" to the end of the cardinal number, creating "fourth" from "four," "fifth" from "five," "sixth" from "six," and so on.

To form the ordinal form of a number in French, simply drop the -e from the end of the cardinal number and add -ième to the end. If the cardinal number does not end in e, simply add the -ième ending to the word. This works for all numbers but these three: *premier*, which is unique when compared to the other ordinal numbers; *cinquième*, which adds a "u" after the "q;" and *neuvième*, which changes the "f" into a "v." These last two changes are quite logical; without the changes, attempts at pronunciation would be nightmarish.

In English, you commonly see ordinal numbers like "first" and "second" abbreviated in writing as "1st" and "2nd." French does this too, but the small characters following the arabic number are different. The number 1 is followed by a small *er* when it is abbreviated in the masculine, and a small *re* when abbreviated in the feminine. All others are followed by a small *e*.

TABLE 2-11

ORDINAL NUMBERS ABBREVIATIONS			
FRENCH	**PRONUNCIATION**	**ABBREVIATION**	**ENGLISH**
premier (m)	pruh-mee-yay	1er	first
première (f)	pruh-mee-aihr	1re	first
deuxième	doo-zee-ehm	2^{e}	second
troisième	twah-zee-ehm	3^{e}	third
dix-huitième	dee-zwee-tee-ehm	18^{e}	eighteenth

You will often encounter these abbreviations in a variety of places: in newspapers, on signs, and in books and magazines. When you come across these abbreviations in written French, know that an ordinal number is intended.

Dates

Face it. There are going to be some words you just have to learn to get by in French—little words, like days of the week and months of the year. You may find it helpful to read these word lists out loud a few times, memorizing them by rote, just like students do in school. When said out loud in a series, these groups have a catchy rhythm, so it shouldn't take you long to have them down pat.

TABLE 2-12

DAYS OF THE WEEK		
FRENCH	**PRONUNCIATION**	**ENGLISH**
lundi	loohn-dee	Monday
mardi	mahr-dee	Tuesday
mercredi	mer-cruh-dee	Wednesday
jeudi	jhoo-dee	Thursday
vendredi	vahn-druh-dee	Friday
samedi	sah-my-dee	Saturday
dimanche	dee-mahnsh	Sunday

TABLE 2-13

MONTHS OF THE YEAR		
FRENCH	PRONUNCIATION	ENGLISH
janvier	jahn-vee-ay	January
février	fayv-ree-ay	February
mars	mahr	March
avril	ah-vreehl	April
mai	may	May
juin	jwehn	June
juillet	jwee-ay	July
août	ah-oot	August
septembre	sep-tahm-br	September
octobre	oc-tob-br	October
novembre	no-vehm-br	November
décembre	day-sehm-br	December

ESSENTIALS

In written French, days of the week and months of the year are not capitalized, unless they happen to be used at the beginning of a sentence.

CHAPTER 3
Developing a Basic Vocabulary

This chapter helps you master the little words that will add up to big results when you begin speaking to native French speakers. The chapter starts with conjunctions (in English, words such as "and," "or," and "but"), and then moves into a series of basic words and phrases that will help you assimilate in no time.

Conjunctions

Conjunctions are words that are used to join parts of a sentence together. In English, common conjunctions are "and," "or," and "but." You can use the following French conjunctions in the same way as English ones:

- *donc* (so, then, therefore)
- *ensuite* (next)
- *et* (and)

- *ou* (or)
- *puis* (then)
- *mais* (but)

Basic Words to Memorize

The following vocabulary list includes a few basic words you can quickly master. They're fairly easy to remember, and you'll probaby find yourself using them extensively whenever you speak French.

TABLE 3-1

BASIC FRENCH WORDS		
FRENCH	PRONUNCIATION	ENGLISH
oui	whee	yes
non	nohn	no
bonjour	bohn-jhoor	hello
excusez-moi	eks-cyoo-zay-mwa	excuse me
s'il vous plaît	seel-voo-play	please
merci	mehr-see	thank you
merci beaucoup	mehr-see bow-coo	thank you very much
Pardon?	pahr-dohn	Pardon me?
Monsieur	mohn-syoor	Mr.
Madame	mah-dam	Mrs.
Mademoiselle	mahd-mwa-zel	Miss

Describing Things and People

You can use a number of different phrases to refer to things and people, depending on the particular situation. This section describes the various constructions you can use.

Il est

In English, we often use the phrase "it is" to describe things: it is blue, it is old, it is hot. In French, this can be done using *il est* or *c'est*. Both forms can mean the same thing, ranging from "he is," "she is," or "it is," depending on the construction of the sentence. Each form, however, is used at a different time.

Il est is the correct choice in the following circumstances. If the subject of the sentence is female, then you may use *elle est* to make it agree.

Using a Single Adjective

When using a single adjective that refers to a specific person or a specific thing, *il est* is the proper construction. The adjective will agree in gender and number with the subject of the sentence. You can also use it in other tenses instead of just in the present.

- *J'ai lu ce livre. Il a été bon.* (I read this book. It was good.)
- *J'aime ce jardin. Il est bon.* (I love this garden. It is nice.)

The phrase *il est bon* could also mean "he is good" in English. When translating, it is important to go to the heart of the meaning of the sentence and translate that, instead of trying to provide a word-for-word translation. Because pronouns are being used, you must determine which actual nouns they represent and derive the meaning from that.

Referring to a Profession

When simply stating that a person is of a certain profession, the phrase *il est* or *elle est* is used, and the noun appears with no article. English tends to use an indefinite article in its equivalent translation (see Chapter 4), so be careful.

- *Elle est médecin.* (She is a doctor.)
- *Il est pharmacien.* (He is a pharmacist.)
- *Il est gendarme.* (He is a police officer.)

Referring to Nationalities

When stating that a person is of a certain nationality, *il est* or *elle est* is used with the adjective, without any article. This more closely resembles the English construction, so it should seem straightforward to you. Remember that when a nationality is used in this fashion, it is not capitalized in French, because the word acts as an adjective. Only when a nationality is used as a noun is it capitalized.

- *Elle est française.* (She is French.)
- *Il est anglais.* (He is English.)

Referring to Religious Beliefs

When you wish to state that a person is of a certain religious belief or denomination, *il est* or *elle est* is used with an adjective, which also appears without an article, like the previous constructions. English normally capitalizes these words, but French does not.

- *Elle est catholique.* (She is Catholic.)
- *Il est protestant.* (He is Protestant.)

C'est

The phrase *c'est* also means "it is," but it is used in different circumstances from *il est*. It is a contraction of *ce* and *est*, and therefore doesn't actually use a subject pronoun (see Chapter 9). Study its uses in this section, and then compare and contrast it with the previous section so you understand the differences between the choices.

With a Proper Name

When you wish refer to someone using his or her proper name, *c'est* is the appropriate choice, rather than *il est*.

- *C'est Yvon Dumont.* (It's Yvon Dumont.)
- *C'est Michel.* (It's Michael.)
- *C'est Monsieur Allard.* (It's Mr. Allard.)

With a Disjunctive Pronoun

When wanting to say things like "it is me," *c'est* is the proper construction. Technically, the proper English translation should be "it is I," because when object pronouns are used with the verb "to be," they are supposed to be identical to the subject. The proper English rules are often not followed, however, so choose the translation that seems to make the most sense.

- *C'est moi.* (It is me.)
- *C'est toi.* (It is you.)
- *C'est elle.* (It is her.)

When Referring to a Situation or Idea

C'est is often used with a singular masculine adjective to refer to states of being or ideas.

- *Oui, c'est vrai.* (Yes, that's right.)
- *J'acheterai le livre, c'est certain.* (I will buy the book, it's certain.)

When Referring to a Noun That Is Modified by Other Words

When a noun is used with adjectives that modify or refine the meaning of the noun, *c'est* is the appropriate choice. Even a single article used with a noun is enough to modify it and make it necessary to use the *c'est* construction.

- *C'est un livre excellent.* (It's an excellent book.)
- *C'est une pomme.* (It's an apple.)

Il y a

In English, we often use phrases like "there is" or "there are" to refer to the general existence of things. In French, this is done with the phrase *il y a*. The French word *y* is an object pronoun (see Chapter 9). In this construction, it is the rough equivalent of the English "there." Even when *il y a* is used with a plural object, the subject and verb don't change. This is a French idiomatic expression that does not translate literally, so don't try to put it in the plural when referring to more than one object. It doesn't change for feminine objects, either; *il* is still used in the construction, even when referring to something feminine.

- *Il y a un bon film au cinéma.* (There is a good film at the theatre.)
- *Il y a une grande vedette en ville.* (There is a big star in town.)

You can also use the construction *il y a* as a question to ask if something exists. You could use the phrase *est-ce que* in front of it to form the question, or you can use inversion (see Chapter 7). When inversion is used, however, the pronoun retains its regular position in front of the verb, so you must insert a "t" in between.

- *Y a-t'il un bon film ici?* (Is there a good film here?)
- *Y a-t'il une femme ici?* (Is there a lady present?)

Voilà

Voilà is used to indicate something specific. It is actually a preposition that means "there is," "there are," or even "that is." Rather than merely pointing out its existence the way *il y a* does, *voilà* points specifically to the item being indicated when used at the beginning of the sentence. It is like actually pointing to an item with your finger; as a general rule, *voilà* should be used only when pointing your finger would be an appropriate gesture to accompany the statement.

If you look at the following sentences carefully, there isn't actually any verb used. *Voilà* takes the place of both the subject and the verb, being used only with the object of the sentence. When translating into English, simply choose the form that makes the most sense.

- *Voilà les enfants.* (There are the children.)
- *Voilà une fenêtre.* (There is a window.)

Because *voilà* doesn't really use a verb, you don't have to worry about agreement with any of the words; any articles must still agree with the nouns, however.

CHAPTER 4

Understanding Articles

In English, we often say things like "the book" or "a library." "The" and "a" are known as articles. The word "the" or "a" introduces a noun and serves a grammatical purpose by showing how the word is to be treated in the sentence—whether it is referring to a specific object or referring to things in a more general sense. It tells you how the noun fits and relates to the other words in the sentence.

Discovering French Articles

French articles work just like English articles, except that the articles change slightly for masculine or feminine nouns, plural or singular nouns, and (like English) nouns that begin with vowels. In English, the definite article can often be dropped or ignored, but in French, articles are very much a necessity to proper communication. French articles usually become a part of the word—before too long, you'll barely even notice them. In some ways, it will be helpful to you to think of articles as a part of the words themselves rather than an additional piece that needs to be memorized. As a matter of fact, when learning a noun, memorize the article along with it—this will save you from looking the gender of nouns up later (see Chapter 5).

FACTS

You can use articles to help you remember the gender of nouns with nouns that begin with a vowel. Because gender is mostly a matter of memorization, the indefinite article will tell you the gender, leaving one less thing to memorize.

"The" is called a definite article, because you use it to indicate a certain, specific item, as opposed to something in general. In French, the definite article can take one of four forms:

- *le*: when used before a word with masculine gender
- *la*: when used before a word with feminine gender
- *l'*: when used before a word that starts with a vowel or silent "h"
- *les*: when used to indicate a group or more than one of an item

With indefinite articles, the exact item is not known; examples of this are "a car" or "an apple." There are three forms of indefinite articles in French:

- *un*: when used before a word with masculine gender
- *une*: when used before a word with feminine gender
- *des*: when used to indicate a group or more than one of an item

The Definite Article

As a general rule, any time the word "the" is used in English, the definite article will be used in French: *le, la,* and *les.* All are the equivalent of "the" in English. *Le* is the masculine form, *la* is the feminine, and *les* is used for plural nouns of either gender.

The definite article should not be translated literally. The rules for article usage differ slightly in each language; sometimes, it will not be required in an English sentence, while its presence is necessary in French.

When translating, never simply replace *le* or *la* with "the." Whenever you see an article being used in either language, look to the noun and translate that. If the noun requires an article in the translated sentence, only then should it be used.

Keep the following points in mind, and you should find that learning and understanding definite articles pose no problems for you at all.

Before a Vowel

Whenever *le* or *la* precedes a word starting with a vowel, it becomes *l'.*

- *l'eau* (f) (pronounced *low*), means "water"
- *l'écran* (m) (pronounced *lay-krahn*), means "screen"
- *l'heure* (f) (pronounced *leur*), means "hour"

Nouns in a Series

When referring to nouns in a series, each noun must have the corresponding definite article:

- *J'ai le lait, le pain, et la moutarde.*
  (I have the milk, the bread, and the mustard.)

People

When using a noun that refers to a person, the definite article is used. If you are addressing that person directly, however, no article is used.

- *Le professeur a un livre.* (The professor has a book.)
- *Monsieur professeur, avez-vous un livre?* (Mr. Professor, do you have a book?)

Seasons

When referring to seasons, the definite article is usually used in front of the noun.

- *la saison* (season)
- *le printemps* (spring)
- *l'été* (m) (summer)
- *l'automne* (m) (autumn)
- *l'hiver* (m) (winter)

Languages

Names of languages are used with a direct article, except with the verb *parler*. Chapter 2 gives you the phrase, *parlez-vous français?* The verb *parler*, which means "to speak," does not use a definite article when referring to a language.

- *le français* (French)
- *l'anglais* (m) (English)
- *l'espagnol* (m) (Spanish)
- *l'allemand* (m) (German)
- *le portugais* (Portuguese)
- *l'italien* (m) (Italian)
- *le chinois* (Chinese)
- *le japonais* (Japanese)
- *le russe* (Russian)

The Indefinite Article

Indefinite articles are used when one is referring in general to an item. In English, the indefinite articles are "a" and "an," and the French indefinite articles are very similar: *un, une,* and **des**. *Un* and *une* are equivalent to "a" in English. *Des*, the plural, can mean "some" or "any" in English, and is used with plural nouns of either gender.

Indefinite articles are pretty well interchangeable with direct articles; the choice depends on the sense in which the noun is meant. If you are referring to something specific, the direct article is the appropriate choice. When you're referring to things in general terms, use the indefinite article.

The Partitive Article

French also has a unique class of articles, known as the partitive, that is used when the exact quantity of an item is not known. It conveys the sense of "some" or "any."

The partitive is a grammatical distinction that doesn't really exist in English, so you may have to watch yourself in the beginning to make sure that you are using the right article. In English, we can say, "He has eggs." Inferred in the statement is the word "some"—in fact, the sentence "He has some eggs" means basically the same thing. In English, the "some" is often omitted entirely.

In French, however, these words cannot be ignored; the partitive article is required to convey proper meaning. It is known as the partitive because it describes only a part of the object and not the object as a whole. Whenever the sense of "some" or "any" is inferred in the sentence, the partitive article must be used.

The partitive is signaled by the word *de* in French. *De* is a preposition that has a great many other uses; you'll learn more about it in the next section. One of its most important uses, however, is in the partitive, along with the definite article. Whenever you see *de* or one of its contractions, ask yourself which sense is meant—whether something in its entirety is meant or only a small part of it. If it's only a small part, the English equivalent is probably "some" or "any," and, therefore, the word takes the partitive in French.

The partitive is formed by combining *de* and the definite article.

- *de* + *le* = *du*: when used before singular nouns with masculine gender
- *de* + *la* = *de la*: when used before singular nouns with feminine gender
- *de* + *l'* = *de l'*: when used before singular nouns that begin in a vowel or silent h
- *de* + *les* = *des*: when used before plural nouns of either gender

Suppose you're talking to a friend who invites you over to her place for coffee. You hope she has milk, so you could ask any of the following in English:

- Do you have any milk?
- Do you have some milk?

- Do you have milk?

Because you are only referring to a small amount of all the milk available, "some" is meant, so the partitive is used in French, as follows: *As-tu du lait?*

Similarly, suppose you are getting together with your friend to bake a triple-layer cake, and you are going over the list of ingredients, deciding who will supply which ingredients. Wondering if she has the milk that the recipe calls for, you want to ask, "Do you have the milk?" Because milk is being referred to in a specific sense, the definite article is used, rather than the partitive article: *As-tu le lait?* You aren't asking whether your friend has some milk, or any milk, or enough milk—you're asking whether she has the specific amount of milk that the recipe calls for. Because you mean it in a specific sense, the partitive does not get used; the direct article is used, instead.

Pay particular attention to the amount when choosing which article to use. If you use a definite article when the partitive is required, native French speakers may become terribly confused, trying to figure out what you mean. For example, if you asked, *As-tu le lait?* when you meant to ask only for some, your listeners will be trying to figure out which milk you mean—whether it's all the milk in the world or another specific amount.

Partitive Article in Negative Expressions

As you may recall from Chapter 2, *ne . . . pas* can be used to make an expression negative. It is the equivalent of the English word "not." There are other ways to make a statement negative (see Chapter 8).

When the partitive is used in a negative expression, *de* appears alone, without the definite article. Whether the noun being used in the partitive is masculine or feminine, the only word appearing before it will be *de*.

- **Masculine:** *As-tu du lait?* (Do you have some milk?) *Non, je n'ai pas de lait.* (No, I don't have any milk.)

- **Feminine:** *As-tu de la farine?* (Do you have any flour?) *Non, je n'ai pas de farine.* (No, I don't have any flour.)

Naturally, there's an exception. When using *être*, the verb "to be," the proper partitive article is always used, whether the sentence is negative or not. Say you wrap some cake up for a friend; when you give it to him, he asks, "What is it?" You could answer this way: *C'est du gâteau.* (It is some cake.)

Remember that in the negative, the verb *être* uses the regular partitive article. Say your friend asks if there is water in your glass: *Ce n'est pas de l'eau. C'est de la bière.* (No, it's not **some** water. It's **some** beer.)

In the negative, notice that *de l'eau* includes both *de* and the definite article, because *l'eau* is a feminine word. The partitive is used in full because it appears with the verb *être*. If another verb were being used in the negative, only *de* would be used.

ALERT

Être is the only verb that uses the regular partitive article in a negative expression; all other verbs, including *avoir*, simply use *de* alone as the partitive article. *in a negative expression.*

Plural Uses of the Partitive Article

Des, you'll remember, is normally the plural indefinite article. In the partitive, it is used only with words that are always plural. Therefore, if you know that a noun can be used in the singular, *des* will always be the plural indefinite article. If the noun only has meaning in the plural, however, *des* will indicate that the noun is being used in the partitive sense.

Say you and a friend are thinking about going on a trip, and he asks if you have any holiday or vacation days: *As-tu des vacances?* (Do you have any holidays?)

Because your friend is referring to vacation days in general, the partitive is used: *Oui, j'ai des vacances.* (Yes, I have some.) If you didn't have any available vacation days, you would answer in the negative: *Non, je n'ai pas des vacances.*

CHAPTER 5
Using Nouns

A noun is the grammatical term for a word that designates a person, place, thing, or idea. In French, a noun is known as a *nom,* which also happens to be the same word for "name." That's actually a good way to remember it—a noun is simply the name of a person, place, thing, or idea.

Understanding Nouns

There are two general types of nouns: concrete and abstract. A noun is concrete when it describes something definite, like a person, place, or thing. Ideas and emotions are also nouns, but these are considered abstract.

Nouns can be used in sentences a number of ways. They can appear as the subject of a verb, performing the action described in the sentence, or they can appear as the object and receive the action of the sentence, either directly or indirectly.

- **Subject:** The **girl** is walking.
- **Direct object:** I found the **girl**.
- **Indirect object:** I gave the puppy to the **girl**.

The same noun can be used to convey a variety of different meanings. French, like English, relies on word order and auxiliary words to show how the noun is affected by the sentence. You'll learn more about the uses of direct and indirect objects in Chapter 9.

There are other kinds of nouns, too. Pronouns are words that replace nouns, such as "him" or "her." Pronouns are used in place of a noun; in the first of the preceding examples, the word "she" could replace "the girl," and the word "her" could be used instead as the direct object or indirect object. Pronouns can be used in all of these instances (see Chapter 9).

In this chapter, you learn some French nouns and how they are used. Don't strain yourself in memorizing all of them. If you read over the vocabulary sections periodically, you should find that you are becoming more and more familiar with the words.

Gender of Nouns

One of the biggest differences you'll notice between French and English is the use of gender. Each noun in French will either have a feminine or masculine gender. This a linguistic trait inherited from Latin, where there could be three categories of gender: masculine, feminine, and neuter. French has only two: masculine and feminine.

The gender designation in French is rather arbitrary. There isn't necessarily much logic as to whether a noun will be masculine or feminine, nor are there any hard-and-fast rules. There are some general pointers, which you can find in this chapter, but in the end, the advice is always the same: Memorize the gender of a word as you learn it.

ALERT

Don't let yourself get confused about the concept of gender in French. It refers only to the noun as a word; it does not necessarily indicate the sex of the person indicated by the noun. Gender is a grammatical concept and has nothing to do with the biological sex of the object or person involved.

The gender of a noun is important to know; it can affect how the word is used and how other words are used along with it. The French Academy has long upheld the use of gender in the French language, and language purists defend its usage on historical grounds. As long as you remember that it's only a grammatical concept, you should have no trouble with it at all.

In this book, nouns are presented with the article (or, if the article is ambiguous, you'll find a small "m" for masculine and a small "f" for feminine nouns). You can also consult a French-English dictionary, which will indicate the gender of a particular word for you.

While there are no hard and fast rules about determining the gender of nouns, the majority of French words follow a consistent gender pattern. In addition to the noun's article, the ending can sometimes help you determine the proper gender of a noun.

The following lists give you the chance to become familiar with some French nouns, their endings, and their gender. This list is only a guideline, of course; there will always be exceptions (some notable ones are included in the list).

Masculine Nouns

This section helps you determine which nouns are masculine by looking at their endings.

TABLE 5-1

NOUNS ENDING IN -AIRE

NOUN	PRONUNCIATION	ENGLISH
le dictionnaire	le deek-syo-nehr	dictionary
le propriétaire	le pro-pree-ay-tehr	owner
le vocabulaire	le vo-cab-yoo-lehr	vocabulary
la grammaire*	la gram-mehr	grammar

* Exception to this ending.

TABLE 5-2

NOUNS ENDING IN -ASME AND -ISME

le sarcasme	le sar-kasm	sarcasm
l'optimisme	lop-tee-meesm	optimism
le pessimisme	le pess-ee-meesm	pessimism
le tourisme	le too-reesm	tourism

TABLE 5-3

NOUNS ENDING IN -É

le blé	le blay	wheat
le café	le kah-fay	coffee
l'employé	lom-ploy-ay	employee
le pavé	le pah-vay	pavement

Many words that end in -té are exceptions.

TABLE 5-4

NOUNS ENDING IN -EAU

le bateau	le bah-tow	boat
le bureau	le boo-row	office
le chapeau	le shah-po	hat
l'eau (f)*	low	water

* Exception to this ending.

TABLE 5-5

NOUNS ENDING IN -ET

l'alphabet	lal-fa-bay	alphabet
le billet	le bee-yay	ticket
le juillet	le jhwee-ay	july
l'objet	lob-jhay	object
le sujet	le soo-jhay	subject

TABLE 5-6

NOUNS ENDING IN -*IEN*		
NOUN	PRONUNCIATION	ENGLISH
le chien	le shee-ehn	dog
le magicien	le mah-jee-syen	magician
le musicien	le moo-zee-syen	musician
le pharmacien	le far-meh-syen	pharmacist

TABLE 5-7

NOUNS ENDING IN -*IN*		
le bain	le behn	bath
le cousin	le koo-zehn	cousin
le juin	le jwehn	june
le magasin	le may-gah-zehn	shop
le matin	le mah-tehn	morning
le vin	le vehn	wine

TABLE 5-8

NOUNS ENDING IN -*NT*		
l'accent	lax-sahn	accent
l'accident	lax-see-dahn	accident
l'argent	lar-jhahn	money

TABLE 5-9

NOUNS ENDING IN -*OIR*		
l'espoir	less-pwar	hope
le miroir	le mee-rawr	mirror
le rasoir	le rah-zwar	razor
le soir	le swahr	evening

ESSENTIALS

In written French, personal titles are often abbreviated.

Singular	Abbreviation	Plural	Abbreviation
Monsieur	M.	Messieurs	Mssrs.
Madame	Mme	Mesdames	Mmes.
Mademoiselle	Mlle	Mesdemoiselles	Mlles.

In spoken French, the full word is always pronounced.

Feminine Nouns

You can often determine which nouns are feminine by looking at the endings.

TABLE 5-10

NOUNS ENDING IN -ADE		
NOUN	PRONUNCIATION	ENGLISH
la limonade	la lee-mo-nad	lemonade
la parade	la pahr-ad	parade
la promenade	la prom-nad	walk
la salade	la sal-ad	salad

TABLE 5-11

NOUNS ENDING IN -AISON		
la maison	la meh-zohn	house
la raison	la rez-ohn	reason
la saison	la sez-ohn	season

TABLE 5-12

NOUNS ENDING IN -ANCE		
l'assistance	lass-ee-stahns	assistance
la balance	la bal-ahnss	balance
la chance	la shahns	chance
la naissance	la ness-ahns	birth
la vacance	la vek-ahns	vacancy

TABLE 5-13

NOUNS ENDING IN -ENCE		
la différence	la dee-fay-rahns	difference
l'essence	less-ahns	gasoline
la science	la see-ahns	science
la sentence	la senn-tahns	sentence
l'excellence (m)*	lex-say-lahns	excellence
le silence*	le see-lahns	silence
* Exception to this ending.		

TABLE 5-14

NOUNS ENDING IN -*ANDE*		
NOUN	**PRONUNCIATION**	**ENGLISH**
la commande	la com-ahnd	command
la demande	la dee-mahnd	request
la viande	la vee-ahnd	meat

TABLE 5-15

NOUNS ENDING IN -*ISE*		
l'église	lay-gleez	church
la fraise	la frez	strawberry
la surprise	la sur-preez	surprise
la valise	la vall-eez	suitcase

TABLE 5-16

NOUNS ENDING IN -*SON*		
la boisson	la bwa-sohn	drink
la prison	la pre-zohn	prison
la chanson	la shahn-sohn	song

TABLE 5-17

NOUNS ENDING IN -*TÉ*		
la beauté	la byoo-tay	beauty
la cité	la see-tay	city
la liberté	la lee-behr-tay	liberty
la nationalité	la nah-see-yo-nal-ee-tay	nationality
le côté*	le ko-tay	side
l'été (m)*	lay-tay	summer
* Exception to this ending.		

TABLE 5-18

NOUNS ENDING IN -*TIÉ*		
l'amitié	lam-ee-tay	friendship
la moitié	la mway-chee-ay	half
la pitié	la pee-chee-ay	pity

TABLE 5-19

NOUNS ENDING IN -*UDE*		
l'étude	lay-tood	study
l'habitude	lab-ee-tood	habit
la solitude	la soll-ee-tood	solitude

TABLE 5-20

NOUNS ENDING IN -*TURE*		
NOUN	PRONUNCIATION	ENGLISH
l'aventure	la vahn-choor	adventure
la ceinture	la sayn-choor	belt
la culture	la cul-choor	culture
la facture	la fak-choor	invoice
la nourriture	la new-ree-choor	food, nourishment

Some Special Gender Notes

As a rule, most French nouns require a specific gender. Some nouns, however, can use either gender but have two different meanings, depending on the particular gender used. In the masculine, the word will have one meaning, but the feminine will mean something else.

TABLE 5-21

NOUNS WITH DIFFERENT GENDER MEANINGS			
MASCULINE	ENGLISH	FEMININE	ENGLISH
le livre (le lee-vruh)	book	*la livre* (la lee-vruh)	pound
le manche (le mahnsh)	handle	*la manche* (la mahnsh)	sleeve
le mode (le muhd)	mode	*la mode* (la muhd)	fashion, manner, way, custom
le poste (le pahst)	post	*la poste* (la pahst)	mail, postal service
le vase (le vahs)	vase	*la vase* (la vahs)	mud, slime
le voile (le vwahl)	veil	*la voile* (la vwahl)	sail

Plural Nouns

Whenever you talk about more than one of something, the noun must be used in the plural. In English, turning most nouns into a plural form is fairly easy—we usually just add an "s" to the end of the word. Some English words, however, change quite a bit when referring to the plural.

TABLE 5-22

ENGLISH PLURAL NOUNS			
SINGULAR	PLURAL	SINGULAR	PLURAL
child	children	phenomenon	phenomena
foot	feet	wolf	wolves
man	men		

You may not even think about these differences—they come naturally as part of the English language. After you know a few nouns in French, though, when you come across a new word, you'll be able to determine its plural form by comparing it to the similar nouns you already know. If you get really stuck on a plural form, you can always check a dictionary.

Fortunately, most nouns follow fairly simple rules for the formation of the plural. Most nouns will simply add an "s" to the end of the noun to make the plural form. Other nouns, however, may pose more difficulty. French nouns can have a great variety of endings, and some of the plural forms are made in unique ways. This section shows the rules for forming the plural and also indicates some exceptions you may encounter.

Nouns Ending in -s, -x, or -z

If the noun already ends in -s, -x, or -z, no change occurs; a plural article is simply used with a word to indicate the plural.

TABLE 5-23

NOUNS ENDING IN -S, -X, OR -Z		
SINGULAR	PLURAL	ENGLISH
le fils (le feece)	*les fils* (lay feece)	son(s)
le repas (le re-pah)	*les repas* (lay re-pah)	meal(s)
la toux (lay too)	*des toux* (day too)	cough(s)
le prix (le pree)	*les prix* (lay pree)	prize(s)
le nez (le nay)	*les nez* (lay nay)	nose(s)

Nouns Ending in -*ail*

Most nouns ending in -*ail* add an "s" at the end of the word to form the plural.

TABLE 5-24

NOUNS ENDING IN -*AIL*		
SINGULAR	PLURAL	ENGLISH
l'éventail (lay-vahn-tie)	les éventails (lay vahn-tie)	fan/fans
le détail (lay day-tie)	les détails (lay day-tie)	detail/details

A few nouns ending in -*ail* don't follow the regular rules, dropping the -*ail* and adding -*aux* to the end instead.

TABLE 5-25

IRREGULAR NOUNS ENDING IN -*AIL*		
SINGULAR	PLURAL	ENGLISH
bail (by)	baux (bo)	lease(s)
corail (ko-rye)	coraux (ko-ro)	coral(s)
émail (ay-my)	émaux (ay-mo)	enamel(s)
soupirail (soo-pee-rye)	soupiraux (soo-pee-ro)	ventilator(s)
travial (tra-vye)	travaux (tra-vo)	work(s)
vitrail (vee-try)	vitraux (vee-tro)	stained-glass window(s)

Nouns Ending in -*eau*

For nouns ending in -*eau*, simply add an "x" to the end of the noun.

TABLE 5-26

NOUNS ENDING IN -*EAU*		
SINGULAR	PLURAL	ENGLISH
le couteau (le coo-tow)	les couteaux (lay coo-tow)	knife/knives
le cadeau (le cah-dew)	les cadeaux (lay cah-dew)	gift/gifts
le gâteau (le gah-tow)	les gâteux (lay gah-tow)	cake/cakes

Nouns Ending in -*eu*

For nouns ending in -*eu*, add an "x" to the end of the noun.

TABLE 5-27	NOUNS ENDING IN -*EU*		
SINGULAR	**PLURAL**		**ENGLISH**
le jeu (la jhoo)	*les jeux* (lay jhoo)		game(s)
le feu (le foo)	*les feux* (lay foo)		fire(s)

Nouns Ending in -*al*

For nouns ending in -*al*, the ending is changed to -*aux*.

TABLE 5-28	NOUNS ENDING IN -*AL*		
SINGULAR	**PLURAL**		**ENGLISH**
l'animal (lay-nee-mahl)	*les animauxl* (lay-zahn-mo)		animal(s)
le canal (le kah-nahl)	*les canaux* (lay kah-no)		canal(s)
le journal (le jhoor-nahl)	*les journaux* (lay jhoor-no)		newspaper(s)

Nouns Ending in -*ou*

For nouns ending in -*ou*, add an "x" to the end of the word.

TABLE 5-29	NOUNS ENDING IN -*OU*		
SINGULAR	**PLURAL**		**ENGLISH**
le bijou	*les bijoux* (lay bi-jo)		jewel(s)
le chou	*les choux* (lay choo)		cabbage(s)
le genou	*les genoux* (lay jhen-oo)		knee(s)
l'hibou	*les hiboux* (lay ibo)		owl(s)

Nouns That Are Always Plural

Some French nouns are always used in the plural sense; the singular either doesn't exist or means something different.

TABLE 5-30	NOUNS THAT ARE ALWAYS PLURAL		
PLURAL NOUN	**PRONUNCIATION**		**ENGLISH**
les gens	lay jhan		people
les mathématiques	lay mah-tay-ma-teek		mathematics

TABLE 5-30

NOUNS THAT ARE ALWAYS PLURAL *(CONTINUED)*		
PLURAL NOUN	PRONUNCIATION	ENGLISH
les vacances	lay vah-kahns	vacation
les frais	lay freh	expenses

When referring to vacations, the term *les vacances* must always be used in the plural. Even if you are only referring to one particular vacation or a single day of vacation, *les vacances* must be used. *La vacance,* the singular form of the word, means "vacancy."

Family Names

When the noun is a family name, nothing is added. It is used on its own, without turning the noun itself into a plural form; the plural is inferred from the article. Other words, such as verbs, that are used with the noun will also be used in the plural sense to agree with it.

- *les Dumont* (the Dumonts; the Dumont family)
- *les Lasalle* (the Lasalles; the Lasalle family)

Irregular Plurals

Some words undergo a bit of a transformation or even change entirely in the plural sense. These are irregular plurals.

TABLE 5-31

IRREGULAR PLURALS		
SINGULAR	PLURAL	ENGLISH
l'œill (loo-ay)	*les yeuxl* (lay yeuh)	eye(s)
Monsieurl (mohn-syeuhr)	*Messieurs* (may-syeuhr)	Mr.
Madame (mah-dahm)	*Mesdames* (mah-dahm)	Mrs.
Mademoiselle (mah-de-mwah-zell)	*Mesdemoiselles* (may-de-mwah-zell)	Miss

CHAPTER 6

Forming Present-Tense Verbs

This chapter gets you into verbs, specifically those in the present tense. Building on the articles and nouns in the two preceding chapters, you can use the information in this chapter to create full sentences! While forming the verb in the present tense is easier than for the past and future tenses, verbs can still be a challenge. This chapter simplifies the process.

Verb Forms: The Infinitive

You've probably noticed that when you refer to verbs in English, the verb is prefaced by the word "to." "To go," "to be," and "to speak" are examples. The "to" tells you that the verb is being used in a general sense, not tied to a particular subject. Because these verbs don't have a subject or object, they are said to be in the infinitive.

- I don't like **to drive**.
- I want **to go**.

- I love **to walk**.

In French, nothing is placed before the word in the infinitive. As a matter of fact, you have likely already learned many infinitive French verbs. The infinitive in French is simply the unconjugated form of the verb you have probably already seen throughout the book:

- *avoir* (to have)
- *être* (to be)
- *parler* (to speak)

- *aimer* (to love)
- *écouter* (to listen)
- *nager* (to swim)

FACTS

Occasionally, you may come across signs in French that say things like *Ne Pas Fumer*. At first, they may seem confusing, as it appears to read "not to smoke." This is just the French way of doing things, but think about it like this: Because the sign doesn't know who is going to be reading it, it keeps the verb in the infinitive; that way, it can apply to everyone.

This construction can also be used with the other negative words. Simply replace *pas* with the proper word and follow it with the infinitive of the verb.

Conjugating Verbs in the Present Tense

In French, the verb changes slightly to reflect the subject of the sentence. This is known as conjugation—putting the correct form of the verb with the subject. The ending of the verb must always match the subject in French.

For example, the verb *courir* means "to run." When using it in a sentence, the verb changes slightly for each different subject it takes. If you wanted to say "I run," you would say, *Je cours. Je* is the subject, meaning "I," and *cours* is the properly conjugated form of the verb *courir.* English verbs sometimes change, too: If you consider the examples "I run" and "he runs," you notice that the verb does in fact change, even if only slightly. In French, the endings of verbs can also help you determine the gender and number of the subject if you're unsure.

Verb Stems

The stem of the verb is the magic key to French verbs. It is the part of the word that does not change when conjugated with various subjects. Constructions in the tenses other than the present tense also utilize the verb stem, adding on special endings to indicate the tense of the verb. (In Chapters 12 through 16, you find out about other verb tenses, so that you can refer to things in the past or in the future.)

To find the stem of a verb, simply drop the ending from its infinitive form. Because the infinitive is not used with a subject, the changes that occur with stem-changing verbs don't affect the infinitive; when a stem-changing verb is used in the infinitive, the stem changes simply do not occur.

It is important to know the infinitive verb form, because it is usually the only one listed in French-English dictionaries. Seldom will you find a conjugated form of the verb in a dictionary. If you want to look up a verb you don't know, and it's in the conjugated form, drop the ending and look for the infinitive of the verb.

Most of the French verbs you'll encounter follow simple rules for conjugation. The word endings follow a predictable pattern, so you have to memorize only the endings for one verb. You can then replace the endings on other verbs with similar endings without having to memorize all of the forms over and over again. Like much of the language, it will become second nature to you. Because the majority of French verbs do follow a regular pattern, you can easily learn new verbs later.

French also has some irregular verbs, where the verb forms seem to follow no logical pattern at all. These will have to be memorized individually. Fortunately, there are only a few of them.

-er Verbs in the Present Tense

Most of the French verbs you'll encounter follow simple rules for conjugation. Verbs that end in *-er* are the most common form of verb in the French language; for the most part, they all follow the same conjugation pattern. This means that you only have to memorize the word endings one time—after that, you can just use the endings of the verbs you already know to come up with the appropriate ending. Verbs that end in *-er* use the following endings when conjugated in the present tense.

TABLE 6-1	ENDINGS OF *-ER* VERBS	
PERSON	**SINGULAR**	**PLURAL**
1st Person	*je* (I) -*e*	*nous* (we) -*ons*
2nd Person	*tu* (you) -*es*	*vous* (you) -*ez*
3rd Person	*il* (he) -*e*	*ils* (they) -*ent*
	elle (she) -*e*	*elles* (they) -*ent*

You may have encountered the verb *parler* in Chapter 2; it means "to speak." Here is how it looks when conjugated.

TABLE 6-2	CONJUGATION OF THE VERB *PARLER* (TO SPEAK)	
PERSON	**SINGULAR**	**PLURAL**
1st Person	*je parle* (jhe parl)	*nous parlons* (noo parlohn)
2nd Person	*tu parles* (tchoo parl)	*vous parlez* (voo parlay)
3rd Person	*il parle* (eel parl)	*ils parlent* (eel parl)
	elle parle (ell parl)	*elles parlent* (ell parl)

Some of the verb endings have distinct sounds, such as *parlons* and *parlez*. The other endings are actually silent, so they all sound the same. You must rely on the subject pronoun to determine what is going on in the sentence. Even though the endings aren't pronounced, however, it's still important to know the spelling of the proper endings, because they are required in written French.

As you've probably gathered, *je parle* means "I speak," *tu parles* means "you speak," *il parle* means "he speaks," and so on. In English, we have a few different ways of speaking in the present tense. For example, in English, we can say:

- I speak.
- I do speak.

- I am speaking.

All these sentences, in essence, mean the same thing. All are conjugated in the first person singular, present tense, and indicate an action that is occurring to a subject (I), describing what that subject is doing: speaking. In English, stylistic factors usually determine which of the three choices is used; French uses fewer words to say the same thing. Any or all of those English meanings can be conveyed by saying *Je parle*.

Remember that the verb *parler*, when used with the name of a language, does not take a definite article. One says, *Je parle français*, not, *Je parle le français*.

This is a unique quality of the verb *parler*. Most other verbs will require an article when followed by a noun.

When translating from French to English, simply choose the translation that makes the most sense, given the situation. Quite often, the answer that sounds right is the correct one. When translating from English to French, however, caution is needed. "Do" and "am" are simply there as a part of the verb in English; do not try to translate these words individually.

When translating "I am speaking," for example, most students will translate the I into *je*, and "am" into *suis*: the proper form of the verb *être*, "to be." At this point, the students have *je suis*, which does indeed mean "I am"—but what do you do with "speaking?"

However, if you remember that the present tense conjugation of *parler* can mean "I speak," "I do speak," or "I am speaking," you'll know just to use the subject pronoun and verb *(je parle)* without adding in any helper words that really shouldn't be there.

Here are a few other *-er* verbs you should know.

- *aimer* (to like, to love)
- *arriver* (to arrive)
- *désirer* (to desire, to want)
- *écouter* (to listen)
- *entrer* (to enter, to come in)
- *envoyer* (to send)
- *étudier* (to study)
- *placer* (to place, to put)
- *porter* (to wear, to carry)
- *rester* (to remain, to stay)
- *retourner* (to return, to go back)

The beauty of most *-er* verbs is that they are all conjugated alike. In order to conjugate a verb ending in *-er*, you simply have to cut off the "er" to get the stem. After you have the stem, you can tack on the appropriate ending. There are a few verbs whose stems also change when conjugated, and they're covered in this section. These changes always affect the spelling and often affect the pronunciation.

Verbs Ending in *-cer*

For verbs ending in *-cer*, the "c" changes to a "ç" when used with *nous* to maintain the soft "s" sound. Other forms follow the regular *-er* conjugation pattern.

TABLE 6-3

CONJUGATION OF THE VERB *EFFACER* (TO ERASE)		
PERSON	**SINGULAR**	**PLURAL**
1st Person	*j'efface* (jheff-ass)	*nous effaçons* (noo-zeff-ass-ohn)
2nd Person	*tu effaces* (tchoo-eff-ass)	*vous effacez* (voo-zeff-ass-ay)
3rd Person	*il efface* (eel-eff-ass)	*ils effacent* (eel-zeff-ass)
	elle efface (ell-eff-ass)	*elles effacent* (ell-zeff-ass)

Verbs conjugated like *effacer* include:

- *agacer* (to irritate)
- *annoncer* (to announce)
- *commencer* (to begin)
- *épicer* (to spice)
- *prononcer* (to pronounce)
- *remplacer* (to replace)

Verbs Ending in -ger

Verbs ending in -ger remain mostly similar, but add an "e" before the -ons when used with *nous* in order to make sure that the "g" sound remains soft. Other forms remain unchanged and follow the regular pattern.

TABLE 6-4

CONJUGATION OF THE VERB *MANGER* (TO EAT)		
PERSON	SINGULAR	PLURAL
1st Person	*je mange* (jhe mahnj)	*nous mangeons* (noo mahn-jhohn)
2nd Person	*tu manges* (tchoo mahnj)	*vous mangez* (voo mahn-jhay)
3rd Person	*il mange* (eel mahnj)	*ils mangent* (eel mahnj)
	elle mange (ell mahnj)	*elles mangent* (ell mahnj)

Verbs conjugated like *manger* include:

- *changer* (to change)
- *charger* (to charge)
- *corriger* (to correct)
- *mélanger* (to mix)
- *nager* (to swim)
- *voyager* (to travel)

Verbs with an é

For -er verbs with an *é*, in order to aid pronunciation, the accent changes to a *grave* (see Chapter 1) in all cases except for *nous* and *vous*. Note that this only affects the accent closest to the ending of the stem.

TABLE 6-5

CONJUGATION OF THE VERB *PRÉFÉRER* (TO PREFER)		
PERSON	SINGULAR	PLURAL
1st Person	*je préfère* (jhe pray-fehr)	*nous préférons* (noo pray-fay-rohn)
2nd Person	*tu préfères* (tchoo pray-fehr)	*vous préférez* (voo pray-fay-ray)
3rd Person	*il préfère* (eel pray-fehr)	*ils préfèrent* (eel pray-fehr)
	elle préfère (ell pray-fehr)	*elles préfèrent* (ell pray-fehr)

Verbs conjugated like *préférer* include:

- *célébrer* (to celebrate)
- *espérer* (to expect, to hope)
- *insérer* (to insert)

Verbs Ending in *-eler*

For verbs ending in *-eler*, the stem changes to include a double "l"; this affects all conjugation forms but *nous* and *vous*.

TABLE 6-6

CONJUGATION OF THE VERB *APPELER* (TO CALL)		
PERSON	**SINGULAR**	**PLURAL**
1st Person	*j'appelle* (jha-pell)	*nous appelons* (noo-zah-pell-ohn)
2nd Person	*tu appelles* (tchoo a-pell)	*vous appelez* (voo-zah-pell-ay)
3rd Person	*il appelle* (ee-la-pell)	*ils appellent* (eel-za-pell)
	elle appelle (el-la-pell)	*elles appellent* (el-za-pell)

Words conjugated like *appeler* include the following:

- *morceler* (to break up, to parcel)
- *rappeler* (to remind)

Verbs Ending in *-eter*

Verbs ending in *-eter* are very similar to *appeler*; these verbs double the "t" in all cases but *nous* and *vous*.

TABLE 6-7

CONJUGATION OF THE VERB *JETER* (TO THROW)		
PERSON	**SINGULAR**	**PLURAL**
1st Person	*je jette* (jhe jhett)	*nous jetons* (noo jet-ohn)
2nd Person	*tu jettes* (tchoo jhett)	*vous jetez* (voo jet-ay)
3rd Person	*il jette* (eel jhett)	*ils jettent* (eel jhett)
	elle jette (ell jhett)	*elles jettent* (ell jhett)

Verbs conjugated like *jeter* include:

- *projeter* (to project)
- *rejeter* (to reject, to throw again)

Verbs Ending in *-ayer*

For verbs ending in *-ayer,* to form the new stem, simply turn the "y" into an "i" in all cases but *nous* and *vous.*

TABLE 6-8

CONJUGATION OF THE VERB *PAYER* (TO PAY)		
PERSON	SINGULAR	PLURAL
1st Person	*je paie* (jhe payy)	*nous payons* (noo pay-ohn)
2nd Person	*tu paies* (tchoo payy)	*vous payez* (voo pay- ay)
3rd Person	*il paie* (eel payy)	*ils paient* (eel payy)
	elle paie (ell payy)	*elles paient* (ell payy)

Verbs conjugated like *payer* include the following:

- *balayer* (to sweep)
- *begayer* (to stammer)
- *effrayer* (to frighten)
- *embrayer* (to couple)
- *enrayer* (to check)
- *essayer* (to try)
- *rayer* (to delete, to scratch, to erase)

Verbs Ending in *-oyer*

Verbs ending in *-oyer,* like verbs ending in *-ayer,* turn the "y" into an "i" in all cases but *nous* and *vous.*

TABLE 6-9

CONJUGATION OF THE VERB *NETTOYER* (TO CLEAN)		
PERSON	SINGULAR	PLURAL
1st Person	*je nettoie* (jhe neh-twa)	*nous nettoyons* (noo neh-twoy-ohn)
2nd Person	*tu nettoies* (tchoo neh-twa)	*vous nettoyez* (voo neh-twoy-ay)
3rd Person	*il nettoie* (eel neh-twa)	*ils nettoient* (eel neh-twa)
	elle nettoie (ell neh-twa)	*elles nettoient* (ell neh-twa)

Verbs conjugated like *nettoyer* include:

- *employer* (to employ)
- *envoyer* (to send)
- *noyer* (to drown)
- *renvoyer* (to return)

Beware of the verb *nettoye r* –it begins with the *ne* sound, which is often used to begin negative expressions. It can sometimes make people search for *pas* or another word used to turn statements into the negative.

Verbs Ending in *-uyer*

Verbs ending in *-uyer* follow the same pattern as the other verbs with endings that include a "y," using an "i" to form the endings in all forms but *nous* and *vous*.

TABLE 6-10

CONJUGATION OF THE VERB *ENNUYER* (TO BORE)		
PERSON	SINGULAR	PLURAL
1st Person	*j'ennuie* (jhahn-wee)	*nous ennuyons* (noo-zahn-wee-yohn)
2nd Person	*tu ennuies* (tchoo ahn-wee)	*vous ennuyez* (voo-zahn-wee-yay)
3rd Person	*il ennuie* (ee-lahn-wee) *elle ennuie* (el-lahn-wee)	*ils ennuient* (ee lahn-wee) *elles ennuient* (el lahn-wee)

Verbs conjugated like *ennuyer* include:

- *appuyer* (to support)
- *essuyer* (to wipe)

ESSENTIALS

When memorizing conjugation forms, rote is often the best method. Repeating them over and over will help emblazon them upon your memory, but this method can seem a little boring at times. If you find it a little monotonous, you can always try putting the words to a tune to make it a little more fun.

-re **Verbs in the Present Tense**

There are two more regular verb forms: verbs that end in *-re* and *-ir*. Like the *-er* verbs, each group follows a predictable pattern. There are, of course, some exceptions for each group, but these irregular verbs also tend to follow similar conjugation patterns when compared to each other, so it should be relatively easy to recall the forms. You'll learn about verbs ending in *-ir* in the next section of this chapter.

Regular verbs ending in *-re* are conjugated slightly differently from other verbs. They use the following endings:

TABLE 6-11	ENDINGS OF *-RE* VERBS		
PERSON	**SINGULAR**	**PLURAL**	
1st Person	*je* (I) -s	*nous* (we)	-ons
2nd Person	*tu* (you) -s	*vous* (you)	-ez
3rd Person	*il* (he)	*ils* (they)	-ent
	elle (she)	*elles* (they)	-ent

The third person singular form merely uses the stem of the verb alone; no extra endings are added. To create the third person singular form in written French, you need only remove the *-re* ending and use the stem alone with the proper subject or subject pronoun.

TABLE 6-12	CONJUGATION OF THE VERB *VENDRE* (TO SELL)	
PERSON	**SINGULAR**	**PLURAL**
1st Person	*je vends* (jhe vahn)	*nous vendons* (noo vahnd-ohn)
2nd Person	*tu vends* (tchoo vahn)	*vous vendez* (voo vahn-day)
3rd Person	*il vend* (eel vahn)	*ils vendent* (eel vahnd)
	elle vend (ell vahn)	*elles vendent* (ell vahnd)

A number of verbs, as follows, are conjugated like *vendre*. Practice conjugating the verbs using different subject pronouns until they become natural to you.

TABLE 6-13

REGULAR VERBS ENDING IN -RE		
FRENCH	PRONUNCIATION	ENGLISH
défendre	day-fahn-druh	to defend, to protect
descendre	day-sahn-druh	to go down, to get off
épandre	ay-pahn-druh	to scatter, to strew
fendre	fahn-druh	to split, to crack, to cut open
fondre	foahn-druh	to melt, to dissolve
mordre	mohr-druh	to bite, to gnaw
pendre	pahn-druh	to hang, to hang up, to suspend
perdre	pehr-druh	to lose, to waste
pondre	pohn-druh	to lay (as in eggs)
rendre	rahn-druh	to return, to restore, to give back, to repay
répondre	ray-pohn-druh	to answer, to reply
tendre	tahn-druh	to stretch, to strain
tondre	tohn-druh	to shear, to clip, to crop, to cut
tordre	tohr-druh	to twist, to wring, to contort

Here are some examples of -re verbs in action. Practice conjugating these verbs on your own by making up sentences, using the vocabulary you have learned in this and previous chapters.

- *Le caissier vend les billets.* (The cashier is selling the tickets.)
- *Les gendarmes défendent la ville.* (The police protect the city.)

ESSENTIALS

You can design your own mini-quizzes and tests by making flash cards with a different verb in the infinitive on the front of each card. You can make up another set of cards with all of the subject pronouns and draw a card from each. Then, practice conjugating each verb with the subject pronoun.

When a "p" appears at the end of an *-re* verb stem, a "t" is added to the ending in the third person. This is an issue of pronunciation—it would be very difficult to pronounce a "p" at the end of a word, so a "t" is added, as follows:

- *corrompre* (*ko-rahmp-ruh*): to corrupt. *Elle corrompt les élèves.* She corrupts the students.
- *interrompre* (*een-teh-rahmp-ruh*): to interrupt. *Il interrompt le film.* He is interrupting the film.
- *romper* (*rahmp-ruh*): to break, to snap, to break off. *Il rompt le crayon.* He is breaking the pencil.

There aren't a whole lot of verbs that end in *-pre*, but you should still know how to use them. Adding the "t" in the third person singular ending also occurs in written French, so remember to make the change when writing, too.

-ir Verbs in the Present Tense

There is one last type of regular French verbs, those that end in *-ir*. There are also a number of irregular verbs that end in *-ir*; these all follow similar conjugation patterns, however, and they are verbs that are quite commonly used in the language. You'll probably find yourself using these words a lot, so it shouldn't take you too long to get used to the conjugation patterns.

TABLE 6-14	CONJUGATION OF THE VERB *FINIR* (TO FINISH)	
PERSON	**SINGULAR**	**PLURAL**
1st Person	*je finis* (jhe fin-ee)	*nous finissons* (noo fin-ee-sohn)
2nd Person	*tu finis* (tchoo fin-ee)	*vous finissez* (voo fin-ee-say)
3rd Person	*il finit* (eel fin-ee)	*ils finissent* (eel fin-ees)
	elle finit (ell fin-ee)	*elles finissent* (ell fin-ees)

Here are some French verbs ending in *-ir* that follow the same pattern as *finir*. You can simply form the stem of the verb by dropping the *-ir* ending and replacing the properly conjugated ending as usual.

TABLE 6-15

REGULAR VERBS ENDING IN -*IR*		
FRENCH	PRONUNCIATION	ENGLISH
accomplir	ack-kom-pleer	to accomplish
accourir	ack-oo-reer	to hasten
accueillir	ack-way-eer	to welcome
agir	ah-jheer	to act
agonir	ah-go-nheer	to insult
applaudir	app-law-deer	to applaud
bâtir	bah-teer	to construct, build
choisir	schwa-zeer	to choose
faillir	fie-yeer	to fail
fleurir	floo-reer	to blossom, to bloom
fournir	foor-neer	to furnish
garantir	gahr-ahn-teer	to guarantee
gésir	jhay-zeer	to lie
mourir	moo-reer	to die
obéir	oh-bay-eer	to obey
rafraîchir	reh-fresh-ear	to refresh
rôtir	roh-teer	to roast

Irregular Verbs

Irregular verbs do not follow the patterns for *-er*, *-re*, and *-ir* verbs. Instead, they have their own patterns that you must memorize for each verb.

Avoir, Être, Faire, and Aller

Two of the most-used irregular verbs, *avoir* and *être*, are an integral part of the French language, as they often get used in conjunction with other verbs when complex sentences are formed. *Avoir* means "to have" or "to hold," and *être* means "to be." *Faire* and *aller* are also common irregular verbs.

TABLE 6-16

CONJUGATION OF *AVOIR* (TO HAVE, TO HOLD)		
CONJUGATION	PRONUNCIATION	ENGLISH
j'ai	jhay	I have
tu as	tcho ah	you have
il a	eel-ah	he has
elle a	ell-ah	she has
nous avons	noo-za-vohn	we have
vous avez	voo-za-vay	you have
ils ont	eel-zohn	they have
elles ont	ell-zohn	they have

TABLE 6-17

CONJUGATION OF *ÊTRE* (TO BE)		
je suis	jhe swee	I am
tu es	tchoo ay	you are
il est	ee-lay	he is
elle est	ell-ay	she is
nous sommes	noo-sum	we are
vous êtes	voo-zett	you are
ils sont	eel sohn	they are
elles sont	ell sohn	they are

Although **être** appears to be a regular -*re* verb, it in fact follows a very different conjugation pattern from other -*re* verbs.

Another commonly used irregular verb, **faire**, means "to make" or "to do."

TABLE 6-18

CONJUGATION OF THE VERB *FAIRE* (TO MAKE, TO DO)		
PERSON	SINGULAR	PLURAL
1st Person	je fais (jhe fay)	nous faisons (noo fay-sohn)
2nd Person	tu fais (tchoo fay)	vous faites (voo fett)
3rd Person	il fait (eel fay)	ils font (eel fohn)
	elle fait (ell fay)	elles font (ell fohn)

Note that the second person plural form, *vous faites*, does not follow the normal pattern of ending in *-ez*; its conjugation is very similar to *être*, as in *vous êtes*. The other forms of *faire*, fortunately, follow a relatively predictable pattern.

The verb *faire* can also be used with the infinitive form of another verb to indicate the sense of "to have something done" or even "make something happen." This is often used when you are having something done by someone else, especially when the person doing it isn't important to the meaning. The someone is inferred. Whenever you aren't doing something yourself, you can use this phrase.

A good example is *Je fais laver mes vêtements*: I am having my clothing washed. An attempt to translate this sentence literally would yield only weird results. Remember that when the verb *faire* is followed by the infinitive form of a verb, this specialized meaning is intended.

Aller is another word that is used extensively in the French language. It means "to go," and like the other verbs that get constant usage, it is irregular.

TABLE 6-19

CONJUGATION OF THE VERB *ALLER* (TO GO)		
PERSON	**SINGULAR**	**PLURAL**
1st Person	*je vais* (jhe vay)	*nous allons* (noo zah-lohn)
2nd Person	*tu vas* (tchoo vah)	*vous allez* (voo zah-lay)
3rd Person	*il va* (eel vah)	*ils vont* (eel vohn)
	elle va (ell vah)	*elles vont* (ell vohn)

Irregular Verbs Ending in *-oir*

Irregular verbs ending in *-oir* don't really make much sense at first glance. Some of the singular endings of words end in "x," while others end in "s," and none of the endings seem to have any inherent logic. With practice, you'll get used to the endings. It may take some memorization, but feel free to refer back to this section as often as you like. These verbs tend to be some of the most widely used words in the French language, so you'll get lots of practice with them.

In addition, you can use some of these verbs with an infinitive to create new and complex sentences, expanding immensely your ability to speak

French. As you read over the lists, pay attention to the third person plural ending; it is usually formed differently from the other plural conjugations. It is actually more similar to the singular endings of the conjugated verb.

Consider the following irregular verbs ending in -oir.

TABLE 6-20

CONJUGATION OF THE VERB *VOULOIR* (TO WANT, TO WISH, TO WILL)		
PERSON	**SINGULAR**	**PLURAL**
1st Person	*je veux* (jhe vhu)	*nous voulons* (noo voo-lohn)
2nd Person	*tu veux* (tchoo vhu)	*vous voulez* (voo voo-lay)
3rd Person	*il veut* (eel vhu)	*ils veulent* (eel vheul)
	elle veut (ell vhu)	*elles veulent* (ell vheul)

TABLE 6-21

CONJUGATION OF THE VERB *POUVOIR* (TO BE ABLE)		
1st Person	*je peux* (jhe puh)	*nous pouvons* (noo poo-vohn)
2nd Person	*tu peux* (tchoo puh)	*vous pouvez* (voo poo-vay)
3rd Person	*il peut* (eel puh)	*ils peuvent* (eel puhv)
	elle peut (ell puh)	*elles peuvent* (ell puhv)

FACTS

When the verb *pouvoir* is used with an infinitive verb, it takes on the English equivalent of "can," as in the following examples:

- *Je peux voir.* (I can see. I am able to see.)
- *Nous pouvons aller.* (We can go. We are able to go.)
- *Ils peuvent payer pour les billets.* (They can pay for the tickets. They are able to pay for the tickets.)

Using "can" as a verb in this way is really an English idiom that means "to be able"; when translating into French, use *pouvoir*.

TABLE 6-22

CONJUGATION OF THE VERB *VOIR* (TO SEE)		
PERSON	**SINGULAR**	**PLURAL**
1st Person	*je vois* (jhe vwah)	*nous voyons* (noo voy-ohn)
2nd Person	*tu vois* (tchoo vwah)	*vous voyez* (voo voy-ay)
3rd Person	*il voit* (eel vwah)	*ils voient* (eel vwah)
	elle voit (ell vwah)	*elles voient* (ell vwah)

TABLE 6-23

CONJUGATION OF THE VERB *RECEVOIR* (TO RECEIVE, TO GET)		
PERSON	SINGULAR	PLURAL
1st Person	*je reçois* (jhe rhe-swah)	*nous recevons* (noo rhe-se-vohn)
2nd Person	*tu reçois* (tchoo rhe-swah)	*vous recevez* (voo rhe-se-vay)
3rd Person	*il reçoit* (eel rhe-swah)	*ils reçoivent* (eel rhe-swahv)
	elle reçoit (ell rhe-swah)	*elles reçoivent* (ell rhe-swahv)

TABLE 6-24

CONJUGATION OF THE VERB *DEVOIR* (TO HAVE TO, TO OWE)		
1st Person	*je dois* (jhe dwah)	*nous devons* (noo dehv-ohn)
2nd Person	*tu dois* (tchoo dwah)	*vous devez* (voo dehv-ay)
3rd Person	*il doit* (eel dwah)	*ils doivent* (eel dwahv)
	elle doit (ell dwah)	*elles doivent* (ell dwahv)

FACTS

The verb *devoir* can also carry the meaning of "ought" when translated into English; many people use the word "should" to indicate this case, too. Using *devoir* is almost like saying you "must" do something, but just a little bit softer in meaning. For example, *Je dois voir le film* can mean "I should see the film," "I ought to see the film," or "I have to see the film." In the same way, *Nous devons acheter des billets* can mean "We ought to buy tickets," "We should buy tickets," or "We have to buy tickets."

TABLE 6-25

CONJUGATION OF THE VERB *SAVOIR* (TO KNOW)		
PERSON	SINGULAR	PLURAL
1st Person	*je sais* (jhe say)	*nous savons* (noo sah-vohn)
2nd Person	*tu sais* (tchoo say)	*vous savez* (voo sah-vay)
3rd Person	*il sait* (eel say)	*ils savent* (eel sahv)
	elle sait (ell say)	*elles savent* (ell sahv)

Irregular Verbs Ending in *-ir*

Some of the following irregular *-ir* verbs can be used with nouns after them to indicate the object that the verb refers to. This is known as a direct object; you will learn more about these in Chapter 9. Memorize the following verbs, and remember not to try to use the regular -ir ending.

TABLE 6-26

CONJUGATION OF THE VERB *COURIR* (TO RUN)		
PERSON	**SINGULAR**	**PLURAL**
1st Person	*je cours* (jhe koohr)	*nous courons* (noo koohr-ohn)
2nd Person	*tu cours* (tchoo koohr)	*vous courez* (voo koohr-ay)
3rd Person	*il court* (eel koohr)	*ils courent* (eel koohr)
	elle court (ell koohr)	*elles courent* (ell koohr)

TABLE 6-27

CONJUGATION OF THE VERB *DORMIR* (TO SLEEP)		
1st Person	*je dors* (jhe dohr)	*nous dormons* (noo dohr-mohn)
2nd Person	*tu dors* (tchoo dohr)	*vous dormez* (voo dohr-may)
3rd Person	*il dort* (eel dohr)	*ils dorment* (eel dohrm)
	elle dort (ell dohr)	*elles dorment* (ell dohrm)

TABLE 6-28

CONJUGATION OF THE VERB *OBTENIR* (TO OBTAIN)		
1st Person	*j'obtiens* (jhob-tee-ehn)	*nous obtenons* (noo-zob-tehn-ohn)
2nd Person	*tu obtiens* (tchoo ob-tee-ehn)	*vous obtenez* (voo-zob-tehn-ay)
3rd Person	*il obtient* (eel ob-tee-ehn)	*ils obtiennent* (eel-zob-tee-ehnn)
	elle obtient (ell ob-tee-ehn)	*elles obtiennent* (ell zob-tee-ehnn)

TABLE 6-29

CONJUGATION OF THE VERB *OFFRIR* (TO OFFER)		
1st Person	*j'offre* (jhahfruh)	*nous offrons* (noo-zoff-rohn)
2nd Person	*tu offres* (tchoo ahfruh)	*vous offrez* (voo-zoff-ray)
3rd Person	*il offre* (eel zahfruh)	*ils offrent* (eel-zahfruh)
	elle offre (ell zahfruh)	*elles offrent* (ell-zahfruh)

TABLE 6-30

CONJUGATION OF THE VERB *OUVRIR* (TO OPEN)		
PERSON	**SINGULAR**	**PLURAL**
1st Person	*j'ouvre* (jhoovruh)	*nous ouvrons* (noo-zoo-vrohn)
2nd Person	*tu ouvres* (tchoo oovruh)	*vous ouvrez* (voo-zoo-vray)
3rd Person	*il ouvre* (eel oovruh)	*ils ouvrent* (eel-zoovruh)
	elle ouvre (ell oovruh)	*elles ouvrent* (ell-zoovruh)

TABLE 6-31

CONJUGATION OF THE VERB *PARTIR* (TO LEAVE, TO DEPART)		
1st Person	*je pars* (jhe pahr)	*nous partons* (noo pahr-tohn)
2nd Person	*tu pars* (tchoo pahr)	*vous partez* (voo pahr-tay)
3rd Person	*il part* (eel pahr)	*ils partent* (eel part)
	elle part (ell pahr)	*elles partent* (ell part)

TABLE 6-32

CONJUGATION OF THE VERB *SERVIR* (TO SERVE)		
1st Person	*je sers* (jhe sehr)	*nous servons* (noo sehr-vohn)
2nd Person	*tu sers* (tchoo sehr)	*vous servez* (voo sehr-vay)
3rd Person	*il sert* (eel sehr)	*ils servent* (eel sehrv)
	elle sert (ell sehr)	*elles servent* (ell sehrv)

TABLE 6-33

CONJUGATION OF THE VERB *SORTIR* (TO GO OUT)		
1st Person	*je sors* (jhe sohr)	*nous sortons* (noo sohr-tohn)
2nd Person	*tu sors* (tchoo sohr)	*vous sortez* (voo sohr-tay)
3rd Person	*il sort* (eel sohr)	*ils sortent* (eel sohrt)
	elle sort (ell sohr)	*elles sortent* (ell sohrt)

TABLE 6-34

CONJUGATION OF THE VERB *TENIR* (TO HAVE, TO HOLD)		
1st Person	*je tiens* (jhe tee-ehn)	*nous tenons* (noo tehn-ohn)
2nd Person	*tu tiens* (tchoo tee-ehn)	*vous tenez* (voo tehn-ay)
3rd Person	*il tient* (eel tee-ehn)	*ils tiennent* (eel tee-ehnn)
	elle tient (ell tee-ehn)	*elles tiennent* (ell tee-ehnn)

TABLE 6-35

CONJUGATION OF THE VERB *VENIR* (TO COME)		
PERSON	SINGULAR	PLURAL
1st Person	*je viens* (jhe vee-ehn)	*nous venons* (noo vehn-ohn)
2nd Person	*tu viens* (tchoo vee-ehn)	*vous venez* (voo vehn-ay)
3rd Person	*il vient* (eel vee-ehn)	*ils viennent* (eel vee-ehnn)
	elle vient (ell vee-ehn)	*elles viennent* (ell vee-ehnn)

There are some other verbs that are conjugated in the same way as *venir*: *devenir* (to become) and *revenir* (to come back). Because these verbs are simply expanded forms of the verb *venir*, they use the same endings when conjugated.

Idiomatic Expressions with *Avoir*

In Chapter 2, you learned about idiomatic expressions—expressions that have meaning only in a particular language. Some phrases using *avoir* have unique translations that don't quite parallel the English usage. Many of these phrases will seem foreign to you, as English uses the verb "to be" for most of them. *Avoir* means "to have" or "to hold," so you may need to spend some time becoming familiar with these expressions.

It is relatively easy to remember these idiomatic expressions when translating from French to English, because they don't make a whole lot of sense if translated literally. When moving from English to French, however, extra caution is needed, as you can easily fall into a trap if you accidentally translate the English words literally to form a French sentence. This can seriously alter the meaning, so pay close attention.

Later in the book, you will learn about other verb tenses; you will then be able to use idiomatic expressions with *avoir* in the past or future tense. Verb tenses are covered in Chapters 12 through 16.

Avoir can be used with different words to describe a variety of physical conditions. In some cases, English has its own verb that functions as the equivalent of the expression; in other cases, it uses an adjective. Included in the following list are tips for remembering the constructions.

Avoir Chaud

Literally, it looks like "to have hot," which does not make sense in English, but the meaning is "to be hot" or "to feel hot."

Avoir Froid

Be very careful with this expression, which means "to be cold" or "to feel cold." If this expression is used with the verb *être* in French, it means "to be frigid," so avoid using *Je suis froid* unless you really mean it.

Avoir Faim

Literally, this means "to have hunger," which makes sense in English, but just sounds rather absurd. Instead, in French, this expression means "to be hungry."

Avoir Soif

This construction, which means "to be thirsty," closely resembles "hunger," so you should find it easy to remember the two of them.

Avoir L'Air

The literal translation of this expression (which means "to seem") is "to have the air," which is very close to "seem" in English.

Avoir Sommeil

You can use this phrase, which means "to be sleepy," when you want to indicate that someone is tired or sleepy, including yourself.

Avoir . . . Ans

You can use this phrase when you want to indicate that you are of a particular age. Literally, it means "to have years," as in *J'ai trente ans.*

which means "I am thirty years old." To remember this expression, it may help you to mentally tack on the phrase "under my belt" to the end of the sentence. "I have twenty years under my belt" is a perfectly acceptable English colloquialism, so this way, it makes sense. Just remember not to say it out loud.

Avoir Mal

This expression is used to describe an ache or pain and is followed by the preposition *à* and a noun with a definite article to indicate the source of the pain. An example is *il a mal à la tête*, which means "He has a headache."

Avoir Tort

There is no separate verb for "wrong." Instead, this idiomatic expression is used, and it means "to be wrong."

Avoir Raison

This phrase is the opposite of *avoir tort* and means "to be right."

Avoir Besoin de

Literally, this phrase would translate as "to have a need for." When translating into English, a close approximation is "to need." The phrase *J'ai besoin de lait* means "I need milk."

Avoir Peur de

When translating this expression, which means "to be afraid," you can also use the verb "to fear."

Avoir Honte de

Honte means shame, so it literally means "to have shame about" something. A more common translation is "to be ashamed of something."

Avoir Envie de

In the English equivalent of this expression that means "to feel like," "feel like" is often followed by a word ending in "-ing," like "reading."

After the French idiomatic expression, the infinitive of the verb is used: *Je n'ai pas envie de manger,* which means "I don't feel like eating."

Avoir Lieu

You can use this phrase to describe the beginning of almost any event—it means "to take place."

Avoir de la Chance

Chance means luck; you can wish someone "good luck" by saying *Bonne chance!* In order to say that someone is lucky, use this idiomatic expression.

Avoir L'occasion de

In English, this phrase usually means "to have the opportunity." It can also be translated as "to have the chance," but be sure not to confuse it with *avoir de la chance.*

The Present Participle

In English, you often use verb forms that end in "-ing" to describe actions; sometimes, these are used as verbs or adjectives, while other times they are used as nouns. We refer to these words as present participles.

ALERT

Do not confuse the present participle with the past participle. The past participle (see Chapter 12) is used in compound tenses such as the *passé composé,* the *plus-qu-parfait,* the subjunctive, and the *futur antérieur.* The present participle in French always has the equivalent of an English verb ending in "-ing," even if the word isn't being used as a verb.

In French, the present participle is based on the *nous* (us) form of the present indicative conjugation. To form the present participle, simply drop the *-ons* ending from the present conjugation of the *nous* form and replace it with *-ant.*

TABLE 6-36	PRESENT PARTICIPLES			
	INFINITIVE	*NOUS* FORM	PRESENT PARTICIPLE	ENGLISH
	parler (pahr-lay)	*parlons* (pahr-lohn)	*parlant* (pahr-lahn)	speaking
	courir (coo-rheer)	*courons* (coo-rhon)	*courant* (coo-rhahn)	running
	voir (vwahr)	*voyons* (vwoy-ohn)	*voyant* (vwoy-ahn)	seeing
	vouloir (voo-lwahr)	*voulons* (voo-lohn)	*voulant* (voo-lahn)	wanting
	étudier (ay-too-dee-ay)	*étudions* (ay-too-dee-ohn)	*étudiant* (ay-too-dee-ahn)	studying
	prendre (prahn-druh)	*prenons* (prahn-ohn)	*prenant* (prahn-ahn)	taking
	entendre (ahn-tahn-druh)	*entendons* (ahn-tahn-dohn)	*entendant* (ahn-tahn-dahn)	hearing
	travailler (trah-vy-ay)	*travaillons* (trah-vy-ohn)	*travaillant* (trah-vy-ahn)	working

Fortunately, there are only three irregular present participles: *avoir*, *être*, and *savoir*.

TABLE 6-37	IRREGULAR PRESENT PARTICIPLES		
	INFINITIVE	PRESENT PARTICIPLE	ENGLISH
	avoir (ah-vwahr)	*ayant* (ay-yahn)	having
	être (eh-truh)	*étant* (ay-tahn)	being
	savoir (sah-vwahr)	*sachant* (sa-shahn)	knowing

In English, we often use the present participle "-ing" form of a verb as the past participle in the present, but we also use it to form other compound tenses. Consider the following examples.

- I was walking to the store.
- I am speaking to the man.
- I will be going to Paris.

Take care not to confuse the French past participle with the English present participle. In compound tenses in French, it is the past participle that is used. English only has one participle, so it must pull double duty. French has two distinct and separate ones, so be careful with them. When translating from English to French, simply determine the actual tense of the verb and translate accordingly. Don't automatically assume that every time you see a word ending in "-ing" in English that the present participle will be used in French.

Present Participle as an Adjective

In English, we often use the participle as an adjective, using it to modify a noun. The present participle does the same thing in French. As an adjective, it must agree in gender and number with the noun it is being used to modify. The present participle is placed immediately after the noun when used in this construction. For example, *Il m'a dit une histoire amusante.* (He told me an amusing story.) *Amusant* is formed from the *nous* form of the verb *amuser.* The *-ons* ending is dropped from *amusons,* to form *amusant.* Because *histoire* is a feminine noun, the adjective must be modified to agree, so an "e" is added to the end.

Remember that, when used as an adjective, the present participle must agree with the noun it modifies, both in gender and in number.

Present Participle as a Noun

As mentioned above, the participle in English can also be used as a noun. Consider the following examples.

- Speaking is my favorite pastime.
- Reading is a fun hobby.
- I love singing songs.

Each of these "-ing" words is technically being used as a noun, even though they appear to be verbs. "Speaking" is the subject of the sentence; only things can be subjects, so a special construction is required. In English, this is accomplished using the participle; when used in this fashion, it is known as a gerund. The definition of a gerund is "a verbal noun," which basically means a verb that is being used in a sentence construction as a noun. Therefore, the participle can be the subject of the sentence or the object, as with "singing." In French, a gerund is represented by the infinitive of the verb, instead of using a participle: *Parler est mon passe-temps favori.* (Speaking is my favorite hobby.)

Of course, you don't have to use a gerund in English; you could also use the infinitive form in the English translation, forming "To speak is my favorite hobby," instead of using a gerund.

Don't worry about the fancy linguistic terms, though. To determine the difference between a participle and a gerund in English, see how it's being used. Whenever you come across a participle in English, run through the following points to determine what function it serves in the sentence:

- Is the participle being used as a verb in a compound construction? If so, then the participle is part of the verb; when translating into French, use the appropriate tense. If it is being used in the present tense, the French verb is conjugated in the present indicative, as the present indicative conjugation encompasses the English present participle in constructions like "I am walking."

    If the English participle is being used in the past tense, an auxiliary verb is required in French, with the past participle. If the participle is being used in the future tense, it will take either the future tense or the *futur antérieur,* depending on the sentence.
- Is the participle being used to modify a noun? If so, then the participle is an adjective, and the French present participle is used. Remember that it must match in gender and in number with the noun it is modifying.
- Is the participle being used as a noun? Does it appear as the subject or object of the sentence? If so, it is a gerund, and a participle is not used in French. Instead, an infinitive is used.
- Does it have the sense of "by," "while," or "upon" doing something? If so, the following construction, using *en,* is required. The preposition *en* is used in French with the present participle to convey the English sense of "by," "while," or "upon." This construction will often appear at the beginning of a sentence to set the mood or context of the sentence, for example: *En lisant, j'ai appris beaucoup d'information.* (By reading, I learned a great deal of information.)

When used in this fashion, the present participle is tied to the subject of the verb. Be careful when translating from English that the participle actually relates back to the subject; English is notorious for "dangling participles," which are participles that don't clearly relate back to a source. Try to determine exactly what is meant in the sentence and translate accordingly.

When translating from French to English, simply choose the form that makes the most sense within the context of the sentence. The preposition *en* can carry any of the three meanings, so use whichever seems appropriate to you to complete the meaning of the sentence.

Participles from the Past—Using Infinitives with *Après*

In English, we often say things like "After having read the first book, I started the second." "After having read" is a special construction that uses the participle in English. In French, instead of using the past or present participle, the infinitive form is used, much like the construction of the French gerund.

The preposition *après,* meaning "after," is used in French to achieve this result, in a construction known as the past infinitive. To form the past infinitive in French, simply use the infinitive of *avoir* or *être* and follow it with the French past participle.

- *Après avoir entendu, j'ai téléphoné à ma mère.* (After having heard, I called my mother.)
- *Après l'avoir vu, il est parti.* (After having seen it, he left.)
- *Après être revenu, je me suis couché.* (After having come back, I went to bed.)

When the auxiliary verb is *être,* even though it may appear before the subject of the sentence, the past participle still must agree in gender and number with the subject: *Après être revenues, elles se sont couchées.* (After having come back, they went to bed.)

Refer to Chapter 12 for more information on the agreement of past participles that use *être* as the auxiliary verb.

CHAPTER 7
Asking Questions and Giving Orders

This chapter helps you ask questions in a variety of ways (something you may need to do a lot of if you're traveling to a French-speaking country!) and give orders or imperatives, such as telling someone to "fetch me that French dictionary."

Asking Basic Questions

In French, there are a few different ways to ask a question. The most common are inversion, *est-ce que*, and intonation.

With Inversion

Inversion is only sometimes seen in written French; in spoken French, however, it is very common. It involves changing the word order in the sentence, putting the verb before the subject pronoun. English does the same thing. For example, "You are going to the store" is a declarative sentence. To create a question, you may ask, "Are you going to the store?"

"You," the subject pronoun, appears first in the declarative sentence, immediately before the verb, "are." In an inverted question, however, the verb begins the sentence and the pronoun directly follows the verb.

- *Comment allez-vous?*
- *Comment vous appelez-vous ?*
- *Parlez-vous anglais?*

In order to ask a question using inversion, the subject and object are reversed. In written French, a hyphen is placed between the two words to indicate their relationship. In spoken French, anytime you hear a verb come before the subject, remember that you're being asked a question.

With *Est-Ce Que*

Literally, *est-ce que* means "is it that," and is often placed at the beginning of sentences as a sort of marker to let listeners know that a question is coming. Unlike inversion, when *est-ce que* (pronounced *esskuh*) is used, there is no change in the order of the words in the rest of the sentence. It should not be translated literally, because it is just a pointer; the best English translation may be nothing more than a question mark. You can use *est-ce que* at the beginning of any sentence to turn it into a question.

With Intonation

It is common in spoken English for questions to end with a rising of the voice, such as when you ask "How are you?" The same happens in French. This is known as intonation.

Intonation is usually combined with other ways of asking a question; most French speakers will ask questions with intonation even when the other methods are used, too. In informal situations, intonation can even be used on its own to turn a regular sentence into a question without changing the word order or adding a phrase like *est-ce que*. In formal situations, however, you're better off using *est-ce que*.

Asking Questions with Interrogative Pronouns

In English, we often begin questions by asking "who" or "what." These are known as interrogative pronouns. French uses a similar set of interrogative pronouns that ask questions about unidentified people or things. The following section outlines their uses.

Asking Questions about People

Qui is the French interrogative pronoun used to ask questions about people. It has the English equivalent of "who" or "whom," depending on how it is used within the sentence. The following list explains the occasions when *qui* is used. Later in this section, you find out how to use similar constructions to ask questions about things.

Qui as the Subject of the Sentence

You can use *qui* to ask a question about someone by using it as the subject of the sentence. When used in this construction, the sentence does not need to be inverted, nor does *est-ce que* need to be used. *Qui* looks after the question for you; simply place it at the beginning of the sentence followed by a verb conjugated in the third person singular.

- *Qui est ici?* (Who is here?)
- *Qui est venu hier soir?* (Who came last night?)

You may also encounter the phrase *qui est-ce qui* used to start a question. This is just a longer way of doing things; the above construction works equally well and is preferred in most circumstances, but be aware that *qui est-ce qui* exists.

Qui as the Direct Object of the Sentence

Qui does not have to be the subject of the sentence; it can also be used as the object. When used in this way, the question must be formed a little differently, because the proper subject and verb must be used, along with one of the traditional ways of forming a question, using either *est-ce que* or inversion of the subject and verb. *Qui* is still placed at the beginning of the sentence, even though it is technically the object of the sentence.

* *Qui regardes-tu?* (Who are you looking at?)
* *Qui est-ce que tu regardes?* (Who are you looking at?)

Both of the above sentences actually mean the same thing; the only difference is in the form of the question. The different translations come from the fact that English can treat the construction a number of different ways. When *qui* is used as the direct object of the sentence, the correct English translation will probably be "whom." Although this is the correct grammatical form in English, it doesn't find popular usage; "who" is often used, especially in spoken English. Pay close attention to determine which is the subject and which is the object, and then position your pronouns appropriately.

Qui Used with a Preposition

When *qui* is used with a verb that normally takes a preposition (see Chapter 9) used with its object, the preposition is placed at the beginning of the sentence, with *qui* immediately following it. The rest of the sentence is then formed the same as if *qui* were simply appearing as the object, using *est-ce que* or inversion.

* *À qui avez-vous parlé?* (Who have you spoken to?)
* *À qui est-ce que tu as besoin de parler?*
  (Who do you need to talk to?)

When *qui* is used with a preposition, it appears as the object and may also translate as "whom" in English. The above sentences could also be translated as "To whom have you spoken?" and "To whom do you need to talk?" Refer to the previous point, *qui* as the direct object, for more information. For more information on prepositions, refer to Chapter 9.

Asking Other Kinds of Questions

When you're not asking specifically about a person, French uses a different construction. Instead of using *qui,* one of the following variations is used. You can use these interrogative pronouns to ask about actions, ideas, situations, and things, but never people.

Qu'est-Ce Qui as the Subject of the Sentence

This one will be relatively easy for you, as it is used whenever "what" is the subject of the sentence in English. Make sure, however, that "what" is in fact the subject of the sentence; if it is actually the object, the construction in the following point, *qu'est-ce que,* is used.

- *Qu'est-ce qui se passe dans le livre?*
  (What happens in the book?)
- *Qu'est-ce qui t'amuse de l'émission?*
  (What amused you about the broadcast?)

Because it is used as the subject of the sentence, the verb must used in the third person singular. Any pronouns you see between this phrase and the verb will be object or reflexive pronouns, not subject pronouns; don't let them confuse you into thinking that they are the actual subject. (See Chapters 9 and 13.)

Que as the Object of the Sentence

You must be careful when using these constructions in French, because English tends to put "what" at the beginning of the sentence, regardless of whether it's the direct object or the subject. Only when the word "what" forms the subject of the sentence is *qu'est-ce qui* used, as outlined above. Many times in English, the "what" that begins the section is actually the direct object. Consider the following English examples:

- What did you do last night?
- What are you doing at the hospital?
- What did you take to the game?

In all of these sentences, "what" is the direct object. "You" is the subject. Be careful not to get them confused, because the direct object interrogative pronoun takes a different form in French. *Que* is used as the interrogative pronoun, which translates in this case as "what." It must be used with either *est-ce que* or inversion; when it appears in front of a subject pronoun that begins with a vowel, it contracts, losing the final "e" and adding an apostrophe.

- *Qu'est-ce qu'il a fait hier soir?*
  (What did he do last night?)
- *Qu'est-ce que tu vas faire demain?*
  (What are you going to do tomorrow?)

In these examples, the subject pronoun is present, so if you come across such a construction, you'll know that it is an object. When *qui* is used immediately followed by a verb, you'll know that it is the subject. Study the English translations to see the difference in how the subject appears; be careful, because there is a verb that follows the word "what." Think of this as an English way of introducing the question, and pay close attention so that you don't try to make "what" the subject in French.

The word *que* doesn't always mean "what"; you will also encounter *que* in different contexts where it has other meanings. You will learn more about this in Chapter 9.

Quoi as the Object of a Preposition

Instead of using *que* as the object of the preposition, *quoi* is used instead. It also translates to "what" when used in this construction; its form follows the same pattern as *qui,* with the preposition appearing at the beginning of the sentence, being followed immediately by the interrogative pronoun. The rest of the sentence is constructed normally, using either *est-ce que* or inversion to complete the question.

- *À quoi as-tu joué la semaine dernière?*
  (What were you playing last week?)
- *De quoi est-ce que Phillipe a parlé?* (What was Phillip talking about?)

The majority of these uses will be idiomatic, as English verbs are often handled differently than in French when it comes to how prepositions are used. Refer to Chapter 6 for more information on verbs that use prepositions with their objects.

Other Uses of *Qu'est-Ce Que*

Qu'est-ce que can also be used to ask other kinds of questions, such as "What is that?" In French, this is done using variations of the French phrase *Qu'est-ce que c'est,* which means "What is it?" This construction can be used to ask for more information about something, when followed with a noun, or can ask for a general definition when used with a pronoun.

- *Qu'est-ce que c'est que ça?* (What is that?)
- *Qu'est-ce que c'est qu'une réponse vraie à la question?*
  (What is a correct response to the question?)
- *Qu'est-ce que c'est que le titre?* (What is the title?)

SSENTIALS

Qu'est-ce que c'est is a very common French phrase; when pronounced, it is completely run together, so it sounds like *kess kuh say.* It's pronounced a lot shorter than it looks, and if you try to pronounce it like it reads, you may not be understood.

Using the Interrogative Adjective *Quel*

In Chapters 9 and 10, you can learn a number of pronouns and adjectives. There is another adjective, *quel,* meaning "what" or "which," that you can also use to ask questions in French. As an adjective, it must agree in gender and number with the noun it is modifying. **TABLE 7-1** includes the available forms.

TABLE 7-1

	FORMS OF QUEL	
GENDER	SINGULAR	PLURAL
Masculine	quel	quels
Feminine	quelle	quelles

In Chapter 9, you can find out about the relative pronoun *lequel*. *Quel* is used in a very similar fashion, but it is used to ask a question meaning "what" or "which." The following list outlines the usage of the interrogative adjective *quel*.

Simple Questions

Quel can be used to begin the sentence and ask the question "what" or "which." The verb *être* is used, and the noun *quel* modifies is placed immediately following the verb.

- *Quel est ton nom?*
  (What is your name?)
- *Quelle est ta couleur préférée?*
  (What is your favorite color?)

Quel Modifying the Subject

Quel can also be used to modify the subject of a sentence. When this happens, *quel* begins the sentence, placed immediately before the noun that's acting as the subject of the sentence. *Quel* forms the question for you; you do not need to add *est-ce que* or use inversion in this construction, for example: *Quelle personne a écrit ce livre?* (Which person wrote this book?)

Quel Modifying the Object

Quel can also modify the object of a sentence. Simply place *quel* at the beginning of the sentence and place the noun it modifies immediately after it. Either *est-ce que* or inversion can then be used to complete the question.

- *Quel livre as-tu lu?*
  (What book did you read?)
- *Quel homme est-ce que vous avez vu?*
  (Which man did you see?)

Quel Modifying the Object of a Preposition

When *quel* is used to modify a noun that's being used as the object of a preposition, the preposition is placed at the beginning of the sentence, with the proper form of *quel* immediately following it. The noun being modified is then placed directly after *quel*, with inversion or *est-ce que* being used to complete the question. (When translating from French to English, you don't need to worry about precise grammar, as long as you're maintaining the meaning of the original French sentence, so a second translation is given.)

- *À quel magasin allez-vous?*
  (To which store are you going? Which store are you going to?)
- *De quel roman est-ce que tu parles?* (About which book are you speaking? Which book are you talking about?)

Each sentence, while not being grammatically perfect, is completely acceptable in English. In English as in French, we like to put the "what" at the beginning of the sentence. Although this ends up leaving prepositions at the end of the sentence, this is commonly done in English, so feel free to translate so that things sound normal and not stilted. For information on *quel*'s cousin, the relative pronoun *lequel*, refer to Chapter 9.

Using Interrogative Adverbs

Interrogative adverbs can be used in French to ask questions about location, time, manner, number, or cause. Normally, these adverbs are placed at the beginning of a sentence and used with *est-ce que*, inversion, or intonation to complete the question. See Chapter 11 for more on adverbs.

- *à quelle heure* (when, at what time): *À quelle heure est-tu parti hier?* (At what time did you leave yesterday?)
- *combien* (how much): *Combien est-ce que tu as payé cette blouse?* (How much did you pay for this blouse?)
- *combien de* (how many): *Combien de romans as-tu achetés?* (How many books did you buy?)
- *comment* (how): *Comment allez-vous aujourd'hui?* (How are you doing today?)
- *où* (where): *Où est la salle de bain?* (Where is the bathroom?)
- *pourquoi* (why): *Pourquoi n'allons nous pas à Paris?* (Why are we not going to Paris?)
- *quand* (when): *Quand est-ce qu'il arrivera?* (When will he get here?)

Giving Orders: The Imperative Verb Form

In English, we can tell people what to do by saying things like "go to the store" or "bring me a drink." Because it's a direct order to someone, there doesn't really need to be a subject pronoun, because you know who's supposed to do what in the conversation. In French, this operates much the same way and is done using the imperative form of the verb.

QUESTIONS?

How do I tell when to use *tu* or *vous* when addressing someone?
As a rule anytime you call someone Mr. or Mrs., use the *vous* form to maintain your level of politeness. As a matter of fact, think of using *tu* as like being on a first-name basis with someone. *Tu* should be used only with people you know well.

The imperative form of the verb is based on the present-tense conjugation (see Chapter 6). There are three possibilities using the imperative form. The first two use either the *tu* or the *vous* form of the verb, and the third uses the *nous* form. To form the imperative, simply drop the subject pronoun from the construction, which turns it into an order.

Tu Form

The *tu* form of the verb is used when you are giving an order to one person; usually, this is someone with whom you are fairly familiar. If you want to give an order to someone you don't know very well, use the *vous* form instead (see the following section). For verbs ending in *-er,* when the verb is used in the imperative, the "s" is dropped from the end of the *tu* form in written French. In spoken French, the "s" in the *tu* form isn't pronounced anyway, so you shouldn't notice much of a difference. This happens only with verbs ending in *-er,* however. The "s" is maintained at the end of the word in verbs ending in *-ir* and *-re.*

- *Porte la chemise rouge.* (Wear the red shirt.)
- *Finis le livre.* (Finish the book.)
- *Apprends la leçon.* (Learn the lesson.)

Nous Form

The *nous* form of the verb is used when saying the English equivalent of "Let's go to the mall" or "Let's go get a soda." This form of the imperative collects everyone together and makes them a group; in fact, the *nous* form is often referred to as the "collective" form in grammatical circles. Because you are included in the group, the *nous* form of the verb is used. If you are telling someone else to go and do something, and you are not included in the action, use the *vous* form in the preceding section.

- *Restons ici.* (Let's stay here.)
- *Partons maintenant.* (Let's go now.)
- *Lisons quelque chose.* (Let's read something.)

Vous Form

The *vous* form of the verb is used when giving an order to a group of people. In addition, it is used as a polite form when speaking with someone to whom you should show deference and respect.

- *Téléphonez à votre maman.* (Call your mother.)
- *Finissez le repas.* (Finish the meal.)
- *Lisez le journal.* (Read the newspaper.)

Negative Imperatives

When the imperative is used with negative expressions, it follows the normal negative construction (see Chapter 8), despite the absence of a subject pronoun. The *ne* is placed before the verb, and the *pas* or other negative modifier immediately after it.

- *Ne lisez pas ce livre-là.* (Do not read that book.)
- *Ne téléphone pas après minuit.* (Do not call after midnight.)

The imperative form of the verb can also be used with object pronouns. When there is only one, it is straightforward; you will have to pay closer attention when more than one is used, however. The pronouns follow a specific order, and each is tacked on to the end of the verb with a hyphen. The pronouns are added in the following order.

1. **Direct object:** When the imperative form is used with a direct object, the pronoun is placed after the verb and separated with a hyphen. This happens often with reflexive verbs, because the verb requires an object pronoun to complete its meaning. If the pronoun is *te,* the pronoun *toi* is used instead after the verb: *Dépêchez-vous* or *Dépêche-toi.* (Hurry up.) See Chapter 9 for the lowdown on pronouns.
2. **Indirect object:** When the imperative form is used with an indirect object pronoun, the pronoun is placed after the direct object but still joined to the verb phrase with a hyphen. If the indirect object pronoun is *me,* the pronoun *moi* is used: *Donne-moi le cahier.* (Give the notebook to me.)
3. **The pronoun** *y:* When the pronoun *y* is used, it is placed after any direct or indirect object pronouns: *Vas-y.* (Go there.)
4. **The pronoun** *en:* When the pronoun *en* is used in the imperative construction, it appears last but is still joined to the other words with a hyphen: *Donne-lui-en.* (Give some to him.)

If the imperative verb is being used with an object pronoun (see Chapter 9) that begins with a vowel, the "s" is kept at the end of the *tu* form: *Manges-en.* (Eat some.) This assists in pronunciation. A "t" is sometimes inserted in between an inverted verb and subject; that rule, however, applies only to inverted questions. When the imperative form appears with a pronoun, it will always be an object pronoun, so the rules for inverted questions do not apply.

FACTS

Remember that when pronouns are used with the imperative, they are object pronouns and not subject pronouns. The *nous* and *vous* forms can be particularly problematic because their forms don't change between the subject and object. You will often encounter this with reflexive verbs (see Chapter 13); the only way you can really distinguish between the pronouns is to recognize the reflexive verb.

Irregular Imperative Verb Forms

The imperative can be used with irregular verbs. This section shows the forms of the four most common irregular verbs, *être, avoir, faire,* and *aller.* Familiarize yourself with them so that you can recognize them on sight. If you forget about one of the forms and don't recognize it when you come across it, the fact that it is used without a subject pronoun should help to jog your memory.

Être

The forms of *être* are completely irregular. Instead of using the present indicative conjugation, the following forms must be used:

- *Tu* form: sois
- *Nous* form: soyons
- *Vous* form: soyez

Avoir

Like *être, avoir* also has unique formations in the imperative.

- *Tu* form: aie
- *Nous* form: ayons
- *Vous* form: ayez

Faire

Faire is unique in that even though it's an irregular verb, it follows the regular conjugation pattern, using the present indicative conjugated form.

- *Tu* form: *fais*
- *Nous* form: *faisons*
- *Vous* form: *faites*

Aller

Aller forms the imperative much like the regular *-er* verbs, dropping the "s" from the end of the *tu* form. When the *tu* form *va* is used with an object pronoun such as *y*, it takes an "s," to form *vas-y*. When pronounced, it sounds like *vazz-ee*.

- *Tu* form: *va*
- *Nous* form: *allons*
- *Vous* form: *allez*

CHAPTER 8

Negating Words and Phrases

If you've read other chapters in this book, you've probably seen *ne . . . pas* used to make negative statements. It is equivalent to the English "not;" it is probably the most common negative expression you will encounter. Naturally, there are more. *Ne* is almost always a part of the construction, but other words can be used in place of *pas* to create other negative expressions.

Negative Expressions

When using a negative expression, *ne* is placed before the verb and *pas* is placed immediately after. If a different negative expression is being used, it also is placed immediately after the verb: *Tu ne parles pas français.* (You are **not** speaking French.)

As a result of elision, if the verb begins with a vowel, the "e" is dropped from *ne* and an apostrophe is used: *Je n'ai pas de lait.* (I **don't** have any milk.)

In spoken French, the *ne* can be left out of the negative expression, which can make a conversation harder to follow. In addition, the *ne* is used only in sentences that have a verb. If the sentences don't have one, the negative word is used on its own:

- *Pas moi.* (Not me.)
- *Pas de problème.* (No problem.)

If you want to make negative expressions other than "not," you can use the following negative expressions after *ne,* in place of *pas.* There are others, but these comprise the most common of the expressions; for now, they're all you need to know.

Jamais

Jamais means "never," as in the following:

- *Je n'ai jamais de stylo.* (I never have a pen.)
- *Nous n'avons jamais raison.* (We are never right.)

Pas Encore

Pas encore means "not yet." Here's an example: *Il n'a pas encore le livre.* (He doesn't have the book yet.)

Que

Que means "only," as in the following: *Il n'a que le dictionnaire.* (He only has the dictionary.)

Plus

Plus means "no longer," as in the following: *Je n'ai plus le cahier.* (I no longer have the notebook.)

Rien

Rien means "nothing," as in: *Je n'ai rien.* (I have nothing; I don't have anything.)

Personne

Personne means "no one," as in: *Je n'aime personne.* (I like no one; I don't like anyone.)

In spoken French, the *ne* can be omitted from negative expressions. Listen for negative expressions. Remember that statements may be negative despite the absence of *ne*, so you can't rely on it as a signpost in a conversation.

Responding to Negative Questions

Normally, *oui* is the word for "yes." After a negative expression, however, French uses a different word, *si*, to answer in the affirmative. *Non* is used to agree with the negative expression. To refute it, use *si*.

TABLE 8-1	RESPONDING TO NEGATIVE QUESTIONS	
QUESTION	ANSWER USING *NON*	ANSWER USING *SI*
Est-ce que tu n'as pas les clefs?	*Non, je n'ai pas les clefs.*	*Si, j'ai les clefs.*
You don't have the keys?	No, I don't have the keys.	Yes, I have the keys.

Negative Conjunctions (Neither . . . Nor)

You can use another construction as the equivalent of the English "neither . . . nor" when referring to more than one thing in the negative. The

French construction uses the word *ni,* which acts like both the English "neither" and "nor." Think of this as an idiomatic expression; when translating, simply insert the English word that seems most appropriate.

As a general rule, expect to see *ni* twice in each sentence. It is used with the negative pointer *ne* as the negative form of conjunctions like *et,* meaning "and," or *ou,* meaning "where," to convey the opposite meaning.

The negative conjunctions can be used with nouns that are acting either as the subject or as the object of the sentence. When used with two nouns that are acting as the subject, a *ni* is placed before each subject, and the *ne* is placed immediately in front of the verb. Because there are two subjects, the verb will be conjugated in the plural: *Ni Alain ni Paul n'est allé ici.* Neither Alain nor Paul came here.

When used with the object, the negative conjunction follows the same predictable pattern as *ne . . . pas* constructions; the *ni* is simply repeated. In addition, you don't have to retain the French negative conjunctions if they don't make a lot of sense in English. Feel free to use an English translation that more appropriately reflects the meaning of the sentence. With *ni . . . ni* expressions, it doesn't always make sense to translate literally.

- *Est-ce que tu as vu ce film-ci ou ce film-là?*
  (Did you see this film or that film?)
- *Je n'ai vu ni ce film-ci ni ce film-là.*
  (I saw neither this film nor that one; I didn't see either film.)

If the negative conjunction *ni . . . ni* is used in front of nouns that take an indefinite article or a partitive article when used in the non-negative sense, the articles disappear when cast into a negative construction. If the partitive is used in the non-negative construction, the English sentence may retain a sense of "some" or "any" when cast in the negative.

- *As-tu de la farine ou du lait?* (Do you have any flour or milk?)
- *Non, je n'ai ni farine ni lait.* (No, I have neither flour nor milk; No, I don't have any flour or milk.)

You can also use *ni . . . ni* with verb actions to indicate that two things were not done, instead of just one. In this construction, the *ni* is used only one time, before the second verb. The subject of the sentence appears only one time, because the conjunction serves to join the second verb to the subject: *Il ne parle ni lit.* (He is not reading or speaking.)

In French, each individual part must be made negative using the *ni*. Consider the example above. The "not" applies both to reading and speaking in English; it is possible to say "he is not reading, nor is he speaking," but "he is not reading nor speaking" sounds absurd. Don't translate literally; use whichever English phrase makes the most sense.

Negative conjunctions can be used with the infinitive form of a verb, too, when used with other verbs. This construction follows the typical negative pattern, with each *ni* being placed before each infinitive form, and the *ne* being placed before the conjugated verb:

Je ne dois ni manger ni dormir en ce moment. (I don't have to eat or sleep right now.)

Negative Pronouns

Negative pronouns operate slightly differently from the negative expressions in the rest of this chapter, because many of the expressions in this section can be used both as a subject and an object of a sentence. When they are used as the subject, the main word is placed at the beginning of the word in the subject position and the *ne* follows it in its regular position after the subject but before the verb.

The following negative pronouns, with the exception of *nul,* can be used as either the subject or the object of the sentence. The main difference between the negative pronouns and the negative adjectives is that the pronouns can stand on their own, while the negative adjectives require a noun to modify them. Remember that when these pronouns (discussed in Chapter 9) are used in the place of the subject of the sentence, they are used with a singular verb, and the *ne* takes its normal position after the subject.

Ne . . . Aucun
This will usually be the primary choice when referring to "no one" or "not one," unless one of the following forms happens to be more appropriate. As a general rule, it is hard to go wrong if you stick with *aucun.*

Ne . . . Nul

When used as a subject pronoun, this expression (which means "no one," "nobody" or "not one") tends to be much more formal than any of the others; as a matter of fact, you may only ever encounter it in formal literary situations. (You are unlikely to encounter this negative pronoun in spoken French.) Remember, also, that this pronoun, when it is used, can be used only as the subject.

Ne . . . Pas Un

This expression, which means "not one" or "not even one," is a much more emphatic form than the previous two pronouns and is used only in rare cases.

Ne . . . Personne

Personne (which means "no one" or "nobody"), when used as an object, is slightly unique compared to the other negative expressions, including adjectives, adverbs, and pronouns. Instead of placing the word immediately after the conjugated verb in tenses like the *passé composé* or *plus-que-parfait* (see Chapter 12), *personne* is placed after the past participle. When it is used as the subject of the sentence, it follows the same pattern as the other negative pronouns.

Ne . . . Rien

This expression, which means "nothing" or "not anything," is usually used as the opposite of *quelque chose*, meaning "something," or *tout*, meaning "all." It can be used as an object, where it follows the regular construction pattern in the negative. If the expression is used with an infinitive, you must place *à* in between the negative expression and the infinitive form of the verb.

Negative Adverbs

Many of the negative expressions in this chapter are actually adverbs, used to modify the verb in a negative sense—in fact, *ne . . . pas* is an adverb! Some are used in special situations or to convey certain meanings, so study the subtleties. For practice, use the following negative adverbs to convert sentences to negative expressions—either make up sentences or practice with the examples in this book, turning those into negative expressions using these adverbs. See Chapter 11 for more on adverbs.

Ne . . . Aucunement

This expression, which means "not at all" or "not in the least," is an emphatic form compared to *ne . . . pas*; use it when you want to make absolutely sure that your listeners appreciate the intensity of your objection.

FACTS

Adjectives can also be used with nouns to create negative expressions, and their construction looks like that of negative pronouns:

- *ne . . . aucun* (none, not one, not any): This is often used to negate statements made using its opposite words, like *quelques* or *tous*. This is by far the most commonly used negative adjective.
- *ne . . . nul* (no, not any, not one): This expression is slightly less emphatic than *ne . . . aucun*; you may not come across it as often.
- *ne . . . pas un* (not one, not even one): This is a much more emphatic form than the previous two negative adjectives. It can be accompanied by *seul*, creating *pas un seul*, meaning "not a one" or "not many."

Ne . . . Guère

This expression, which means "not much," "not very," or "only a little," is the rough equivalent to such French phrases as *pas beaucoup, pas très, peu de, presque pas*, and *à peine*. Whenever those meanings are intended, you can use *ne . . . guère* to achieve the same result.

Ne . . . Jamais

While *ne . . . jamais* means "never," when *jamais* is used without the *ne* in French, it holds the opposite meaning of "ever;" be careful not to get them confused. It can be used as the opposite of *toujours, quelquefois, parfois, souvent, de temps en temps*, and *de temps à autre*.

Ne . . . Nulle Part

This expression, which means "nowhere," is the opposite of *partout* or *quelque part*; when used in sentences with a past participle, the negative adverb is placed after the past participle, instead of before it, like the other negative adverbs. When used to negate an infinitive expression, *nulle part* is placed after the infinitive; again, unlike the others, they are placed before the infinitive.

Ne . . . Nullement

This expression, which means "not at all" or "by no means," is like *ne . . . aucunement*: an emphatic form of *ne . . . pas* that can be used to express an absolute disagreement with a statement or an out-and-out denial of some point made by another speaker.

Ne . . . Pas du Tout

This expression, which means "not at all," is nearly identically to *ne . . . aucunement* and *ne . . . nullement*. It can also be used as an emphatic form of *ne . . . pas*.

Ne . . . Pas Encore

This expression, which means "not yet," is the opposite of *déjà*, which means "already." This negative adverb is very close in meaning to *ne . . . toujours pas*, covered later in this section.

Ne . . . Pas . . . Non Plus

This construction, which means "no longer," can also be used in response to a negative question posed using *pas*. In that case, it is the opposite of *aussi*, meaning "also" or "too." When used in this sense, the best English equivalent is probably "either," as in "not me, either."

Ne . . . Plus

This expression, which means "no longer," is basically an opposite construction of *encore* or *toujours*. As a matter of fact, it will often be the appropriate choice when responding in the negative to a question asked with *encore* or *toujours*. It can also be used to indicate an action, event, or circumstance that existed in the past but has since ceased.

Ne . . . Point

Point tends to be an archaic negative adverb, used seldom in modern French. When it is used, however, it is more emphatic than *pas*, even though it means close to the same thing: "no," "not at all," or "none." This tends to be a literary adverb; you may encounter it in written French, especially French from an earlier time period.

Ne . . . Que

This is technically not a negative statement (it means "only"), but rather a limiting one that uses *ne*, so it certainly looks like a negative construction. It basically carries the same meaning as *seulement*. If the word *que* is already used in the sentence for another purpose, however, you cannot use *ne . . . que* to denote "only;" you must use *seulement*.

Sans

While this isn't technically a negative expression (it means "without"), it can end up with that result. As a matter of fact, it can even replace the expression *ne . . . pas* to negate the sentence. To add to the confusion, *sans* can also be used instead of the *ne* with all of the other negative expressions, so watch for its usage and remember that it sometimes has the effect of making the sentence negative, even when no other negative expressions appear. In such a case, making the sentence negative may be a preferable English construction when you're trying to translate from the French.

Ne . . . Toujours Pas

While this basically shares the same meaning as *ne . . . pas encore*, it also carries with it a sense of impatience or apprehension: "not yet." It does not carry the same meaning as *pas toujours*, which means "not always," so don't confuse the two expressions.

CHAPTER 9
Utilizing Objects, Prepositions, and Pronouns

This chapter covers a potluck meal of French grammar: direct and indirect objects, prepositions, and four types of pronouns: subject, object, demonstrative, and relative. Not sure what any of this means? That's okay. This chapter explains these concepts both in terms of English grammar and your newly acquired French skills.

Direct and Indirect Objects

The subject of the sentence (see Chapter 5 for the lowdown on nouns) is the person or thing that performs the action indicated by the verb (see Chapter 6). There is another component to the sentence—the object, or the thing that receives the action of the verb.

There are two kinds of objects—direct objects and indirect objects.

Direct objects receive the action of the verb directly; whatever is being described by the verb is happening to the direct object. To understand how the direct object works, consider the following example: *Il a une auto.* (He has **a car**.)

The verb used in this sentence is *avoir,* or "to have." The subject, as indicated by *il,* is the person who is performing the action of the verb. "The car," placed after the verb, is the thing receiving the action of the verb "to have." It is the thing being affected by the verb.

The indirect object is usually fairly easy to determine in French. It always appears with a preposition (see the following section), which will be your major clue: *Il a donné le cadeaux à moi.* (He gave the present **to me**.) In English, however, determining the indirect object can pose more difficulties. Consider the following example: I gave her the present.

Where is the indirect object in this sentence? It's actually hidden in an English linguistic quirk; quite often, the indirect object is placed directly after the verb; with this construction, no preposition is needed. (Restructure the sentence as "I gave the present to her," and the indirect object becomes more visible.)

In French, however, this never happens, because a preposition is always placed before the indirect object, even when there is no actual direct object used in the sentence, as often happens with some verbs: *Elle a parlé à Pierre.* (She spoke to Pierre.) In the preceding example, the direct object is, in a way, inferred; you could insert *français* or even *mots,* meaning words in general; when the verb is used, this meaning is understood, or assumed.

When translating from French to English, you should have no problem with direct and indirect objects; when translating from English to French, however, extra caution is needed. In English, you have to break the sentence down to make sure that you are conveying the proper meaning when translating into French. You cannot simply rely on word order to determine direct or indirect objects.

As noted, *parler* is a verb that can be used with an indirect object and still make sense despite the absence of a direct object: *Elle a parlé à Pierre.* (She spoke to Pierre.) The direct object is understood to be *français* (French) or *mots* (words). Verbs that can be used without a direct object are known as intransitive verbs.

Avoir (to have) on the other hand, cannot be used in this way. It is a transitive verb and, therefore, requires a direct object. If you think about it, you have to have something "to have" before you can do anything with it indirectly.

QUESTIONS?

Why can't I directly translate English and French transitive verbs?
The English equivalents of transitive verbs are not always used in the same manner as in French, so be careful with them. Never try to translate word for word; instead, take apart the meaning of the sentence and translate that.

TABLE 9-1 gives you some common transitive verbs that take a direct object. In order to remember that they are transitive, try to imagine them being used without a direct object as you read over the list.

TABLE 9-1

FRENCH TRANSITIVE VERBS		
VERB	**PRONUNCIATION**	**ENGLISH**
aider	eh-day	to help (someone)
attendre	ah-tahn-druh	to wait (for something or someone)
chercher	sher-shay	to look (for something or someone)
écouter	ay-koo-tay	to listen (to something or someone)
entendre	ahn-tahn-druh	to hear (something or someone)
regarder	rhuh-gahr-day	to watch (something or someone)
voir	vwahr	to see (something or someone)

TABLE 9-2 contains some verbs that can be used in an intransitive sense. All will affect something indirectly (the indirect object) and are indicated with the preposition *à* (see the following section). These verbs may not function in the same way as their English counterparts, so don't translate word for word. In order to help you remember these verbs, the preposition is listed along with the verb; say them out loud together as you read the list.

TABLE 9-2

FRENCH INTRANSITIVE VERBS		
VERB	PRONUNCIATION	ENGLISH
obéir à	oh-bay-ear ah	to obey (someone)
parler à	par-lay ah	to speak (to someone)
plaire à	plehr ah	to please (someone)
ressembler à	ruh-sahm-blay ah	to look like, to resemble (someone)
téléphoner à	tay-lay-fohn-ay ah	to telephone (someone)

Prepositions

Prepositions are small words that are used in front of nouns and articles. English words like "to," "with," "in," and "on" are prepositions. When prepositions are used in a sentence, they take an object, which basically means that the preposition must have a noun following it. In other words, the preposition must have a noun to complete its meaning.

English grammar tells you never to end a sentence with a preposition, but this rule is often ignored in common usage. In French, a preposition cannot be used without a noun following it, so if you find yourself using a preposition at the end of a sentence, you'd better find a noun to put after it.

In English, many verbs, when used with a preposition, take on a slightly different meaning, such as "to go out."

Like English, French has a number of prepositions. This section lists some common ones.

The Preposition À

The preposition *à* ("ah," like the "a" sound in "hat") is one of the most versatile in the language. It can have a wide variety of meanings, including "at," "to," "in," "of," and "by"; the meaning will usually be associated with the noun, as follows:

- *à Paris* (in Paris)
- *à pied* (on foot)
- *à la pharmacie* (at the pharmacy)

The preposition *à* sometimes contracts when used with a definite article. The following table shows how the various definite articles are used with the preposition.

TABLE 9-3

DEFINITE ARTICLES USED WITH *À*			
ARTICLE	RESULT	ARTICLE	RESULT
le	*au*	*l'*	*à l'*
la	*à la*	*les*	*aux*

The following list illustrates the different functions *à* can perform, including the English equivalents to the constructions.

Location or Destination

Use *à* to indicate a location or destination, as in the following examples:

- *J'habite aux Etats-Unis.* (I live in the United States.)
- *Nous avons été au magasin.* (We were at the store.)
- *Je suis allé à Paris.* (I went to Paris.)

Distance

À can also be used to indicate a degree of separation in either time or space, as follows:

- *Il habite à un kilomètre de moi.* (He lives one kilometer from me.)
- *Je suis à dix minutes de l'école.*
  (I am ten minutes away from the school.)

Specific Points in Time

À can be used to refer to specific hours or moments, including calendar dates, as follows: *Il arrivera à dix heures.* (He will arrive at ten o'clock.)

Characteristics or Manner

À can be used to indicate the fashion in which something is done or the characteristics of something that exists:

- *J'ai vu le garçon aux cheveux blonds.* (I saw the boy with blond hair.)
- *Elle fait la cuisine à la française.* (She is cooking in the French way.)

Possession

When the preposition *à* is used to indicate possession, it is a little more emphatic than when a possessive pronoun or the preposition *de* is used to indicate the owner. Use this construction only when you want to make absolutely certain that everyone understands what you mean, because it can carry that much gravity, as the following examples illustrate:

- *Cette voiture est à moi, pas lui.* (This car is mine, not his.)
- *Non, je lis le roman à Pierre.* (No, I am reading Pierre's book.)

To Describe How the Action of a Verb Is Performed

Use *à* to describe exactly how verbs are performed: *Ils font leurs devoirs à la main.* (They are doing their homework by hand.)

To Describe Weights and Measures

Use *à* for weights and measures:

- *J'avais acheté la farine au kilo.* (I used to buy flour by the kilogram.)
- *Ils boivent la bière au verre.* (They drink beer by the glass.)

To Describe the Function or Purpose of an Item

Use *à* to describe the function or purpose of an item:

- *Je porterai mon sac à dos.* (I will be wearing my backpack.)
- *La recette prend un cuillère à soupe de beurre.* (The recipe takes a tablespoon of butter.)

Après

Après (*ap-reh*) means "after," when referring to time, either in a direct or indirect sense, as follows:

- *après dîner* (after dinner)
- *après 5h00* (after 5:00)

Après can sometimes be used with verbs; you can find out more about this in Chapter 6. The *grave* accent isn't pronounced, but think of it as a reminder not to turn the ending into an "ay" sound.

ESSENTIALS

In French, time is referred to differently than in English. Instead of saying "five o'clock," the French simply say "five hours," or *cinq heures*. When the time is written, rather than use a colon, a small *h* is used to indicate the *heures*.

Avant

Avant (*avahn*) means "before," when referring to time. It also gets combined with other words, such as *avant-bras*, to make "forearm," and *avant-première* to become "dress rehearsal." Note the following other examples:

- *avant le dîner* (before dinner)
- *avant midi* (before noon)

Avec

Avec (*avek*) means "with" and functions very closely to the usage of the English preposition: *avec un sourire* (with a smile).

Chez

Chez (*shay*) is a convenient little French word that often takes a number of English words to translate. It is used with names or personal pronouns, and conveys a sense of habitual residence. Possible English translations include "at the home of" and "at the office of." In less formal speech, *chez Pierre* could even be translated as "at Pierre's place."

Dans

Dans (*dahn,* like the beginning of "dawn") means "in." When translating from English to French, however, be careful, because *à* can sometimes be the proper choice. When referring to time, it can also mean "during." Note the following examples:

- *dans la voiture* (in the car)
- *dans la journée* (during the day)

De

De (*de,* similar to the pronunciation of *le*) is another versatile French preposition. Normally, it means "of" or "from," as in *de Paris* (from Paris), but it also has other uses, including being used as the partitive article (see Chapter 4). *De* is used extensively throughout the French language.

Depuis

Depuis (*de-pwee*) is used to indicate a sense of time. It can mean "since" or "for" and is used with events that began at some point in the past but are still occurring, as in the following examples:

- *depuis cinq ans* (for five years)
- *depuis hier* (since yesterday)

En

En (*ahn,* with a very soft "n") is another versatile preposition. Because it can be used in such a wide variety of situations, it can be difficult to translate. Its meanings include "in," "on," "to," "as," "like," and "by," depending on its usage. In addition to the following examples, see Chapter 7 for more uses of *en.*

- *en huit jours* (in eight days)
- *en enfant* (like a child)
- *en avion* (by plane)
- *en pied* (by foot)

Pendant

Pendant (*pehn-dahn,* with the final "t" silent), which means "during" or "while," can be easily confused with *depuis* or the following preposition in this list, *pour*. *Pendant* is used only when speaking about events in the past or future. It is not used in the present tense.

- *pendant mes vacances* (during my vaction)
- *pendant deux ans* (for two years)

Pour

Pour (*poohr*) also means "for" and will be the most common translation for "for" in English. It can also be used to refer to time, but only when used with events that will occur in the future. Note the following examples:

- *pour vous* (for you)
- *pour trois ans* (for three years)

When making French sentences involving concepts of time, be careful not to confuse the prepositions *pour, depuis,* and *pendant.* Each has a specific meaning and is used for a particular purpose. Using the wrong preposition will likely cause confusion amongst your listeners.

Sans

Like its opposite *avec, sans* (*sahn*), which means "without," is used much the same as in English, as in the following examples:

- *sans amour* (without love)
- *sans toi* (without you)

Sur

Sur (*soohr,* like "sure" without the "sh" sound) normally means "on," but can sometimes translated as "at," "in," or "about," as in the following examples:

- *sur le bureau* (on the desk)
- *deux dentistes sur cinq* (two in five dentists)

Vers

Vers (*vehr*) can mean "toward" or "around" and can be used in both a physical sense and to convey a sense of time, as in the following examples:

- *vers New York* (toward New York)
- *vers Boston* (around Boston)
- *vers midi* (around noon)

Subject Pronouns

Sentences in French are formed, for the most part, in the same way that they are formed in English. Every sentence must have a subject to do something and a verb to indicate what the subject is doing. You can always find your way around the sentence when you know who's doing what. Sentences can get more complex when other words, like prepositions or direct objects, are added, but if you can identify the subject and verb, the other words fall into place.

There are three kinds of subjects—first person, second person, and third person. The following sentences demonstrate the English subject pronouns in action. Reviewing these will help you better understand the French subject pronouns.

- First person: **I** am going to the store.
- Second person: **You** are going to the store.
- Third person: **She** is going to the store.

Each of the above also has a plural form. In English, the plural forms would be:

- **First person: We** are going to the store.
- **Second person: You** are going to the store.
- **Third person: They** are going to the store.

In a sense, French uses the exact same subject pronouns as English, but they're spelled and pronounced differently. Maybe that seems silly, but this is one of the only times that French and English operate in a nearly identical fashion. There are some subtle things to remember about French subject pronouns, which you'll learn about in this section, but for the most part, when you see one, you can pretty well just replace the corresponding English word. Luckily, subjects will be one of the easiest topics you'll learn.

TABLE 9-4

FRENCH SUBJECT PRONOUNS		
PERSON	SINGULAR	PLURAL
1st Person	*je* (jhe), I	*nous,* (noo), we
2nd Person	*tu* (tchoo), you	*vous* (voo), you
3rd Person	*il* (eel), he	*ils* (eel), they
	elle (ell), she	*elles* (ell), they

FACTS

In French, the subject of a sentence usually ends up being a pronoun; this often happens in English, too. "We," "you," "they," "I," "he," "she," and "it" are all examples of English pronouns that commonly get used as subjects in sentences. If you think about it, most of our conversations take place using pronouns, without ever using an actual noun. The same is true in French.

Note the following slight differences between the way these pronouns are used in English and French:

- English doesn't have a separate second person form to distinguish between singular and plural. French does, so when formulating sentences, you will have to be careful that you make the appropriate choice. *Tu* is singular, so it is used when talking to one other person. *Vous* is plural and is used for two or more people.

- *Vous* can also be used when speaking to a single person. In formal situations, *vous* is a polite way of addressing another individual. It's a good rule of thumb to use *vous* to address people; it is considered polite and courteous. Use *tu* only when speaking to people with whom you share some level of familiarity. Strangers should be addressed using *vous*.

- *Il*, the masculine singular subject pronoun, is equivalent to the English word "he," and is used when referring to a masculine subject. *Elle* is used when referring to a female subject.

- In the plural, *elles* is only used when referring to more than two female subjects. If all the members of the group to which you are referring are not female or if the sex is not known, *ils* is used as the subject pronoun. It may help to think of *ils* as "they" in general, including but not limited to males, while *elles* can only be used when the pronoun is replacing female subjects.

Whenever the plural subject pronouns are used with a verb that begins with a vowel, the "s" sound gets tacked on to the beginning of the next word. This is a result of liaison, which is discussed in Chapter 1.

Object Pronouns

Just like subject pronouns are used to represent subjects, you can use object pronouns to represent objects, too. This way, you don't have to repeat the proper words of nouns over and over in conversation. You can use object pronouns to represent these nouns, in some cases making your sentences considerably shorter. Naturally, when pronouns are used, you have the potential for some ambiguity, but you can usually figure out who's talking about what fairly easily.

In English, the most common object pronoun is "it." It is used in a variety of senses, and sometimes, you don't even realize that it's being used. It represents a noun and in the sentence becomes a shorthand way of referring to that noun so you don't have to keep repeating the same words over and over. Object pronouns make your sentences more economical.

Object pronouns are often used both in written and spoken French, but they cannot be used until a noun is introduced in the conversation to replace. Otherwise, the pronoun has no meaning. Remember that a pronoun has to link back to another noun in some way, in order to define it; a pronoun used without this relationship has no meaning at all.

Direct Object Pronouns

When a noun is being used in a sentence as the direct object, the following object pronouns are used.

TABLE 9-5	FRENCH DIRECT OBJECT PRONOUNS	
PERSON	SINGULAR	PLURAL
1st Person	*me* (muh), me	*nous* (noo), us
2nd Person	*te* (tuh), you	*vous* (voo), you
3rd Person Masculine	*le* (le), him, it	*les* (lay), them
3rd Person Feminine	*la* (la), her, it	*les* (lay), them

When these pronouns are used to replace a noun in a sentence, they are inserted before the verb. This is much different from English, which tends to maintain the normal word order and places the pronoun after the verb: *As-tu conduis cette auto?* (Do you drive **this car**?) *Oui, je le conduis.* (Yes, I drive **it**.)

When a singular object pronoun appears before a verb that begins with a vowel, it contracts with the verb; simply drop the vowel from the end of the pronoun and add an apostrophe: *Avez-vous vu mon père?* (Have you seen **my father**?) *Non, nous ne l'avons pas vu.* (No, we have not seen **him**.)

When the object pronoun is used with an infinitive (see Chapter 6), the pronoun is placed directly before it. Be careful that you don't distort the meaning of sentences by accidentally placing your object pronoun with a conjugated verb, instead of with the infinitive where it should be: *Vas-tu finir tes devoirs?* (Are you going to finish **your homework**?) *Oui, je vais les finir.* (Yes, I am going finish **it**.)

Remember that you can't translate object pronouns directly from one language to the other; the preceding example is a good illustration of one of the reasons it doesn't work.

Some French verbs handle objects differently than English does. Therefore, you have to get to the heart of the true meaning of the sentence before you can start translating any words. You can get away with it when translating a lot of sentences that use actual nouns, but when object pronouns are used, sentences get a little more complicated. As long as you remember to identify which noun is which before you translate, you should have few problems.

Indirect Object Pronouns

In English, we tend to use the same object pronouns for both the direct and indirect object, using prepositions or word order to convey the intended meaning. This is not the case in French. The object pronouns differ slightly and are not interchangeable, but the only actual difference is in the third person formation.

TABLE 9-6

FRENCH INDIRECT OBJECT PRONOUNS		
PERSON	**SINGULAR**	**PLURAL**
1st Person	*me* (muh), me	*nous* (noo), us
2nd Person	*te* (tuh), you	*vous* (voo), you
3rd Person Masculine	*lui* (lwee), him	*leur* (leuhr), them
3rd Person Feminine	*lui* (lwee), her	*leur* (leuhr), them

As you can see, there is really no gender distinction in the third person for indirect object pronouns; the same word suffices for both. In addition, the other forms don't modify to agree with gender, just like the subject pronouns. Don't confuse the object pronouns with possessive adjectives (see Chapter 10), which must agree in gender and number with their counterpart nouns.

If you try to translate the sentences below word for word, it doesn't work. You have to study the sentence to determine which word is the direct object and which is the indirect object. The word order doesn't help you in French; all object pronouns follow a certain order, no matter what they are being used to represent. The meaning comes from the verb and the context of the sentence.

Normally, the preposition *à* is used to introduce the noun that represents the indirect object in the sentence. When a pronoun is used instead before the conjugated form of the verb, it replaces both the noun and the preposition, so the preposition disappears from the sentence.

- *Mon copain le donne à moi.* (My friend is giving it **to me**.)
- *Mon copain me le donne.* (My friend is giving it **to me**.)

The indirect object pronoun replaces the preposition entirely. Other prepositions follow different constructions when used with object pronouns.

Uses of Disjunctive Pronouns

Disjunctive pronouns are another set of object pronouns. They are similar to the other object pronouns, but vary in the formation of the third person. These pronouns are often used with prepositions placed after the noun.

TABLE 9-7

FRENCH DISJUNCTIVE PRONOUNS		
PERSON	SINGULAR	PLURAL
1st Person	*moi* (mwah), me	*nous* (noo), us
2nd Person	*toi* (twah), you	*vous* (voo), you
3rd Person Masculine	*lui* (lwee), him	*eux* (euh), them
3rd Person Feminine	*elle* (ell), her	*elles* (ell), them

If the disjunctive pronoun happens to be used before the conjugated verb, *me* and *te* are used for the first person and second person singular forms, instead. You shouldn't need to worry about the kind of pronoun being used; for the most part, the meaning should be fairly obvious, becomes it comes into play only with "me" or "you." From the way these words are used, you should be able to tell easily how each person fits in the sentence.

This may seem confusing, because so many of the different types of pronouns seem to use all the same words. Knowing what kind of pronoun is required isn't as important as knowing which one to use, so don't worry if you can't figure out whether a pronoun is an object or disjunctive pronoun. It really only becomes an issue in the third person, and after you get used to using the proper pronouns, you fall into it quite naturally.

In addition to being used as object complements, disjunctive pronouns can be used in other cases, too. The following list describes some of these uses, showing the wide variety of places you may come across these pronouns.

For Emphasis

Inserting the disjunctive pronoun in the sentence can emphasize the subject or the object. When used in this sense, the pronoun doesn't actually replace the subject or object that it modifies; it is used in addition to it.

- *Avez-vous vu le film?* (Have you seen the film?) *Nous, nous ne l'avons pas vu, mais Sara l'a vu.* (**Us**? No, we haven't seen it, but Sara has seen it.)
- *Moi, je n'aime pas regarder la télé.* (**Myself**, I don't like watching TV.)

Literally, this looks like "Me, I don't like watching TV," but this translation just doesn't make that much sense in English. Rather than translate the words, try to translate the sentiment involved. Perhaps the most appropriate choice in English for the above sentence is "I don't like watching TV, myself."

In addition, when used to complement the subject, these pronouns may be placed either at the beginning or the end of the sentence. When used to complement an object, however, the disjunctive pronoun used for emphasis is always placed at the end. The fact that either the subject or the object can appear at the end of the sentence shouldn't cause too much of a problem for you. To tell which is which, simply look at the subject. If the disjunctive pronoun matches it in gender and number, the emphasis is on the subject; if they don't, then you'll find that they match the object.

- *Je ne l'ai pas vu, moi.* (I didn't see him, myself.)
- *Oui, je l'ai vu, lui.* (Yes, I saw him.)

To Form Compound Subjects or Objects

The disjunctive pronoun can be used with another noun at the beginning of a sentence. When this happens, the noun is placed first, with the disjunctive pronoun following it. In the first or second person, the subject pronoun is used with the verb, separated from the preceding noun and disjunctive pronoun with a comma. They are joined together using the conjunction *et*:

- *Jean et moi, nous allons au cinéma.*
  (John and I, we are going to the movies.)
- *Moi et toi, nous étions toujours les amis vrais.*
  (You and I, we have always been true friends.)

When used as an object, the noun is placed first, with the pronoun placed after it:

- *Il a téléphoné à Jacques et moi.* (He called me and Jacques.)
- *Il a donné le cahier à Sara et moi.*
  (He gave the notebook to me and Sara.)

You can also use two disjunctive pronouns to form a compound subject or object; these, like the others, are joined with the conjunction *et*: *Je vais aller à Paris avec toi et lui.* (I am going to go to Paris with you and him.)

In the third person, the subject pronoun is omitted, and the compound subject stands as the subject for the verb. Remember that in the first and second person, however, the subject pronoun is required: *Lui et elle ont une maison à Québec.* (He and she have a house in Quebec.)

Alone in Response to a Question

The subject pronoun can never appear without a verb, but a disjunctive pronoun can. For that reason, when responding to a question when you just want to answer something like "me" or "him," the disjunctive pronoun is the appropriate choice: *Qui fait ça?* (Who is doing that?) *Moi.* (Me.)

In Conjunction with Certain Verb Phrases, When Used to Indicate a Person

The disjunctive pronoun is placed after the preposition *à*. See the "Prepositions" section earlier in this chapter for the lowdown on *à*.

- *être à* (to belong to someone)
- *faire attention à* (to pay attention to someone)
- *penser à* (to think about someone)
- *présenter à* (to give something to someone)
- *tenir à* (to be attached to someone, to be related to someone)

Here are some examples:

- *Mon chien est à moi.* (My dog belongs to me.)
- *Je n'aime pas le professeur. Il ne fait jamais attention à moi.* (I don't like the professor. He never pays attention to me.)
- *Je pense souvent à lui.* (I often think about him.)

The disjunctive pronoun can be used with only the preceding verbs when a person is the object. If the object happens to be a thing, a different pronoun, *y*, is used.

To Make Comparisons Between People

When used in this sense, the disjunctive pronoun is used with the conjunction *que*, which carries the meaning of "than," and placed at the end of the sentence, after the verb: *Il est plus intelligent que moi.* (He is smarter than I.)

English comparative phrases follow a different construction than French. You will often hear phrases in English like "he is smarter than me," but these are not grammatically correct. In English, the subject pronoun must be used; the verb ("am") is inferred. The French construction is very similar to the wrong English one, so you'll probably find yourself getting it right anyway, but it's still a good idea to learn the proper way to construct English sentences!

To Indicate "Myself" or Its Equivalent

The disjunctive pronoun can be used with *-même* added to the end of it to represent the English usage of words like "myself" or "himself." This isn't an exact equivalent; rather, the *-même* ending reinforces and amplifies the disjunctive pronoun, so the most appropriate English translation is usually a variation of "myself": *Il est allé à Québec lui-même.* (He went to Quebec himself.)

In English, we also use words like "myself" or "yourself" in conjunction with verbs to indicate that an action is being performed by the subject, on the subject; "I am washing myself" is an example. In French, these are known as reflexive verbs—see Chapter 13.

After the Preposition *De*

When the object of the preposition *de* is a person, the preposition uses the corresponding disjunctive pronoun. The preposition remains in the sentence, retaining its usual location after the verb, and the disjunctive pronoun is placed immediately after it. If the disjunctive pronoun begins with a vowel, *de* contracts to *d'*.

- *Est-ce que tu as parlé de Sara?* (Did you talk about Sara?)
- *Oui, j'ai parlé d'elle.* (Yes, I talked about her.)

Remember that the disjunctive pronoun can be used only when referring to actual people. If things, locations, ideas, or anything else that isn't a person are used in the sentence, a disjunctive pronoun cannot be used; instead, the object pronoun *en* is used.

The Object Pronoun *En*

When the preposition *de* is used with an object to indicate a thing, the object pronoun *en* is used to replace the preposition and the noun. *En* is never used in the place of people; only the disjunctive pronouns can be used if the object of the preposition *de* is a person: *Est-ce que tu as beaucoup de stylos?* (Do you have a lot of pens?) *Oui, j'en ai beaucoup.* (Yes, I have many of them.)

FACTS

If the sentences use an expression of quantity, as with *assez de* or *beaucoup de,* or even uses a number, *en* replaces the noun. If the preposition *de* is used in the sentence, *en* replaces it, but if a number is used, the number remains in the sentence, in its regular position, without the noun. Here's an example: *Il a écrit deux romans.* (He wrote two novels.) *C'est vrai? Il en a écrit deux?* (Is that right? He wrote two of them?)

If *de* is being used in the partitive sense, to indicate the English equivalent of "some" or "any," it is not a preposition; instead, it behaves like an article. Don't confuse the preposition *de* with the plural indefinite article *des,* either; if you see *des* being used, you know that it is not the preposition. For more information on indefinite and partitive articles, refer to Chapter 4.

The Object Pronoun Y

The direct object pronoun **y** is a versatile French word. For that reason, it can sometimes be confusing, because it can be hard to link back to a noun to give it meaning. If you keep the following points in mind, deciphering the actual intended meaning of **y** should be much easier for you.

Y is used only when the object it represents is a thing. It can never be used to represent an actual person or even an animate object, for that matter. If you come across the object pronoun **y** being used in either spoken or written French, you know that it must refer to some inanimate object or place that has already been referred to in the conversation or passage.

The appropriate English translation of **y** is usually either "there" or "it," depending on the particular context of the sentence. The object pronoun **y** is used to replace both the preposition *à* and a noun, much as in the way the indirect object pronouns work for people.

*   *Est-ce que tu es allé au magasin?* (Did you go **to the store**?)
    Oui, j'y suis allé. (Yes, I went **there**.)
*   *Avez-vous répondu à la lettre?* (Did you reply **to the letter**?)
    Non, je n'y ai pas répondu. (No, I have not replied to **it**.)

When the object pronoun y represents a feminine noun, the past participle agrees if the verb is conjugated using *avoir*; the same holds true when it is used to replace plural nouns. Because y is an object pronoun, the past participle must agree both in gender and in number when the pronoun appears before the conjugated auxiliary verb.

The object pronoun y doesn't stop there, either. It can also be used to replace other prepositions, such as *dans, sous,* and *devant,* that indicate location. When used in this fashion, it replaces both the preposition and noun, in the same way as with *à*: *Dormirez-vous dans la chambre?* (Will you be sleeping **in the bedroom**?) *Oui, nous y dormirons.* (Yes, we will be sleeping **there**.)

Demonstrative Pronouns

You can use demonstrative adjectives in French to demonstrate the concept of "this" or "that" in English. Instead of having to repeat the noun over and over, French also has demonstrative pronouns you can use to indicate "this one" or "that one." French demonstrative pronouns can never be used on their own; they must be used in a construction with other words. **TABLE 9-8** shows they basic demonstrative pronoun forms. Note their similarities to the object pronouns covered earlier in the chapter.

TABLE 9-8

FRENCH DEMONSTRATIVE PRONOUNS		
GENDER	SINGULAR	PLURAL
Masculine	*celui* (seh-lwee)	*ceux* (seuh)
Feminine	*celle* (sehll)	*celles* (sehll)

Demonstrative pronouns can be used with *-ci* and *-là* to indicate "this one" or "that one." This usage follows the same pattern as with the demonstrative adjectives; the *-ci* or *-là* is simply added to the end of the appropriate demonstrative pronoun:

- *Veux-tu ce livre-ci ou ce livre-là?* (Do you want this book or that book?)
- *Je veux celui-ci, s'il vous plaît.* (I would like this one, please.)
- *Je veux celui-là, s'il vous plaît.* (I would like that one, please.)

Relative Pronouns

A relative pronoun is a pronoun that relates back to something else already mentioned. This sounds a little like all pronouns, except that relative pronouns relate back to something already mentioned within the sentence. Other pronouns are normally used when nouns have been mentioned within the conversation, but not necessarily that sentence.

In English, we encounter relative pronouns all the time, in the form of "that," "who," "whom," "what," and "which." In French, relative pronouns operate differently. Instead of having many separate words, the same ones are used, with the meanings depending on the construction of the sentence.

Relative pronouns are normally used to introduce another thought or idea into the sentence. Consider the following English sentence: The boy **who lives down on the farm** is my friend. If you strip this sentence to the bare essentials, it boils down to "the boy is my friend." The "who lives down on the farm" is included as explanation, expanding the meaning of the sentence and clarifying (in this case) the subject. This part of the sentence is known as a subordinate clause; the word in the sentence that it modifies ("boy") is known as the antecedent.

The subordinate clause is not necessarily integral to the meaning of the sentence; it is a separate idea but included for more information. The sentence can stand alone without it. When you encounter such sentences, isolate the phrase that can be stripped out: This is your subordinate clause. To translate it into French, you must use the correct French relative pronoun, which may not be obvious from the construction of the English sentence.

Relative pronouns in English are often omitted, so you may have to do a bit of detective work in breaking down the sentence in order to translate it. English is notorious for dropping the word "that" from the sentence, but the presence of its equivalent is very much a necessity in French. Other English relative pronouns get omitted, too, but not nearly as frequently as with "that." No matter which relative pronoun you are using in English, in French it cannot be omitted.

Like the interrogative pronouns in Chapter 7, the appropriate English translation is based on how the relative pronoun is used in the subordinate clause, depending on whether it is being used as the subject or the object of the clause. This section outlines the combinations that can occur.

Relative Pronoun as the Subject of the Clause

When the relative pronoun is used as the subject of the clause, the pronoun *qui* is used in French to represent both people and things. An easy way to find out whether the English relative pronoun is the subject of the clause is to see if the clause already has a subject and verb inside it. If it does not, *qui* is used as the subject of the clause, with the verb and the rest of the clause immediately following it. The entire clause is then placed after the noun it modifies in the sentence. Note the following examples:

- *Il est l'homme qui m'a donné un cadeau.*
  (He is the man who gave me a present.)
- *Une femme qui était ma voisine est allée ici.*
  (A woman who used to be my neighbor came here.)

Relative Pronoun as the Object of the Clause

If the subordinate clause has a subject already, there's a good chance that the relative pronoun is going to appear as the object. You can also check the clause by seeing whether the person represented by the pronoun is performing the action or receiving it. If the person represented by the pronoun is performing the action, the pronoun is the subject of the clause. Receiving the action puts the relative pronoun into the object class: *La jeune fille que j'ai rencontrée à Paris est venue ici.* (The young lady whom I met in Paris came here.)

In the above example, the pronoun "whom" may sound a little stilted; many English speakers now just (incorrectly) say "who" or drop the relative pronoun entirely, saying "The young lady I met in Paris came here," which is also perfectly acceptable. In French, these pronouns cannot be ignored. They must be included or the sentence won't have a complete meaning.

Relative Pronouns as the Object of a Preposition

When the relative pronoun is used as the object of a preposition, a number of things can occur. If the relative pronoun is being used to represent a person, *qui* is the correct form to place after the preposition, which retains its normal place in the sentence. You don't have to rearrange any words in the sentence; you can simply insert the subordinate clause immediately after the preposition: *Il est le copain avec qui j'ai travaillé.* (He is the friend with whom I used to work; he is the friend I used to work with.)

When the relative pronoun is being used to represent a thing, however, an alternate form is used. The pronoun *lequel* is simply a combination of a definite article and the word *quel.* When put together, they mean "which" or "that."

TABLE 9-9

THE RELATIVE PRONOUN *LEQUEL*		
GENDER	SINGULAR	PLURAL
Masculine	*lequel* (le-kell)	*lesquels* (lay-kell)
Feminine	*laquelle* (la-kell)	*lesquelles* (lay-kell)

ESSENTIALS

Here's an example: *C'est la chemise pour laquelle j'ai payé beaucoup d'argent.* (It's the blouse for which I paid a lot of money; it's the blouse I paid a lot of money for.)

If the pronoun *lequel* is being used after the preposition *à*, the following contractions occur, following the same rules used for the contraction of the preposition *à* and the definite article.

TABLE 9-10

CONTRACTIONS OF *LEQUEL* WITH *À*		
GENDER	SINGULAR	PLURAL
Masculine	*auquel* (oh-kell)	*auxquels* (oh-kell)
Feminine	*à laquelle* (ah la-kell)	*auxquelles* (oh-kell)

Consider this example: *Le golf est le jeu auquel j'ai toujours aimé.* (Golf is the game that I have always loved; golf is the game I have always loved.)

The English language seems to love placing prepositions at the end of sentences; it happens all the time. In French, it cannot happen, especially when using relative pronouns. The preposition is very much required. It must retain its place in the sentence, and the subordinate clause must be placed with it or the proper meaning is not conveyed. When translating from English, you may have to take a moment to figure out what the preposition is actually modifying to get a proper translation.

The preposition *de* also takes a unique form when used with relative pronouns that represent things. Instead of using one of the regular relative pronouns, *dont* is used. This looks very much like the English word "don't," but it is not a negative word. It can mean "that" or "which," depending on how it is used in the sentence; because it replaces all forms, it can also mean "who" or "whom." Check out these examples:

- *Je n'ai pas vu l'homme dont tu parlais.* (I did not see the man you were speaking of; I did not see the man you were talking about.)
- *Donnez-moi le livre dont j'ai besoin.* (Give me the book that I need; give the book I need.)

Relative Pronouns Without an Antecedent

Sometimes, you may want to use a relative pronoun when there is nothing for it to relate back to. When this occurs, simply insert the demonstrative adjective *ce* before the relative pronoun. It is the English equivalent of "that which," which basically just provides a word for the relative pronoun to relate to so it isn't lost on its own, as in the following:

- *Achetez ce dont vous avez besoin.* (Buy what you need.)
- *Ce dont il a peur est un mystère.* (What he fears is a mystery.)

Ce can be used with any of the relative pronouns in this section. Simply place it before the relative pronoun. For more information on the demonstrative adjective *ce,* refer to Chapter 10.

The Relative Pronoun *Où*

Whenever the antecedent involves time, the relative pronoun *où* must be used, instead of any of the others. It will most often be translated as "when," but in English, the relative pronoun may be omitted entirely. In French, remember that it must be present: *Je me rappelle du jour où je l'ai rencontré.* (I remember the day when I met him; I remember the day I met him.)

The relative pronoun *où* looks a lot like the conjunction *ou*, which means "or." Don't confuse the two. In written French, the accent must appear over the *u* when the word is used as a relative pronoun, because they are two different and distinct words. In spoken French, you cannot hear any difference in the pronunciation.

If the relative pronoun is being used with a preposition and the pronoun represents something that can be interpreted as a location, the relative pronoun *où* replaces the preposition. In English, this can be translated a number of ways; "in which," "where," "at which," and "from which" are examples. If the antecedent is a place where something else occurs, you'll want to use the pronoun *où*: *J'ai vu le magasin où tu as acheté ces livres.* (I saw the store at which you bought these books; I saw the store where you bought these books.)

Just because the antecedent is a location, however, doesn't always mean that the relative pronoun *où* will be used. Only when the relative pronoun is being used to represent a location and is preceded by a preposition does the pronoun *où* get used. When there is no preposition in front of the relative pronoun, you must use the regular *que* or *qui* form, depending on whether it represents the direct object or indirect object of the subordinate clause.

Reported Speech

Sometimes, you want to construct a sentence in which you say what someone else said, but without quoting that person directly. This is known as reported speech, because you're simply recounting the events, rather than using the words that were actually spoken. In English, we do this using the word "that": "He said that he was going to the store."

In French, speech is reported using the relative pronoun *que*. Simply begin the sentence with something that introduces the phrase, like *il m'a dit* for "he told me," and continue with your sentence. Here are some examples:

- *Il a dit que je suis leur copain.* (He said that I am their friend.)
- *Elle m'a dit que le film commence à deux heures.* (She told me that the film starts at two o'clock.)

Remember that you are reporting this speech and not quoting directly. All pronouns should be from your perspective and not from the perspective of the person whose speech you're reporting. If you use a phrase like "he asked me" to begin the sentence, remember that it is not a question anymore. You are simply reporting that the person asked it. As a result, no question mark is placed at the end of the sentence. A simple period is used.

CHAPTER 10

Using Adjectives

Adjectives, from a grammatical perspective, are words that are used to modify nouns. They are the words that help describe a noun, adding depth and meaning. Words like "blue," "big," "bold," and "brilliant" are all examples. Adjectives can be used to create rich and colorful sentences; their addition to your arsenal of French words will allow you to create much more complex—and interesting—sentences.

Basic Adjective Use

Most French adjectives are similar to our English ones, but some operate in quite a different fashion. As with much of the French language, a literal translation is not always appropriate, but don't worry. Because they receive such frequent usage, you will quickly get used to them.

Adjectives are versatile words that can attach themselves to nouns. They modify their endings to agree with the noun in number and in gender, so an adjective used with a masculine noun will have a different ending than one used with a feminine noun, and plural nouns will have a special form, too. Some adjectives follow simple patterns for matching the number or gender, but some follow very irregular patterns, too. As with the rest of the language, the more you practice and use adjectives, the more natural it will all seem to you.

Gender Agreement of Adjectives

Naturally, there are rules for adjectives and their agreement with other words. **TABLE 10-1** contains a number of special formations used by different adjectives to agree with the nouns they are modifying, showing how the different kinds of adjectives found in French change to agree with the gender of the noun.

As a basic rule, to make an adjective agree with a feminine noun, you simply add an "e" to the end of the masculine form. This works with the majority of adjectives.

TABLE 10-1

GENDER AGREEMENT OF ADJECTIVES			
MASCULINE	**FEMININE**	**PRONUNCIATION**	**ENGLISH**
grand	*grande*	grahn, grahnd	large, big
court	*courte*	koor, koort	short, brief, concise,
courtois	*courtoise*	koor-twah, koor-twahz	courteous, polite
fermé	*fermée*	fehr-may, fehr-mayy	closed
intelligent	*intelligente*	in-tel-ee-jhan, in-tel-ee-jhant	intelligent, smart

MASCULINE	FEMININE	PRONUNCIATION	ENGLISH
vrai	*vraie*	vreh, vreh	true, real, right
français	*française*	frahn-seh, frahn-sez	French
amusant	*amusante*	ah-moo-zahn, ah-moo-zahnt	amusing, entertaining

Consider the following examples:

- *Il est grand.* (He is tall.)
- *Elle était courtoise.* (She was polite.)
- *Elles sont françaises.* (They are French.)

ALERT

Note that when the masculine form of an adjective ends in é, another "e" is added to make it agree with a feminine noun. To help you remember this, consider the common English practice of referring to a male about to be wed as a *fiancé* and his future wife as his *fiancée*. Remember that if the masculine form ends in "e," however, nothing is added to the feminine form.

Masculine Adjectives Ending in *-e*

If the masculine form of the adjective already ends in an "e," nothing is added in the feminine; the word is simply used with the same ending.

TABLE 10-2

MASCULINE ADJECTIVES ENDING IN *-E*			
MASCULINE	FEMININE	PRONUNCIATION	ENGLISH
calme	*calme*	kahm	tranquil, quiet, calm
moderne	*moderne*	maw-dern	modern, up-to-date
riche	*riche*	reesh	rich, wealthy, valuable
tranquille	*tranquille*	trahn-keel	quiet, calm, tranquil, peaceful
utile	*utile*	oo-teel	useful, beneficial

Pay attention to these types of adjectives; when the other kinds of adjectives are modified to agree with a feminine noun, it makes it easier to determine which noun the adjective is modifying. When the form doesn't change, it can introduce an element of ambiguity, so be careful.

- *Ma maison est moderne.*
  (My house is modern.)
- *J'ai acheté un livre utile.*
  (I bought a useful book.)

Masculine Adjectives Ending in *-er*

Most masculine adjectives that end in *-er* change their endings to *-ère* to agree in the feminine. This is also a very common form, appearing frequently throughout the French language. The ***accent grave*** that is added to the end of word to form the feminine ensures that the "r" sound is distinctly pronounced, lingering much longer than in the masculine, so that you can actually hear the difference and tell by the sound which gender is intended.

TABLE 10-3

MASCULINE ADJECTIVES ENDING IN -ER			
MASCULINE	**FEMININE**	**PRONUNCIATION**	**ENGLISH**
cher	*chère*	shaihr	dear, precious, expensive
dernier	*dernière*	daihr-nee-yay, daihr-nee-aihr	last, latest
étranger	*étrangère*	ay-trahn-jhay, ay-trahn-jhaihr	foreign, unknown, strange
premier	*première*	pruh-mee-ay, pruh-mee-aihr	first

Review the following examples:

- *Nous avons regardé un film étranger.*
  (We watched a foreign film.)
- *Il a mangé le premier morceau de gâteau.*
  (He ate the first piece of cake.)

Masculine Adjectives Ending in *-f*

Adjectives that end in *-f* change their endings to *-ve* in the feminine; this is very similar to the English pattern of forming plurals, such as turning "wolf" into "wolves." Remember that in French, this change occurs with the gender, not the number. Watch that you don't accidentally change the "f" to "ve" when creating a masculine plural; you'll find out about forming the plural of adjectives in the following section.

TABLE 10-4

MASCULINE ADJECTIVES ENDING IN *-F*			
MASCULINE	**FEMININE**	**PRONUNCIATION**	**ENGLISH**
actif	*active*	ak-teef, ak-teev	active, busy, energetic
bref	*brève*	brhef, brhev	short, brief, concise
neuf	*neuve*	noof, noove	new, brand-new
vif	*vive*	veef, veev	alive, live, living

Examples are as follows:

- *L'enfant est actif.*
  (The child is energetic.)
- *Avez-vous vu mon stylo neuf?*
  (Did you see my new pen?)

Watch out for the word *neu f* —it can mean "nine," but when it is used as an adjective to modify another noun, it means "new." If the form *neuve* is used, that's a dead giveaway that the word definitely isn't meant to indicate "nine," but take care not to confuse the masculine form *(neuf)* with the number "nine."

Masculine Adjectives Ending in *-teur*

Many masculine adjectives that end in *-teur* change their endings to *-trice* to agree in the feminine. Note, however, that some adjectives ending in *-teur* form the feminine by following the *-eur* rules, covered in the following section.

TABLE 10-5

MASCULINE ADJECTIVES ENDING IN -TEUR			
MASCULINE	FEMININE	PRONUNCIATION	ENGLISH
admirateur	admiratrice	ahd-mee-rah-tuhr, ad-mee-rah-treece	admirer
conservateur	conservatrice	kon-sehr-va-tuhr, kon-sehr-va-treece	conservative, preserving
créateur	créatrice	kray-ah-tuhr, kray-ah-treece	creative, inventive
évocateur	évocatrice	ay-vok-ah-tuhr, ay-vok-ah-treece	evocative

The following examples show these endings in action:

- *Pierre est mon ami conservateur.* (Pierre is my conservative friend.)
- *Il porte des vêtements évocateurs.* (He is wearing evocative clothing.)

Masculine Adjectives Ending in *-eur*

Although there are exceptions, a great deal of adjectives that end in -eur change their endings to -euse to agree in the feminine.

TABLE 10-6

MASCULINE ADJECTIVES ENDING IN -EUR			
MASCULINE	FEMININE	PRONUNCIATION	ENGLISH
flatteur	flatteuse	flah-tuhr, flah-tooze	flattering, complimentary
menteur	menteuse	mahn-tuhr, mahn-tooze	lying, false, deceitful
trompeur	trompeuse	trahm-puhr, trahm-pooze	deceitful, false, misleading
voleur	voleuse	vo-luhr, vo-looze	thief, robber, person who steals

The following examples show the -eur ending in action:

- *Il est voleur.* (He is a thief.)

- *Elle est une femme menteuse.* (She is a deceitful woman.)
- *Tu portes des vêtements flatteurs.* (You are wearing flattering clothes.)

Some relatively rare adjectives that end in *-eur* that will take the form *-eresse* in the feminine. While these are not all that common, you should still be able to recognize the feminine form when you come across it, such as the following: *J'ai vu une femme enchanteresse.* (I saw an enchanting woman.)

TABLE 10-7

MASCULINE ADJECTIVES ENDING IN -*EUR* THAT TAKE THE FORM -*ERESSE*			
MASCULINE	**FEMININE**	**PRONUNCIATION**	**ENGLISH**
enchanteur	*enchanteresse*	ahn-shahn-tuhr, ahn-shahn-tuh-ress	enchanting
pécheur	*pécheresse*	pay-shuhr, pay-shuh-ress	sinning

The following adjectives that end in *-eur* are slightly irregular, in that they simply add an "e" to form agreement in the feminine. Familiarize yourself with these adjectives, as the feminine forms do not use an "s" anywhere in the construction.

TABLE 10-8

MASCULINE ADJECTIVES ENDING IN -*EUR* THAT ADD AN -*E*			
MASCULINE	**FEMININE**	**PRONUNCIATION**	**ENGLISH**
antérieur	*antérieure*	ahn-tay-ree-er, ahn-tay-ree-uhr	anterior, earlier, previous, former
extérieur	*extérieure*	eks-tay-ree-er, eks-tay-ree-uhr	exterior, external
inférieur	*inférieure*	ahn-fay-ree-er, ahn-fay-ree-uhr	inferior, lower
intérieur	*intérieure*	ahn-tay-ree-er, ahn-tay-ree-uhr	interior, inner, internal
majeur	*majeure*	may-jhehr, may-jhuhr	major, main, chief, greater

TABLE 10-8

MASCULINE ADJECTIVES ENDING IN -EUR THAT ADD AN -E (CONTINUED)			
MASCULINE	FEMININE	PRONUNCIATION	ENGLISH
meilleur	meilleure	may-er, may-uhr	better
mineur	mineure	mee-ner, mee-nuhr	lesser, minor
postérieur	postérieure	pah-stay-ree-er, pah-stay-ree-uhr	posterior, later, behind
supérieur	supérieure	soo-pay-ree-er, soo-pay-ree-uhr	superior, upper, higher

Note the following examples:

- *La salade est le choix meilleur.* (The salad is the better choice.)
- *Il a reçu l'emploi supérieur.* (He received the superior job.)
- *Nous avons fini la parte majeure.* (We have finished the major part.)

SSENTIALS

If you're having trouble with the feminine forms of certain adjectives, try looking up the adjective in a French-English dictionary. It will spell out the proper feminine ending for you. Remember that when looking up adjectives, dictionary entries will be found under the masculine form of the word.

Masculine Adjectives Ending in -et

Masculine adjectives that end in -*et* become -*ète* to agree in the feminine, also changing the "e" before the "t" to an "e" with an *accent grave*. This results in a more distinct pronunciation of the last syllable, so the final "t" sound is easier to hear when the adjective is used to agree in the feminine.

TABLE 10-9

MASCULINE ADJECTIVES ENDING IN -ET			
MASCULINE	FEMININE	PRONUNCIATION	ENGLISH
complet	complète	com-pleh, com-plett	complete, whole
concret	concrète	con-creh, con-crett	concrete, solid
discret	discrète	dis-creh, dis-crett	discreet, cautious, shy

MASCULINE	FEMININE	PRONUNCIATION	ENGLISH
inquiet	*inquiète*	ahn-kee-eh, ahn-kee-ett	anxious, restless
replet	*replète*	reh-pleh, re-plett	obese, stout

Take a look at the following examples:

- *J'ai vu le film complet.* (I saw the whole film.)
- *Il a posé une question discrète.* (He asked a discreet question.)
- *Il est un homme replet.* (He is a stout man.)

Masculine Adjectives Ending in a Single Consonant

For some masculine adjectives that end in a single consonant, the final consonant is doubled, and an "e" added to the end to form the feminine.

TABLE 10-10

MASCULINE ADJECTIVES ENDING IN A SINGLE CONSONANT			
MASCULINE	FEMININE	PRONUNCIATION	ENGLISH
tel	*telle*	tehl, tell	such
actuel	*actuelle*	ak-choo-el, ak-choo-ell	present, current
cruel	*cruelle*	kroo-el, kroo-ell	cruel, merciless
culturel	*culturelle*	kul-tuhr-el, kul-tuhr-ell	cultural
essentiel	*essentielle*	ess-ahn-chee-el, ess-ahn-chee-ell	essential
habituel	*habituelle*	ah-bee-choo-el, ah-bee-choo-ell	habitual
naturel	*naturelle*	nah-tuhr-el, nah-tuhr-ell	natural
nouvel	*nouvelle*	noov-el, noov-ell	new
traditionnel	*traditionelle*	trah-dee-see-ohn-el, trah-dee-see-ohn-ell	traditional
universel	*universelle*	ooh-nee-vehr-sel, ooh-nee-vehr-sell	universal

TABLE 10-10	MASCULINE ADJECTIVES ENDING IN A SINGLE CONSONANT (CONTINUED)		
MASCULINE	**FEMININE**	**PRONUNCIATION**	**ENGLISH**
usuel	usuelle	oo-zoo-el, oo-zoo-ell	usual
gentil	gentille	jhahn-tee, jhahn-teey	kind, gentle
pareil	pareille	pehr-ay, pehr-ayy	similar, equal
ancien	ancienne	ahn-see-yehn, ahn-see-yenn	ancient, antique
canadien	canadienne	can-ah-dee-ehn, can-ah-dee-enn	Canadian
égyptien	égyptienne	ay-jhip-shehn, ay-jhip-shenn	Egyptian
européen	européenne	oohr-op-ay-ehn, oohr-op-ay-enn	European
israélien	israélienne	iz-ray-lee-en, iz-ray-lee-enn	Israeli
italien	italienne	eet-ahl-ee-en, eet-ahl-ee-enn	Italian
moyen	moyenne	mwoy-en, mwoy-enn	middle
parisien	parisienne	pahr-ee-zee-en, pahr-ee-zee-enn	Parisian
quotidien	quotidienne	kwo-ti-dee-en, kwo-ti-dee-enn	daily
bon	bonne	bohn, bonn	good, kind, favorable
bas	basse	bah, bass	low, inferior
épais	épaisse	ay-peh, ay-pess	thick, dense
gras	grasse	grah, grahss	fat, greasy, rich
gros	grosse	groh, gross	big, large, bulky
las	lasse	la, lass	tired, weary, bored

The following gives examples for several different adjective endings:

- *J'ai assisté à événement culturel à Paris.*
(I attended a cultural event in Paris.)
- *L'amour est la langue universelle.* (Love is the universal language.)
- *Le français est une langue essentielle.*
(French is an essential language.)
- *Ma mère est européenne.* (My mother is European.)
- *David est un homme canadien.* (David is a Canadian man.)
- *J'étais l'enfant moyen.* (I was the middle child.)
- *J'ai entendu un bruit dans la forêt épaisse.*
(I heard a noise in the dense forest.)

Masculine Adjectives Ending in *-eux*

Masculine adjectives that end in *-eux* change their endings to *-euse* to agree in the feminine.

TABLE 10-11

MASCULINE ADJECTIVES ENDING IN *-EUX*			
MASCULINE	FEMININE	PRONUNCIATION	ENGLISH
amoureux	amoureuse	ah-mhu-rhoo, ah-mhu-rhuze	loving, enamored, in love
douloureux	douloureuse	doo-loo-rhroo, doo-loo-rhuze	painful, hurting, sore
ennuyeux	ennuyeuse	ahnn-wee-ooh, ann-wee-ooze	boring, tedious, dull, tiresome
heureux	heureuse	ehrr-oo, ehrr-ooze	happy, blissful
jaloux	jalouse	jha-loo, jha-looze	jealous, envious
nombreux	nombreuse	nom-broo, nom-brooze	numerous, harmonious

Consider the following examples:

- *Je suis heureux.* (I am happy.)
- *Elle est jalouse.* (She is jealous)
- *Pierre est un homme amoureux.* (Pierre is a man in love.)

Masculine Adjectives Ending in *-gu*

When the masculine form of an adjective ends in *-gu*, an "e" with a *tréma* is added to the end, to form *-guë*. This results in distinct pronunciations for the masculine and feminine forms, sounding a lot like *goo-ay*.

TABLE 10-12

MASCULINE ADJECTIVES ENDING IN *-GU*			
MASCULINE	FEMININE	PRONUNCIATION	ENGLISH
aigu	aiguë	ay-goo, ay-goo-ay	pointed, sharp, keen, acute
ambigu	ambiguë	am-bee-goo, am-bee-goo-ay	ambiguous
contigu	contiguë	con-tee-goo, con-tee-gay	adjoining, contiguous

The following examples demonstrate this ending:

- *Il a un crayon aigu.* (He has a sharp pencil.)
- *Elle a posé une question ambiguë.* (She asked an ambiguous question.)

Irregular Adjectives

Some adjectives have completely irregular feminine forms. Although the feminine forms of these adjectives will have to be memorized individually, they tend to be fairly commonly used, so it shouldn't take you too long to become familiar with them.

TABLE 10-13

IRREGULAR ADJECTIVES			
MASCULINE	FEMININE	PRONUNCIATION	ENGLISH
blanc	blanche	blahnc, blahnsh	white, clean, blank
doux	douce	doo, dooce	sweet, gentle, calm, fresh
grec	grecque	grehk, greck	Greek, Grecian
faux	fausse	foe, foess	false, wrong, untrue, fake, forged
favori	favorite	fah-vo-ree, fah-vo-reet	favorite

MASCULINE	FEMININE	PRONUNCIATION	ENGLISH
frais	*fraîche*	freh, frehsh	cool, fresh, new, youthful
long	*longue*	lohng, longg	long, slow, tedious, drawn out
malin	*maligne*	mal-ehn, mal-ehnn	malicious, malignant, mischievous
public	*publique*	poo-blee, poo-bleek	public
roux	*rousse*	rhoo, rhooss	reddish, red-haired
sec	*sèche*	sek, sesh	dry, arid, plain

Take a look at the following examples:

- *Elle a porté une blouse blanche.*
  (She wore a white blouse.)
- *J'ai lavé la blouse avec du savon doux.*
  (I washed the blouse with some mild soap.)

Plural Agreement of Adjectives

The majority of adjectives in French simply add an "s" at the end to agree with a plural noun, whether masculine or feminine. This is very important in written French, but there is not usually too much of a difference in pronunciation in the plural forms of adjectives. If the adjective is being used to agree with a masculine noun, simply add the "s" to the end of the masculine form. If it is being used to agree with a feminine noun, add the feminine ending, and then add the "s."

TABLE 10-14

PLURAL AGREEMENT OF ADJECTIVES				
MASCULINE SINGULAR	MASCULINE PLURAL	FEMININE SINGULAR	FEMININE PLURAL	ENGLISH
amusant	*amusants*	*amusante*	*amusantes*	amusing, entertaining
bleu	*bleus*	*bleue*	*bleues*	blue
content	*contents*	*contente*	*contentes*	content, satisfied, pleased, glad

TABLE 10-14

	PLURAL AGREEMENT OF ADJECTIVES *(CONTINUED)*			
MASCULINE SINGULAR	MASCULINE PLURAL	FEMININE SINGULAR	FEMININE PLURAL	ENGLISH
large	*larges*	*large*	*larges*	broad, wide, large, extensive
petit	*petits*	*petite*	*petites*	little, small
réel	*réels*	*réelle*	*réelles*	real, actual, genuine

If a masculine adjective already ends in "s" or "x," there is no change in the masculine plural form. The exact same word is used, whether singular or plural. Because the feminine form will have an "e" at the end, it takes an "s" in the plural, following the regular rules.

Remember that if an adjective is used with two feminine nouns, it will take a feminine plural form. If it is used to modify both a masculine and a feminine noun, however, it will take the masculine plural form, as it would if it modified two masculine nouns.

TABLE 10-15

	PLURAL AGREEMENT OF ADJECTIVES THAT END IN -*S* OR -*X*			
MASCULINE SINGULAR	MASCULINE PLURAL	FEMININE SINGULAR	FEMININE PLURAL	ENGLISH
dangereux	*dangereux*	*dangereuse*	*dangereuses*	dangerous
frais	*frais*	*fraîche*	*fraîches*	cool, fresh, new
gros	*gros*	*grosse*	*grosses*	big, large, bulky
heureux	*heureux*	*heureuse*	*heureuses*	happy, blissful
mauvais	*mauvais*	*mauvaise*	*mauvaises*	bad, ill, evil, mischievous
malheureux	*malheurueux*	*malheureuse*	*malheureuses*	unhappy, unlucky, unfortunate

Check out the following examples:

- *Elle achetait des petites voitures grosses.*
  (She used to buy small cars.)
- *Je ne pense pas que les avions sont dangereux.*
  (I don't think that planes are dangerous.)
- *Les enfants étaient heureux.* (The children were happy.)

Like conjugating verbs with *ils* and *elles*, the masculine gender kind of trumps the feminine when it comes to agreement of adjectives in the plural. If an adjective appears with two nouns, it must be used in the plural, because it is referring to the two of them together. If both nouns are feminine, the adjective will take the feminine plural form, because it is agreeing with the two nouns collectively. If one is masculine and one is feminine, the masculine plural form is used by convention, as shown in the following example:

- *Sara et Michel sont amusants.* (Sara and Michael are amusing.)
- *Marie et Louise sont amusantes.* (Marie and Louise are amusing.)

Here's another way of looking at this: An adjective will be used in the feminine plural only when it is used with a plural feminine noun or two singular feminine nouns; but if a masculine noun is present, a masculine plural would be the correct choice, because it breaks that rule. At any rate, however you remember it, it's important that your adjectives agree with the nouns they modify, both in gender and number.

Placement of Adjectives

For the most part, place adjectives directly after the nouns they modify. Keep in mind that when you hear adjectives in spoken French, they are usually meant to modify the nouns that precede them. When two adjectives modify a noun, they are joined with a conjunction, such as *et*.

- *J'ai parlé avec un homme gros et heureux.*
  (I spoke with a large and happy man.)
- *Pierre a un chien dangeureux et mauvais.*
  (Pierre has a dangerous and bad dog.)

A few French adjectives usually appear before the noun, however. The following adjectives, when used to modify a noun, are placed directly before it; if the noun is being used with an article, the adjective is inserted between the article and the noun.

TABLE 10-16

ADJECTIVES PLACED BEFORE NOUNS		
ADJECTIVE	PRONUNCIATION	ENGLISH
autre	oh-truh	other, another, different
beau	bo	beautiful, fine, handsome, pretty
court	koor	short, brief, concise
gentil	jhan-tee	noble, gentle, pretty, nice
gros	gro	big, large, bulky
haut	oh	high, tall, upper, haughty
jeune	jhoon	young, youthful, early
joli	jho-lee	pretty, pleasing, neat, fine, nice
long	long	long, slow, tedious, drawn out
mauvais	moh-veh	bad, ill, evil, naughty
meilleur	may-ehr	better, preferable
nouveau	noo-vo	new, recent, novel
petit	peh-tee	little, small, short, very young
vieux	vee-yuh	old, ancient, aged, advanced in years

Some adjectives have an alternate masculine form that's used in front of singular masculine nouns that begin with a vowel.

TABLE 10-17

ALTERNATE MASCULINE FORMS			
MASCULINE	ALTERNATE	FEMININE	ENGLISH
beau	*bel*	*belle*	beautiful, fine, handsome
fou	*fol*	*folle*	mad, demented, wild, foolish
mou	*mol*	*molle*	soft, limp, flabby, weak
nouveau	*nouvel*	*nouvelle*	new, recent, additional
vieux	*vieil*	*vieille*	old, aged, ancient

The following examples show the alternate spellings:

- *Il était un bel ami.* (He was a fine friend.)
- *Mon voisin est un vieil homme.* (My neighbor is an old man.)

If two adjectives are used together and are used before the noun, no conjunction is used, so don't try to insert an *et*. A conjunction is used only when the adjective is in its normal position, immediately following the noun.

- *Elle a un petit nouveau bébé.* (She has a new little baby.)
- *Il a pris une décision fausse et folle.*
  (He made a wrong and foolish decision.)

In English, the adjective is usually placed before the noun, so be careful about where you place them in French, because some adjectives can actually carry different connotations, depending on their position in the sentence. With some adjectives, if they appear before the noun, a figurative meaning is intended and should not be taken literally. When placed after the noun, however, the adjective is meant to be interpreted literally. **TABLE 10-18** contains many of these idiomatic adjectival constructions. Be careful that you don't use any of these adjectives in the wrong position, because you can seriously alter the meaning of the sentence.

TABLE 10-18

ADJECTIVES AND THEIR MEANINGS
ADJECTIVE: *ancien / ancienne*
BEFORE THE NOUN: *Un ancien élève travaillera avec moi.* (A former student will be working with me.)
AFTER THE NOUN: *J'ai acheté la voiture d'un homme ancien.* (I bought the car from an old man.)
ADJECTIVE: *bon / bonne*
BEFORE THE NOUN: *J'ai vu un bon film.* (I saw an enjoyable film.)
AFTER THE NOUN: *Jacques est un homme bon.* (Jacques is a kind man.)
ADJECTIVE: *brave*
BEFORE THE NOUN: *Un brave chat est venu ici.* (A nice cat came here.)
AFTER THE NOUN: *Mon grand-père était un homme brave à la guerre.* (My grandfather was a courageous man in the war.)

TABLE 10-18

ADJECTIVES AND THEIR MEANINGS *(CONTINUED)*

ADJECTIVE: *certain*

BEFORE THE NOUN: *J'ai lu un certain livre.* (I read a unique book.)

AFTER THE NOUN: *Il a dit que le projet est un fait certain.*
(He said that the project is a guaranteed fact.)

ADJECTIVE: *cher / chère*

BEFORE THE NOUN: *Marie est une chère amie.* (Marie is a dear friend.)

AFTER THE NOUN: *Elle a acheté un diamant cher.*
(She bought an expensive diamond.)

ADJECTIVE: *dernier / dernière*

BEFORE THE NOUN: *Demain, il écrira le dernier examen.*
(Tomorrow, he will write the last exam.)

AFTER THE NOUN: *Monsieur Allard est venu ici la semaine dernière.*
(Mr. Allard came here last week.)

ADJECTIVE: *différent*

BEFORE THE NOUN: *Il a beaucoup de différents amis.* (He has many differen
kinds of friends; he has diverse friends.)

AFTER THE NOUN: *Elle a vendu un bâtiment différent.*
(She sold a different building.)

ADJECTIVE: *drôle*

BEFORE THE NOUN: *Il a dit qu'il avait lu un drôle roman.*
(He said that he had read a bizarre novel.)

AFTER THE NOUN: *Nous devons regarder un film drôle.*
(We ought to watch a funny film.)

ADJECTIVE: *grand / grande*

BEFORE THE NOUN: *Edith Piaf était une grande chanteuse.*
(Edith Piaf was a great singer.)

AFTER THE NOUN: *La tour Eiffel est une édifice grande.*
(The Eiffel Tower is a tall structure.)

ADJECTIVE: *même*

BEFORE THE NOUN: *Le professeur a dit la même chose.*
(The teacher said the same thing.)

AFTER THE NOUN: *Cette recette prend ce montant même du beurre.*
(This recipe takes this exact amount of butter.)

ADJECTIVE: *nouveau*

BEFORE THE NOUN: *Elle a trouvé un nouvel emploi.* (She found an additional job.)

AFTER THE NOUN: *Elle a trouvé un emploi nouveau.* (She found a new job.)

TABLE 10-18

ADJECTIVE: *pauvre*

BEFORE THE NOUN: *Je connais beaucoup des pauvres gens.*

(I have known many unfortunate people.)

AFTER THE NOUN: *Nous avons regardé un film d'un homme pauvre.*

(We watched a film about a penniless man.)

ADJECTIVE: *prochain / prochaine*

BEFORE THE NOUN: *Il est venu chez moi la prochaine journée.*

(He came to my house the following day.)

AFTER THE NOUN: *Je ferrai mes devoirs la fois prochaine.*

(I'll do my homework the next time.)

ADJECTIVE: *propre*

BEFORE THE NOUN: *J'aime dormir dans mon propre lit.*

(I like to sleep in my own bed.)

AFTER THE NOUN: *J'aime avoir une chambre propre.*

(I like to have a clean room.)

ADJECTIVE: *sale*

BEFORE THE NOUN: *Le garçon a dit un sale mot à son père.*

(The boy said a bad word to his father.)

AFTER THE NOUN: *Je dois laver ces enfants sales.*

(I have to wash these dirty children.)

ADJECTIVE: *seul*

BEFORE THE NOUN: *Il a perdu son seul dollar.* (He lost his only dollar.)

AFTER THE NOUN: *Je prendrai un avion seule; je ne devrai pas transférer.*

(I will be taking a single plane; I do not have to transfer.)

FACTS

Normally, an adjective is placed after a noun. There are some adjectives that are used before, and some that can be used in either position. These adjectives's position are not interchangeable. When used before a noun, these adjectives have a figurative meaning, not to be interpreted literally. If the adjective appears after the noun, it should be interpreted literally.

Possessive Adjectives

In English, we often use phrases like "my book" or "your hair." These are known as possessive adjectives. They are used to modify the word that follows, telling you more about the noun itself, indicating who owns the thing the noun describes, so to speak. The French equivalents of these pronouns are usually used in the same way an article is used, placed before the noun to modify it.

These adjectives replace the definite or indefinite article. When you use it, you are changing the meaning to "my" or "your" or "his," instead of "the" or "an." You are indicating something specific, something owned by someone, so possessive adjectives replace articles entirely. (See Chapter 4 for more.) Here are examples of possessive adjectives:

- *J'échove mon examen.* (I am failing my test.)
- *Elle ment sur son âge.* (She lies about her age.)
- *Est-ce que vous meublez votre maison?* (Are you furnishing your home?)

The following possessive adjectives correspond to *je, tu,* and *il* or *elle* respectively. They are used when you wish to indicate that only one person possesses the item in question.

TABLE 10-19

| | | MASCULINE | FEMININE | |
PERSON	ENGLISH	SINGULAR	SINGULAR	PLURAL
1st Person	my	*mon* (mohn)	*ma* (mah)	*mes* (may)
2nd Person	your	*ton* (tohn)	*ta* (tah)	*tes* (tay)
3rd Person	his or hers	*son* (sohn)	*sa* (sah)	*ses* (say)

POSSESSIVE ADJECTIVES—ONE PERSON

The forms that correspond to *nous, vous,* and *ils* or *elles* are formed slightly differently. In the singular, the word is the same, whether used with a feminine or masculine noun.

TABLE 10-20

POSSESSIVE ADJECTIVES—MORE THAN ONE PERSON			
PERSON	ENGLISH	SINGULAR	PLURAL
1st Person	our	*notre* (not-truh)	*nos* (no)
2nd Person	your	*votre* (vot-truh)	*vos* (vo)
3rd Person	their	*leur* (leuhr)	*leurs* (leuhr)

The following samples show some possessive adjectives in action.

- *J'ai besoin de votre aide.* (I need your help.)
- *Il aime son chat.* (He loves his cat.)
- *Ils habitent dans ma ville.* (They live in my city.)
- *J'achète leur livre.* (I am buying their book.)
- *Est-ce que tu étudies pour nos examens?* (Are you studying for our tests?)

Demonstrative Adjectives

In English, we use the words "this," "that," "these," and "those" with nouns to indicate specific items. They are known as demonstrative adjectives because they clearly indicate, or demonstrate, exactly what is meant.

TABLE 10-21

FRENCH DEMONSTRATIVE ADJECTIVES		
GENDER	SINGULAR	PLURAL
Masculine	*ce* (suh), *cet* (set)	*ces* (say)
Feminine	*cette* (set)	*ces* (say)

In the singular, the meaning will be "this" or "that," depending on the context of the individual sentence. The plural form, *ces,* represents "these" or "those."

When the singular demonstrative adjective *ce* is used in front of a masculine noun that begins with a vowel, elision does not occur; no vowel is dropped, and no contraction is formed. Instead, a "t" is added to the end of the adjective, and *cet* is used to separate the vowels. As a result, the linguistic challenge of pronouncing two vowels is addressed with liaison, with the final "t" sound running into the beginning of the noun. For more information on liaison and elision, flip to Chapter 1.

In English, the correct choice between "this" and "that" is contextual. The meaning is determined from the circumstances in which the words are used. The French demonstrative adjective covers both meanings. When translating from English into French, use the correct form of *ce,* making sure that it matches the noun it modifies both in gender and in number.

However, when referring to two objects in relation to each other, a slightly different construction is used. In English, we can say "this book or that book" in a single sentence. Because the French adjective *ce* can have either meaning, some modification is needed to show which is which. To translate an English sentence into French, translate the nouns. Preface each noun with the proper form of *ce,* so that it agrees in gender and number. With the noun you wish to indicate as "this," just put *ci* after the noun, and put a hyphen between them. To indicate "that," use *là* after the noun instead, also with a hyphen: *J'ai acheté ce livre-ci, mais j'ai reçu ce livre-là de ma mère.* (I bought this book, but I received that book from my mother.)

You need only worry about adding *ci* or *là* when comparing two nouns in the same sentence. If you come across a sentence that uses the demonstrative adjective only one time, it can appear alone before the noun. The correct translation choice between "this" or "that" in English will just depend on what makes the English sentence sound best.

CHAPTER 11

Understanding Adverbs

While adjectives are used to modify nouns, adverbs can be used to modify other kinds of words, including verbs, adjectives, or even other adverbs. They are used to describe the manner in which something occurs, or, in other words, how it happens.

Forming Adverbs

Luckily, you get a bit of a break when learning about adverbs, because you don't have to worry about agreement. Adverbs are never modified to agree with anything.

If you think of adjectives as modifying and describing the physical aspects of a thing, adverbs then describe the style or fashion about how something is done. Adverbs set the circumstances of the sentence.

Most French adverbs are formed by adding *-ment* to the end of an adjective, much the same way as English adds "-ly" to the end of adjectives to turn them into adverbs. Not all adverbs use this ending, however, so be careful not to confuse them with other kinds of words. Also, there are some other ways to form French adverbs; some words make special changes to assist in pronunciation, while others are completely irregular.

Here are the basic rules for forming adverbs:

* Add *-ment* to the feminine form of the adjective.
* For adverbs formed from adjectives ending in *-i*, add *-ment*.
* For adverbs formed from adjectives ending in *-u*, simply add the ending *-ment*.
* For adjectives ending in *-ant*, change to *-amment*.
* For adjectives ending in *-ent*, change to *-emment*.

TABLE 11-1

FORMING ADVERBS FROM ADJECTIVES			
ADJECTIVE	ADVERB	PRONUNCIATION	ENGLISH
vrai	*vraiment*	vreh-mahn	truly, in truth, indeed, really
absolu	*absolument*	ab-so-loo-mahn	absolutely, arbitrarily
évident	*évidemment*	ay-vee-deh-mahn	evidently
fréquent	*fréquemment*	fray-kay-mahn	frequently
patient	*patiemment*	pah-tee-ehm-mahn	patiently

There are also some adverbs that have irregular stems; some change only slightly from the adjectival form, but others change completely.

TABLE 11-2

	FORMING ADVERBS WITH IRREGULAR STEMS FROM ADJECTIVES		
ADJECTIVE	ADVERB	PRONUNCIATION	ENGLISH
bref	brièvement	bree-ev-mahn	briefly, succinctly, in short
bon	bien	bee-yehn	well, rightly, finely, much, very, entirely, completely
gentil	gentiment	jhan-tee-mahn	prettily, gracefully
mauvais	mal	mahl	wrong, badly
meilleur	mieux	mee-yeuh	better, correctly, more comfortably
petit	peu	peuh	little, not much, few, not very, not many

Memorizing Adverbs

Adverbs in French can be broken out into a number of categories; this may make it easier for you to remember different kinds of adjectives. In addition, if you find yourself forgetting some of the adverbs in the categories, refer back to this section to review these adverbs with similar uses.

TABLE 11-3

	ADVERBS USED TO DESCRIBE MANNER	
ADVERB	PRONUNCIATION	ENGLISH
aisément	eh-zay-mahn	easily, readily, freely, comfortably
bien	bee-yehn	well, much, very
constamment	con-stah-mahn	steadily, continually, constantly
convenablement	con-vehn-ab-le-mahn	suitably, becomingly, decently
ensemble	ahn-samb	together, at the same time
mal	mahl	wrong, badly

TABLE 11-4

	ADVERBS USED TO DESCRIBE TIME	
aujourd'hui	oh-jhoor-dwee	today
demain	deh-mehn	tomorrow
hier	ee-aihr	yesterday

TABLE 11-4

ADVERBS USED TO DESCRIBE TIME		
ADVERB	PRONUNCIATION	ENGLISH
longtemps	lohn-tahm	long, a long while
maintenant	mehn-te-nahn	now, at this moment, at present
tard	tahr	late
tôt	toe	soon, quickly, early
vite	veet	quick, quickly, fast, rapidly

TABLE 11-5

ADVERBS USED TO DESCRIBE FREQUENCY		
déjà	day-jha	already, before, previously
enfin	ahn-fehn	at last, finally, after all, lastly, in short
jamais	jha-meh	ever; with *ne*, never
quelquefois	kel-kuh-fwa	sometimes
souvent	soo-vahn	often, frequently
toujours	too-jhoor	always, ever, forever

TABLE 11-6

ADVERBS USED TO DESCRIBE PLACE		
dehors	dhore	out, outside, out of doors
derrière	dehr-ee-aihr	behind, after
devant	deh-vahn	in front, ahead
ici	ee-see	here, in this place, now, this time
là	lah	there
loin	l'whehn	far, distant, at a distance
où	oo	where
près	preh	by, near

TABLE 11-7

ADVERBS USED TO DESCRIBE AN AMOUNT OR QUANTITY		
aussi	oh-see	also, as, likewise, too, besides
assez	ass-ay	enough
beaucoup	bo-koo	much, many
moins	mwhehn	less, fewer

TABLE 11-7

ADVERBS USED TO DESCRIBE AN AMOUNT OR QUANTITY		
ADVERB	**PRONUNCIATION**	**ENGLISH**
peu	peuh	few, little, not much
tout	too	all, whole, every
très	treh	very, most, very much
trop	troe	too, too much, too many

FACTS

Many of the adverbs you'll encounter can also be used in other ways, such as prepositions. For example, the adverb *aussi* can also be used as a conjunction to join parts of a sentence together; when used in this fashion, the meanings of *aussi* can include "accordingly," "and so," "therefore," and "consequently."

TABLE 11-8

OTHER HANDY ADVERBS TO KNOW		
ADVERB	**PRONUNCIATION**	**ENGLISH**
oui	whee	yes
si	see	so, so much, yes, but yes
naturellement	nah-tuhr-ell-mahn	naturally
probablement	prah-ba-bluh-mahn	probably
peut-être	peuh-te-truh	perhaps, maybe

Adverbial Phrases

The following adverbial phrases can be used in sentences to convey a specific meaning. In a sense, these are idiomatic expressions, so don't try to translate them literally, even though some of the literal approximations come close. Learn the English equivalents, because you'll probably hear these relatively frequently in spoken French.

TABLE 11-9

ADVERB	PRONUNCIATION	ENGLISH
en attendant	ahn att-ahn-dahn	in the meantime
à la longue	ah lah lohng	in the long run
à peu près	ah peuh preh	nearly, about
à propos	ah pro-poe	by the way, at the right time
en même temps	ahn mem tahmp	at the same time
quelque part	kell-kuh pahrd	somewhere
par hasard	pahr haz-ahrd	by accident, by chance
bien sûr	bee-yehn soor	of course
tout de suite	tootd-sweet	immediately
sans doute	sahn doot	doubtless
à moitié	ah mway-ih-tee-yay	half

Table title: ADVERBIAL PHRASES

Positioning and Using Adverbs

In French, the natural position of an adverb is immediately following the verb. Remember that adverbs can't modify a noun, so they must modify something else in the sentence. When the adverb requires a verb to make any sense, the adverb must be placed immediately after the verb. This is especially noticeable with expressions of quantity.

- *J'ai aussi un chat.* (I also have a cat.)
- *Nous avons assez vu.* (We have seen enough.)

When an adverb that denotes an amount or quantity is used to modify a noun, *de* is used with it. Note in the above examples, however, that when an adverb is used to modify a verb, *de* is not used; the adverb appears alone.

- *Ils ont trop de devoirs.* (They have too much homework.)
- *Avez-vous vu beaucoup de films?* (Have you seen many films?)

With expressions of frequency, manner, place, and time, you can put the adverb at the beginning, before the subject, or at the absolute end of the sentence. Never, however, place an adverb between the subject and the verb. Watch carefully, because this placement is very common in English. Avoid it at all costs it—the sentence won't make sense.

CHAPTER 12
Forming
Past-Tense Verbs

Everything prior to this chapter has been limited to the present tense, referring to events that occur "now." In this chapter, you find out how to use verbs in the past tense. The past tense is very different from the present-tense conjugated verb forms, but with a little practice and patience, you'll learn the concepts with ease.

English Past-Tense Constructions

When referring to events that occurred in the past, you have a few choices. You can refer to a single event that happened in the past; in English, we call this the simple past. This tense is used to indicate a specific event that was begun in the past and is now completely finished. The action is sometimes referred to as being in the perfect past because the action is "perfected"—it happened in the past and is now done and completed.

The English past tense works as follows:

- I **went** to the store
- I **have gone** to the store.
- I **did go** to the store.

Sometimes, you want to refer to past events that don't have a concrete beginning or ending or something that was ongoing over a period of time. In English, this tense is often known as the past progressive, because it indicates an event that occurred progressively. In French, this tense is known as the *imparfait,* or the "imperfect" tense, because the event can't be isolated at any one particular point in time. In this chapter and book, we use the term "imperfect" to describe this tense. It should help you keep things straight.

The imperfect past tense looks like this:

- I **used to work** at the library.
- I **would go** for walks in the summer.

You can also refer to events in the distant past; we call this tense the pluperfect in English. It is used to describe an event that occurred before another past event. It is often used in conjunction with the simple past to indicate events that took place, but the construction can appear alone. When it does, however, a more recent past event is still inferred. The pluperfect must have another point of reference in the past to give it meaning.

The distant past tense works as follows:

- I **had gone** to the store.
- I **had left** the restaurant.

To keep these tenses straight in your mind, think of the old story of the son who received a letter from his mother; he opened and read it, and at the end of the letter, it said, "I tried to send you some money with this letter, but I had already sealed the envelope."

This is completely absurd, of course, because of the events described by the tenses. "I had already sealed the envelope" is a pluperfect construction, indicating that it occurred before the other event—the mother's attempt at sending the money with the letter. If she had already sealed the letter, though, how did she write that line?

After you learn the verb tense lessons in this chapter, pay close attention when translating verb tenses. You don't want to inadvertently construct an absolutely ridiculous phrase!

The Simple Past Tense: *Le Passé Composé*

If you recall from the explanation of English tenses, the past is often formed using auxiliary verbs. French also uses auxiliary verbs (either *avoir* or *être*) to form the *passé composé* (or simple past). So to form the *passé composé*, a verb uses either *avoir* or *être* conjugated in the present tense (see Chapter 6), depending on the particular verb. Most verbs use *avoir* to form the past tense, but a few use *être*. The present tense conjugation of *avoir* or *être* is then followed by the past participle (the "-ed" form of the verb).

SSENTIALS

The *passé composé* is always a compound tense, meaning that it's made up of two elements: the conjugated form of *avoir* or *être* and the past participle, which is formed by dropping the infinitive endings (see the following sections for more on past participles).

Uses of the *Passé Composé*

Like the present indicative tense in French, the *passé composé* can carry a number of meanings: *J'ai parlé* means "I spoke," "I did speak," and "I have spoken."

When translating from English to French, do not translate these auxiliary words directly; instead, use the past participle of the verb in French with the proper French auxiliary verb.

ALERT

Remember that English and French don't always treat verbs the same when referring to events in the past tense. When translating sentences using the *passé composé*, be careful not to translate the verbs literally. Recognize that a past construction is being used, and then choose the appropriate auxiliary verb to use with the past participle.

As mentioned in the review of English tenses, the *passé composé* is used to indicate specific events that occurred in the past. In order to be referred to with the *passé composé*, the event must have occurred in the past, usually within a specified time period. If the time period is indefinite, the *imparfait* is probably the better choice; you will learn more about the *imparfait* in the next major section of this chapter.

You will often see the *passé composé* used in the following cases. It can also be used in conjunction with the other past tenses in French to establish the chronology of events, telling you exactly when each event happened in relation to the others.

Simple Completed Actions

The *passé composé* is used to describe an event that occurred at some concrete point in the past, and whose action is now completed. The *passé composé* is also used when a physical or emotional state changes as a result of an event that can be fixed in a specific point in the past. Here are two examples:

- *Je suis né à l'hôpital.*
  (I was born at the hospital.)
- *Il a gagné le jeu.*
  (He won the game.)

Actions with a Specified Time Period

When referring to a specific time in the past, the *passé composé* is used.

- *Le film a commencé à six heures.* (The film started at six o'clock.)
- *J'ai lu le livre pendant une heure.* (I read the book for an hour.)

A Series of Actions

You use the *passé composé* when referring to a series of events, each of which occurred in the past: *Il a écrit une lettre, a mis la lettre dans une enveloppe, et puis a mis la lettre à la poste.* (He wrote a letter, put the letter in an envelope, and then mailed the letter.)

Past Participles Conjugated with *Avoir*

The formation of the past participle for most regular verbs tends to follow a predictable pattern, depending on the ending of the verb. The following rules apply for most verbs; in the next section, you'll also learn about some verbs that follow irregular formation patterns for the past participle.

-er Verbs

To form the past participle, simply drop the *-er* ending and replace it with é. To form the *passé composé*, conjugate *avoir* before the past participle. **TABLE 12-1** shows the verb *parler* conjugated in the *passé composé*.

TABLE 12-1

PARLER CONJUGATED IN THE PASSÉ COMPOSÉ		
PERSON	**SINGULAR**	**PLURAL**
1st Person	*j'ai parlé* (jhay pahrlay)	*nous avons parlé* (noo-zahvohn parlay)
2nd Person	*tu as parlé* (tchoo ah parlay)	*vous avez parlé* (voo-zahvay parlay)
3rd Person	*il a parlé* (eel ah parlay) *elle a parlé* (ell ah parlay)	*ils ont parlé* (eel-zohn parlay) *elles ont parlé* (ell-zohn parlay)

Take a look at the following examples:

- *Les Dumont ont acheté une maison.* (The Dumont family bought a house.)
- *Je n'ai pas téléphoné.* (I did not call.)
- *Nous avons aimé le repas hier.* (We loved the meal yesterday.)
- *Il m'a appelé «Fred.»* (He called me "Fred.")
- *Ils n'ont pas changé le poste.* (They did not change the channel.)

FACTS

You'll recall that some -*er* verbs change stems in present-tense conjugations. When creating the past participle, however, the regular -*er* verb rules for the formation of the past participle apply. Don't change the stem; simply add *é* after dropping the -*er*. For more information on stem-changing verbs, refer to Chapter 6.

-*re* Verbs

To form the past participle, simply drop the -*re* ending and replace it with "u." Place the past participle after the conjugated version of *avoir* to create the *passé composé*.

TABLE 12-2

PERSON	SINGULAR	PLURAL
PERDRE CONJUGATED IN THE *PASSÉ COMPOSÉ*		
1st Person	*j'ai perdu* (jhay pehr-doo)	*nous avons perdu* (noo-zahvohn pehr-doo)
2nd Person	*tu as perdu* (tchoo ah pehr-doo)	*vous avez perdu* (voo-zahvay pehr-doo)
3rd Person	*il a perdu* (eel ah pehr-doo)	*ils ont perdu* (eel-zohn pehr-doo)
	elle a perdu (ell ah pehr-doo)	*elles ont perdu* (ell-zohn pehr-doo)

Here are some examples:

- *Nous n'avons pas répondu au téléphoné.* (We didn't answer the telephone.)
- *Elle a entendu de la musique.* (She heard some music.)

- *La télévision a corrompu le garçon.* (Television corrupted the boy.)
- *J'ai vendu la voiture.* (I sold the car.)
- *Avez-vous perdu le livre?* (Did you lose the book? Have you lost the book?)

-ir Verbs

To form the past participle with most *-ir* verbs, simply drop the "r" from the end, so the verb ends in an "i."

TABLE 12-3

	FINIR CONJUGATED IN THE *PASSÉ COMPOSÉ*	
PERSON	**SINGULAR**	**PLURAL**
1st Person	*j'ai fini* (jhay fee-nee)	*nous avons fini* (noo-zahvohn fee-nee)
2nd Person	*tu as fini* (tchoo ah fee-nee)	*vous ont fini* (voo-zahvay fee-nee)
3rd Person	*il a fini* (eel ah fee-nee) *elle a fini* (ell ah fee-nee)	*ils ont fini* (eel-zohn fee-nee) *elles ont fini* (ell-zohn fee-nee)

Take a look at these examples:

- *Nous avons beaucoup accompli aujourd'hui.*
  (We accomplished a lot today.)
- *Le professeur n'a pas enseigné hier.*
  (The teacher did not teach yesterday.)
- *Il n'a rien choisi.* (He did not choose anything.)
- *Elles ont fini l'examen.* (They have finished the test.)

Irregular Past Participles

Just as there are a number of verbs with irregular conjugations in the present indicative tense, there are a number of exceptions with the past participle, too. The verbs that use these irregular past participles don't have any easy rules, so they will have to be memorized.

ALERT

While most French verbs follow predictable patterns for forming the past participle, remember that there are irregular verbs that use completely different constructions. Memorize these exceptions in addition to the regular rules for the past participle formation.

Because many of the past participles of some verbs use the same ending, it may be helpful to memorize these verbs in groups. As you review the tables of similarly irregular verbs in this section, study the English equivalents closely so that you become adept at recognizing the different English constructions that can be used when translating from the *passé composé*.

TABLE 12-4

IRREGULAR VERBS		
VERB	PAST PARTICIPLE	ENGLISH
avoir	*eu* (ooh)	had, did have, have had
être	*été* (ay-tay)	was
faire	*fait* (fayh)	did, did do, have done

The following examples show irregular verbs in sentences:

- *J'ai eu deux billets.* (I had two tickets.)
- *Ils ont eu une classe.* (They had a class.)
- *Nous avons été petits.* (We were small.)
- *Ils ont été chez Pierre.* (They were at Pierre's place.)
- *Elles ont fait leurs devoirs.* (They did their homework.)
- *As-tu fait un bruit?* (Did you make a noise?)

TABLE 12-5

PAST PARTICIPLES ENDING IN -*ERT*		
VERB	PAST PARTICIPLE	ENGLISH
découvrir	*découvert*	discovered, did discover, have discovered
offrir	*offert*	offered, did offer, have offered
ouvrir	*ouvert*	opened, did open, have opened
souffrir	*souffert*	suffered, did suffer, have suffered

Consider the following examples:

- *Il a ouvert la porte.* (He opened the door.)
- *Nous avons souffert.* (We have suffered.)
- *J'ai offert de l'argent.* (I offered some money.)

TABLE 12-6

PAST PARTICIPLES ENDING IN -*I*		
VERB	**PAST PARTICIPLE**	**ENGLISH**
sourire	*souri*	smiled, did smile, have smiled
suivre	*suivi*	followed, did follow, have followed

Note the following examples:

- *Il a suivi les signes.* (He followed the signs.)
- *J'ai souri.* (I smiled.)

TABLE 12-7

PAST PARTICIPLES ENDING IN -*IS*		
VERB	**PAST PARTICIPLE**	**ENGLISH**
apprendre	*appris*	learned, did learn, have learned
comprendre	*compris*	understood, did understand, have understood
mettre	*mis*	placed, did place, have placed
prendre	*pris*	took, did take, have taken

The following examples demonstrate this ending:

- *Il a appris le français.* (He learned French.)
- *Nous avons pris les clefs.* (We took the keys.)

TABLE 12-8

PAST PARTICIPLES ENDING IN -*IT*		
VERB	**PAST PARTICIPLE**	**ENGLISH**
conduire	*conduit*	drove, did drive, have driven
dire	*dit*	said, did say, have said
écrire	*écrit*	wrote, did write, have written

Take a look at the following examples:

- *J'ai dit, «Oui.»* (I said, "Yes.")
- *Il a conduit un camion chez Alain.* (He drove a truck to Alain's place.)

TABLE 12-9

PAST PARTICIPLES ENDING IN -*U*		
VERB	**PAST PARTICIPLE**	**ENGLISH**
boire	*bu* (boo)	drank, did drink, have drunk
connaître	*connu* (connoo)	knew, did know
devoir	*dû* (doo)	had to, needed to
falloir	*fallu* (fah-loo)	was necessary
lire	*lu* (loo)	read, did read, have read
plaire	*plu* (ploo)	pleased, did please, have pleased
pleuvoir	*plu* (ploo)	rained, did rain, has rained
pouvoir	*pu* (poo)	was able to
recevoir	*reçu* (re-soo)	received, did receive, have received
savoir	*su* (soo)	knew, did know, have known
voir	*vu* (voo)	saw, did see, have seen
vouloir	*voulu* (voo-loo)	wanted, did want, have wanted

Here are some examples:

- *J'ai bu du lait.* (I drank some milk.)
- *As-tu lu le livre?* (Did you read the book?)
- *Avez-vous pu aller au cinéma?* (Were you able to go to the movies?)
- *Je n'ai pas vu le film.* (I did not see the film.)
- *Elle a voulu un stylo.* (She wanted a pen.)

FACTS

The verb *connaître* means "to know" or "to be acquainted with" someone and is always used to refer to a person; the verb *savoir* is used to refer to knowing other things. Remember that the *passé composé* is used to refer to events that are completed.

Object Pronouns and Past Participles

Note that when a direct object pronoun (see Chapter 9) appears before the conjugated verb, the past participle conjugated with *avoir* must agree with the object, both in gender and in number. It is not merely the presence of an object pronoun that makes the past participle agree; it is the fact that the pronoun appears before the verb that kicks the past participle into gear. When this happens, an "e" is added to the end of the past participle to make it agree in the feminine, and an "s" is added to make it agree in the plural, much like the formation of adjectives.

- *Avez-vous vu la voiture?* (Have you seen **the car**?) *Oui, nous l'avons vue.* (Yes, we have seen **it**.)
- *Est-ce que vous avez regardé les films?* (Have you watched **the films**?) *Oui, nous les avons regardés.* (Yes, we have watched **them**.)

If an object pronoun is used after the verb, then no agreement occurs: *Pourquoi est-ce que tu n'as pas donné le roman à moi hier soir?* (Why didn't you give **the novel** to me last night?) *Je n'avais pas fini de lire.* (I hadn't finished reading **it**.)

Verbs That Use *Être* as the Auxiliary

Instead of using *avoir*, some verbs use *être* instead as the auxiliary verb to conjugate in tenses other than the present. While the majority of French verbs use *avoir*, there are a number that must use *être*; if you slip up and use the wrong auxiliary verb, there's a good chance that you won't be understood.

SSENTIALS

To help with the memorization of past participles, instead of memorizing the form alone, use it in a phrase and memorize that: *j'ai eu* (I had; I did have) or *je suis allé* (I went; I did go). Like memorizing nouns with an article to remember the gender, using this method will help you remember which verbs use *être* as the auxiliary verb.

Here is a list of common verbs that use *être*. Many of the verbs follow regular rules for the formation of the past participle, but note that there are some exceptions, such as *mourir* and *naître*. The more you practice French, the more adept you will become at using these verbs. With time, using *être* where required will become second nature to you. For now, familiarize yourself with these verbs and memorize the past participle.

TABLE 12-10

VERBS THAT USE *ÊTRE* AS THE AUXILIARY VERB		
VERB	**PAST PARTICIPLE**	**ENGLISH**
aller	*allé*	went, did go, have gone
arriver	*arrivé*	arrived, did arrive, have arrived
descendre	*descendu*	descended, did descend, went downstairs
entrer	*entré*	entered, did enter, have entered, came in
monter	*monté*	climbed, did climb, have climbed, went up
mourir	*mort*	died, did die, has died
naître	*né*	was born
partir	*parti*	left, did leave, has left
passer	*passé*	spent time, did spend time, have spent time
rester	*resté*	stayed, did stay, have stayed
retourner	*retourné*	returned, did return, has returned
sortir	*sorti*	went out, did go out, has gone out
tomber	*tombé*	fell, did fall, has fallen
venir	*venu*	came, did come, has come

Keep the following examples in mind:

- *Nous ne sommes pas allés.* (We did not go.)
- *Ils ne sont pas retournés hier.* (They did not return yesterday.)
- *Nous sommes partis à six heures.* (We left at six o'clock.)
- *Je suis passé chez Henri.* (I spent time at Henry's place.)
- *Êtes-vous tombé?* (Did you fall?)

The following verbs are derived from shorter French verbs; many of them are modified with a prefix and use the same past participle as the shorter verb. Study the following table and note how prefixes can change the meaning of verbs. That way, if you come across new verbs that have prefixes, you will be more likely to be able to decipher the meaning without having to reach for your dictionary. In the beginning, though, remember that it's a good exercise to guess first, and then check to see whether you're right.

TABLE 12-11

DERIVATIVE VERBS		
VERB	PAST PARTICIPLE	ENGLISH
devenir	devenu	became, did become, have become
parvenir	parvenu	attained, did attain, has succeeded
redescendre	redescendu	came down again, has come down again
remonter	remonté	went up again, did go up again
renaître	rené	was born again, has been revived
rentrer	rentré	returned, came in again, did return
repartir	reparti	went out again, has gone away again
ressortir	ressorti	came out again, has come out again
retomber	retombé	fell again, has fallen again
revenir	revenu	came back, did come back, has returned

You may have noticed that some of the verbs that use *être* as the auxiliary are the complete opposite to other ones that also use *être* with the past participle. You can use this to your advantage in memorizing which verbs use *être* as the auxiliary verb; remember them in pairs, and each will be easier to recall.

- *arriver* and *partir*: The first means "to arrive"; the second means "to leave."
- *entrer* and *sortir*: The first means "to enter"; the second means "to go out."
- *monter* and *descendre*: The first means "to go up"; the second means "to go down."
- *naître* and *mourir*: The first means "to be born"; the second means "to die."

There is an odd—but very important—quirk with verbs that use *être* as the auxiliary: The past participle must agree with the subject in number and gender.

Remember from Chapter 2 that nouns can have a masculine or feminine gender and also be used in the plural. The past participle, when used with the verb *être*, operates in much the same fashion. The ending of the past participle must change to agree with the subject of the sentence, both in gender and in number.

If you get into the habit now, these endings will come naturally with some practice. Save yourself some time later and learn the proper endings from the beginning. Some people benefit from visualizing the past participle written out on an imaginary blackboard with the proper ending attached. Try it with spoken French and see if it helps you!

Fortunately, agreement of past participles conjugated with *être* is fairly straightforward. If the subject is feminine, simply add an "e" to the end of the past participle. If the subject is plural, add an "s." If the subject is both feminine and plural, add *-es* to the end of the word to make it agree.

When a female person is speaking in the first person, the subject *je* is technically used in the feminine, even though it does not modify itself. This can happen with all subject pronouns, when they are used to indicate female subjects.

> Frank: *Je suis allé.* (I went.)
> Ellen: *Je suis allée aussi.* (I went, too.)
> Ellen and Sarah: *Nous sommes parties.* (We left.)

Agreement of the past participle can be difficult at first, because the subject pronouns can be misleading. *Elle* and *elles*, obviously, are always used to designate females and will therefore agree in the feminine, but *je, tu, nous,* and *vous* can also represent female subjects; if this is the case, the participle must agree. Agreement comes up in other areas, too, like objects and adjectives, which are covered in Chapters 9 and 10, respectively. As a rule, agreement is important only in written French, because you don't often hear a whole lot of difference in the pronunciation.

The Imperfect Past Tense: *L'Imparfait*

The imperfect past, or *imparfait,* is less definite than the *passé composé,* referring to events without a specific duration. It is relatively easy to understand and remember, because it follows very simple formation rules. The *imparfait* is an important tense in French and can be used in a variety of ways, including the formation of other tenses.

Uses of the *Imparfait*

One of the most common uses of the *imparfait* in French is to indicate actions or events that occurred habitually in the past. Because one cannot place these events within a specific time period, the *imparfait* is used to place these actions or events in an indefinite period. English equivalents include using words like "would" or "used to" to indicate the events that occurred over time in the past. Here are some examples:

- *J'écoutais la radio chaque matin.* (I used to listen to the radio every morning.)
- *Quand j'étais jeune, j'étais heureux.* (When I was young, I was happy.)
- *Nous mangions à la maison.* (We used to eat at the house.)

You will often encounter the *imparfait* in written French to set tone or setting, describing the general conditions that existed, as follows:

- *Il pleuvait.* (It was raining.)
- *Il n'aimait pas les visiteurs.* (He didn't like visitors.)

You can also use the *imparfait* to describe the existence of past states or conditions:

- *Je voulais aller.* (I wanted to go.)
- *J'avais peur.* (I used to be afraid.)

The following verbs, which are used to describe circumstances or states, can't often be tied to a specific occurrence in the past. Events described by these verbs tend to have happened over the course of time, so the *imparfait* is usually used.

- *avoir*: to have, to hold
- *être*: to be
- *penser*: to think
- *désirer*: to want, to desire
- *préférer*: to prefer
- *détester*: to hate

- *croire*: to believe
- *trouver*: to find
- *songer*: to dream, to imagine
- *savoir*: to know
- *aimer*: to like, to love

- *espérer*: to hope, to wish
- *regretter*: to regret, to grieve
- *pouvoir*: to be able
- *vouloir*: to want

The *imparfait* is also used with *depuis* to indicate something that occurred for a period of time before another event occurred:

- *J'attendais depuis deux heures quand il est arrivé.*
  (I had been waiting for two hours when he arrived.)
- *Nous habitions à Paris depuis un an quand nous avons acheté le magasin.* (We had been living in Paris for a year when we bought the store.)

Verbs with Special Meanings in the *Imparfait*

The *imparfait* is often used in specific circumstances to convey certain subtleties of time in past events. Because the tense is used to indicate an ongoing period in the past, some verbs take on a unique meaning when cast in the hazy time period indicated with the *imparfait*.

Être

When used in the imperfect, *être* takes on the meaning of "was," because it indicates an ongoing event. When used in the *passé composé*, the verb carries the sense of "became," because it indicates a specific time when the event occurred.

Savoir

Because knowledge is assumed to be something held over a long period of time, the imperfect carries the sense of the English word "knew." When used in the *passé composé*, *savoir* tends to indicate that you "found out" something, as we would say in English, to convey the sense of coming upon the knowledge at some particular point in time.

Devoir

In the present tense, *devoir* means "to have to" do something. In the *passé composé*, the correct translation would be "had to." In the *imparfait*, however, it carries a slightly different sense, instead carrying the sense of "supposed to." This actually makes sense, because the *imparfait* is used to indicate events that you cannot pinpoint in time. Because the action or event was something that had to be done, as indicated by the verb *devoir*, putting it in the *imparfait* indicates that it didn't happen at a certain time. Therefore, it carries the sense that the obligation was something that occurred over a period of time in the past; "we were supposed to" is the best English approximation.

Vouloir

When *vouloir* is used to indicate a past state of mind, such as "wanted to write," the *imparfait* is the appropriate choice in French. The *passé composé* is used when you wish to show that the actual act of wanting occurred at a specific point in time, as in "I wanted to write this morning" versus a general state of mind.

Venir de

When *venir de* is used in the present, it conveys the sense of having just done something. It is used in the *imparfait* to convey the sense of "had just done something." This usage is rather idiomatic, so remember to choose the *imparfait* to avoid confusion.

Pouvoir

When used in the *imparfait*, *pouvoir* is much like saying "could have" in English. In the *imparfait*, it tends to indicate that it was a possible state of events, but no attempt was ever actually made to achieve the objective. Using *pouvoir* in the *passé composé* indicates that an attempt was actually made, because it can be tied to a specific point in time.

FACTS

Remember that *pouvoir* in the *passé composé* indicates something that was actually tried or attempted, while the *imparfait* is used to indicate a general possibility that something could happen. In my opinion, if the movie *On the Waterfront* had been in French, Marlon Brando's famous line "I coulda been a contender" would surely have been phrased in the *imparfait*.

Formation of the *Imparfait*

Instead of using an auxiliary verb, the *imparfait* is indicated by a special verb ending, so you don't need to watch for extra words. The *imparfait* is based on the present tense conjugation of the verb (see Chapter 6); to form the imperfect, instead of using the verb stem, you use the first person plural present-tense conjugation—the form of the verb used with *nous*. Simply drop the *-ons* ending and add the correct *imparfait* ending, as shown in **TABLE 12-12**.

TABLE 12-12

IMPARFAIT VERB ENDINGS		
PERSON	**SINGULAR**	**PLURAL**
1st Person	-ais	-ions
2nd Person	-ais	-iez
3rd Person	-ait (m)	-aient (m)
	-ait (f)	-aient (f)

The good news is that all French verbs follow this conjugation pattern to form the imperfect tense, with the exception of *être*, making the *imparfait* one of the easiest forms to learn. Because it is based on the present-tense *nous* form, it also has a unique sound from present-tense conjugations, so you will quickly learn to recognize it when you hear it.

Like the present tense indicative, the pronunciation for the verb when conjugated with *je, tu, il, elle, ils,* and *elles* is the same. In spoken French, there is no discernible difference in the pronunciation. In written French, however, the spelling is important, so spend some time learning the endings of the harder spellings, especially in forms conjugated with *ils* and *elles*.

Verbs Ending in *-er*

Verbs ending in *-er* all follow the same format.

TABLE 12-13

REGARDER CONJUGATED IN THE IMPARFAIT		
PERSON	SINGULAR	PLURAL
1st Person	*je regardais* (jhe rhe-gar-day)	*nous regardions* (noo rhe-gar-dee-ohn)
2nd Person	*tu regardais* (tchoo rhe-gar-day)	*vous regardiez* (noo rhe-gar-dee-ay)
3rd Person	*il regardait* (eel rhe-gar-day) *elle regardait* (ell rhe-gar-day)	*ils regardaient* (eel rhe-gar-day) *elles regardaient* (ell rhe-gar-day)

Sometimes, when forming the *imparfait,* you will end up with a stem that ends in *-i.* The *nous* and *vous* endings begin with an "i," so you end up with two. Don't accidentally drop the second "i" in written French.

TABLE 12-14

ÉTUDIER CONJUGATED IN THE IMPARFAIT		
PERSON	SINGULAR	PLURAL
1st Person	*j'étudiais* (jhay too-dee-ay)	*nous étudiions* (noo-zay-too-dee-ohn)
2nd Person	*tu étudiais* (tchoo ay-too-dee-ay)	*vous étudiiez* (voo-zay-too-dee-ay)
3rd Person	*il étudiait* (eel-lay-too-dee-ay) *elle étudiait* (ell-lay-too-dee-ay)	*ils étudiaient* (eel-lay-too-dee-ay) *elles étudiaient* (ell-lay-too-dee-ay)

Verbs Ending in -re

Verbs ending in -re all follow the same format.

TABLE 12-15

DIRE CONJUGATED IN THE IMPARFAIT		
PERSON	**SINGULAR**	**PLURAL**
1st Person	*je disais* (jhe dee-zay)	*nous disions* (noo dee-zee-ohn)
2nd Person	*tu disais* (tchoo dee-zay)	*vous disiez* (voo dee-zee-ay)
3rd Person	*il disait* (eel dee-zay) *elle disait* (ell dee-zay)	*ils disaient* (eel dee-zay) *elles disaient* (ell dee-zay)

Verbs Ending in -ir

Verbs ending in -ir all follow the same format.

TABLE 12-16

DEVOIR CONJUGATED IN THE IMPARFAIT		
PERSON	**SINGULAR**	**PLURAL**
1st Person	*je devais* (jhe de-vay)	*nous devions* (noo dev-ee-ohn)
2nd Person	*tu devais* (tchoo de-vay)	*vous deviez* (voo dev-ee-ay)
3rd Person	*il devait* (eel de-vay) *elle devait* (ell de-vay)	*ils devaient* (eel de-vay) *elles devaient* (ell de-vay)

Irregular Verbs

Irregular verbs actually follow the regular formation pattern of the *imparfait*, using the regular present-tense *nous* ending. You don't have to memorize any special words or endings for the *imparfait*, with the exception of *être*. For all other verbs, you can simply drop the *-ons* present-tense ending and add the proper form to conjugate the *imparfait*.

TABLE 12-17

AVOIR CONJUGATED IN THE *IMPARFAIT*		
PERSON	SINGULAR	PLURAL
1st Person	*j'avais* (jha-vay)	*nous avions* (noo-zah-vee-ohn)
2nd Person	*tu avais* (tchoo avay)	*vous aviez* (voo-zah-vee-ay)
3rd Person	*il avait* (eel avay) *elle avait* (ell avay)	*ils avaient* (eel ah-vay) *elles avaient* (ell lah-vay)

TABLE 12-18

ALLER CONJUGATED IN THE *IMPARFAIT*		
1st Person	*j'allais* (jha-lay)	*nous allions* (noo-zall-ee-ohn)
2nd Person	*tu allais* (tchoo allay)	*vous alliez* (voo-zall-ee-ay)
3rd Person	*il allait* (eel allay) *elle allait* (ell allay)	*ils allaient* (eel lall-ay) *elles allaient* (ell lall-ay)

TABLE 12-19

FAIRE CONJUGATED IN THE *IMPARFAIT*		
1st Person	*je faisais* (jhe feh-zay)	*nous faisions* (noo feh-zee-ohn)
2nd Person	*tu faisais* (tchoo feh-zay)	*vous faisiez* (voo feh-zee-ay)
3rd Person	*il faisait* (eel feh-zay) *elle faisait* (ell feh-zay)	*ils faisaient* (eel feh-zay) *elles faisaient* (ell feh-zay)

Être follows a different conjugation pattern in the imperfect. Instead of using the *nous* form *sommes,* which doesn't have an *-ons* ending to drop anyway, it uses *ét-* at the beginning as the stem, with the same endings as the other verbs tacked on at the end.

TABLE 12-20

ÊTRE CONJUGATED IN THE *IMPARFAIT*		
PERSON	**SINGULAR**	**PLURAL**
1st Person	*j'étais*	*nous étions*
	(jhay-tay)	(noo-zay-tee-ohn)
2nd Person	*tu étais*	*vous étiez*
	(tchoo ay-tay)	(voo-zay-tee-ay)
3rd Person	*il était* (eel ay-tay)	*ils étaient* (eel ay-tay)
	elle était (ell ay-tay)	*elles étaient* (ell ay-tay)

Stem-Changing Verbs in the *Imparfait*

You may recall from Chapter 6 that some verbs change stems when conjugated in the present tense. Because the *imparfait* is formed using the *nous* conjugation, some stem-changing -*er* verbs will use the modified stem when conjugated in the imperfect. This, of course, happens only with verbs whose *nous* form is affected in the conjugation.

TABLE 12-21

AGACER (TO WORRY) CONJUGATED IN THE *IMPARFAIT*		
PERSON	**SINGULAR**	**PLURAL**
1st Person	*j'agaçais*	*nous agacions*
	(jhah-gah-say)	(noo-zah-gah-see-ohn)
2nd Person	*tu agaçais*	*vous agaciez*
	(tchoo ah-gah-say)	(voo-zah-gah-see-ay)
3rd Person	*il agaçait*	*ils agaçaient*
	(eel ah-gah-say)	(eel ah-gah-say)
	elle agaçait	*elles agaçaient*
	(ell ah-gah-say)	(ell ah-gah-say)

TABLE 12-22

NAGER (TO SWIM) CONJUGATED IN THE *IMPARFAIT*		
1st Person	*je nageais*	*nous nagions*
	(jhe nahj-ay)	(noo nahj-ee-ohn)
2nd Person	*tu nageais*	*vous nagiez*
	(tchoo nahj-ay)	(voo nahj-ee-ay)

PERSON	SINGULAR	PLURAL
3rd Person	*il nageait* (eel nahj-ay) *elle nageait* (ell nahj-ay)	*ils nageaient* (eel nahj-ay) *elles nageaient* (ell nahj-ay)

The Pluperfect Tense: *Le Plus-Que-Parfait*

The *plus-que-parfait* is used in French to go back in time as far as possible from the present. It is more distant than both the *passé composé* and the *imparfait*; in a sense, you can think of it as French's "oldest" tense. In English, this tense is usually achieved by using "had" as the auxiliary word in front of the verb.

QUESTIONS?

What do pluperfect and *plus-que-parfait* **mean?**
The name for both the English "pluperfect" and the French *plus-que-parfait* actually comes from the Latin phrase *plus quam perfectum,* which means "more than perfect." It indicates an event that occurred in the past, before a "perfect" event that occurred in the past. The perfect simple past tense (or *passé composé*) is more recent than the pluperfect (or *plus-que-parfait*).

Now that you have learned the *passé composé* and the *imparfait,* the *plus-que-parfait* should be relatively easy for you. In a sense, it's a combination of both the other tenses. It uses the same past participle as is used to construct the *passé composé,* but instead of using the present-tense conjugation of the auxiliary verb, it uses the *imparfait*. Verbs conjugated in the *plus-que-parfait* will use the same auxiliary verb as if it had been conjugated in the *passé composé*.

For those reasons, the *plus-que-parfait* is fairly easy to construct after you have mastered the other past tenses. Note the following examples:

* *J'avais déjà vu le film.* (I had already seen the film.)
* *Il était tombé quand je suis arrivé.* (He had already fallen when I arrived.)

- *Nous avons mangé.* (We had already eaten.)
- *Est-ce que tu avais écrit ton roman?* (Had you written your novel?)
- *Ils étaient déjà nés quand leur mère est arrivée à l'hôpital.* (They had already been born when their mother arrived at the hospital.)

As a rule, the *plus-que-parfait* is used to indicate a time relationship, so you almost never find it used on its own. When you do come across it, it will usually be used to show chronology: that some event took place before another, more recent event, whether it was a continuous state as indicated by the *imparfait* or a specific action or event that took place at a discernible moment in time, as indicated by the *passé composé.*

Choosing the Appropriate Past Tense

You have to be careful when translating from English to French to make sure that you are choosing the appropriate past tense. Sometimes, in spoken English, the auxiliary words are dropped, so you have to pay a little extra attention to your choices in French.

As long as you keep the following points in mind, you should be well on your way to keeping the past tense choices straight.

- *Passé composé:* The *passé composé* is used to indicate events that have a concrete beginning and ending at some point in the past.
- *Imparfait:* The *imparfait* is used for actions or events that don't have a definite beginning or end, but happened over a course of time in the past.
- *Plus-que-parfait:* The *plus-que-parfait* is used in relation with other tenses to show that something occurred at an even earlier point in time, further back in the past.

Literary Tenses

In written French, it can become cumbersome to use the *passé composé* all the time, over and over, especially when telling a story in the past tense, like most novels do. In French, to avoid this problem, there are special tenses known as literary tenses. These appear only in literature, as a rule, although you never know when you'll run across them. The only thing you can know for sure is that you won't hear anyone speak them.

You may encounter these literary tenses in books or magazines or anywhere you come across written French. Even though you may not ever actually use them, you should at least be able to recognize them, so the formations are outlined here.

Le Passé Simple

The *passé simple*, or simple past tense, is used like the *passé composé* to refer to events that occurred in the past. There is a major difference, however; while the *passé composé* uses either *avoir* or *être* as an auxiliary verb, the *passé simple* does not take any auxiliary; instead, the following endings are added to the stem of verbs ending in *-er*. Note the accents over the plural forms.

TABLE 12-23

PASSÉ SIMPLE WITH -ER VERB ENDINGS		
PERSON	**SINGULAR**	**PLURAL**
1st Person	-ai	-âmes
2nd Person	-as	-âtes
3rd Person	-a (m)	-èrent (m)
	-a (f)	-èrent (f)

TABLE 12-24

PASSÉ SIMPLE CONJUGATION OF PARLER	
SINGULAR	**PLURAL**
je parlai (jhe pahrl-ay)	nous parlâmes (noo pahr-lam)
tu parlas (tchoo pahrl-ah)	vous parlâtes (voo pahr-latt)
il parla (eel pahrl-ah)	ils parlèrent (eel pahrl-aihrr)
elle parla (ell pahrl-ah)	elles parlèrent (ell parhl-aihrr)

With verbs ending in *-ir* and *-re*, the *passé simple* is formed a little differently, adding the endings in **TABLE 12-25**, instead. Unlike the endings of *-er* verbs, only the *nous* and *vous* forms have accents in the conjugated verb endings.

TABLE 12-25

PASSÉ SIMPLE -RE AND -IR VERB ENDINGS		
PERSON	SINGULAR	PLURAL
1st Person	-is	-îmes
2nd Person	-is	-îtes
3rd Person	-it (m)	-irent (m)
	-it (f)	-irent (f)

TABLE 12-26

PASSÉ SIMPLE CONJUGATION OF PARTIR	
SINGULAR	PLURAL
je partis (jhe pahr-tee)	nous partîmes (noo pahr-teem)
tu partis (tchoo pahr-tee)	vous partîtes (voo pahr-teet)
il partit (eel pahr-tee)	ils partirent (eel pahrt-eer)
elle partit (ell pahr-tee)	elles partirent (ell part-eer)

TABLE 12-27

PASSÉ SIMPLE CONJUGATION OF RIRE	
SINGULAR	PLURAL
je ris (jhe rhee)	nous rîmes (noo rheem)
tu ris (tchoo rhee)	vous rîtes (voo rheet)
il rit (eel rhee)	ils rirent (eel rheer)
elle rit (ell rhee)	elles rirent (ell rheer)

You will need to be careful that you don't confuse -ir and -re verbs conjugated in the *passé simple* with the conditional or future forms of the words. Normally, the presence of an "r" is a great pointer to the tense. Fortunately, you won't have to worry about hearing these verbs conjugated in this tense; however, you may encounter them in books, magazines, or even on commemorative plaques. Best to be prepared.

If you come across a formation of the *passé simple*, remember that it is being used to refer to past events. The *passé simple* appears to be a present tense conjugation, because it uses no auxiliary verb, but it is not. It is simply a more convenient way for writers to refer to happenings in the past.

As an example of the *passé simple* in action, you can see it used in the following ancient French proverb: *Le savant n'est pas l'homme qui fournit la vraie réponse, mais celui qui pose les vraies questions.* (The wise person is not the man who has given the right answers, but the one who asks the right questions.)

Pay close attention to the *passé simple* conjugation of the verb *être* in the first person plural. The *nous* form, *fûmes*, is reminiscent of the verb *fumer*, "to smoke." If you come across it, recognize the *circonflexe* accent over the "u," and remember that it means "we were," not "we smoke."

The following irregular verbs have completely irregular formations in the *passé simple*, as they do in most other tenses, too. *Avoir* and *être* are used in the construction of another literary tense, called the *passé antérieur*, which is covered in the following section. While you don't need to memorize these forms to be able to use them in any great capacity, you should be able to recognize them so that you're not completely lost should you stumble across them somewhere.

TABLE 12-28

PASSÉ SIMPLE CONJUGATION OF *AVOIR*	
SINGULAR	**PLURAL**
j'eus (jhoo)	*nous eûmes* (noo oom)
tu eus (tchoo oo)	*vous eûtes* (voo oot)
il eut (eel oo)	*ils eurent* (eel oohr)
elle eut (ell oo)	*elles eurent* (ell oohr)

TABLE 12-29

PASSÉ SIMPLE CONJUGATION OF *ÊTRE*	
SINGULAR	**PLURAL**
je fus (jhe foo)	*nous fûmes* (noo fuhm)
tu fus (tchoo foo)	*vous fûtes* (voo fuht)
il fut (eel foo)	*ils furent* (eel foohr)
elle fut (ell foo)	*elles furent* (ell foohr)

The following verbs, *tenir* and *venir*, also have irregular conjugations in the *passé simple*. The verbs are not readily recognizable from the conjugation; as a matter of fact, you may find yourself confusing them with a number of words, so familiarize yourself with the forms.

TABLE 12-30

PASSÉ SIMPLE CONJUGATION OF TENIR	
SINGULAR	PLURAL
je tins (jhe tehn)	*nous tînmes* (noo tahm)
tu tins (tchoo tehn)	*vous tîntes* (voo tahnt)
il tint (eel tehn)	*ils tinrent* (eel tahn-rh)
elle tint (ell tehn)	*elles tinrent* (ell tahn-rh)

TABLE 12-31

PASSÉ SIMPLE CONJUGATION OF VENIR	
je vins (jhe vehn)	*nous vînmes* (noo vahm)
tu vins (tchoo vehn)	*vous vîntes* (voo vahnt)
il vint (eel vehn)	*ils vinrent* (eel vahn-rh)
elle vint (ell vehn)	*elles vinrent* (ell vahn-rh)

Le Passé Antérieur

If the *passé simple* is similar in use to the *passé composé*, then the *passé antérieur* is similar to the *plus-que-parfait*. It is used to refer to events that happened before the action described using the *passé simple*. However, in formation, it is very much like the *passé composé*. It uses *avoir* or *être* conjugated in the *passé simple* as the auxiliary verb, along with the past participle. As usual, the past participle will agree with any necessary preceding object pronouns. Refer to earlier in this chapter for information on agreement with verbs conjugated with *être* as the auxiliary verb and for agreement with verbs using *avoir* as the auxiliary.

While the *passé antérieur* looks like a simple past construction, it is not. In literary works, it is used to indicate events that happened before the events described using the *passé simple*. In its formation, the *passé antérieur* looks a lot like the *passé composé*, but its meaning is actually closer to the *plus-que-parfait*.

Idiomatic Expressions—the Recent Past

In English, we often use constructions like "I just got back from the store." While technically this refers to a past event, we don't really put this in the past tense; instead, we use the recent past construction, using the word "just." This is an English idiomatic expression.

In French, you can do the exact same thing with the verb *venir,* following it with the preposition *de.* When used in the present indicative, the verb has the exact same meaning as the English "just" construction, being conjugated in the present tense: *Je viens de retourner du magasin.* (I just got back from the store; I just returned from the store.)

When used with reflexive verbs (see Chapter 13), the reflexive pronoun is placed immediately before the infinitive form of the verb. Remember to use an appropriate English translation and don't try to translate word for word, or you will end up with absurd results.

Anytime you would use the "just" construction in English, you can create the same meaning in French using *venir de,* followed by an infinitive. It's a very common expression, and it's much easier to use instead of trying to cast things in the *passé composé* or another past tense. Use it whenever you think it's appropriate. It is widely used in the French language, so you should feel completely comfortable using it, for example: *Je viens de me lever.* (I just got up; I just woke up.)

CHAPTER 13

Using Reflexive Verbs

Reflexive verbs are used to indicate an action that the subject performs on his or her own self. In English, the words "himself" or "herself" point back to the subject. In French, this is done with a reflexive pronoun. The reflexive pronoun shows that the action goes back to the subject; this is important, because the verb will probably have another meaning if it's used without the reflexive pronoun.

Understanding Reflexive Verbs

Reflexive pronouns bear great similarity to the pronouns discussed in Chapter 9. The only difference is in the third person, where there is no gender distinction and, thus, the same word is used for both masculine and feminine subjects.

TABLE 13-1

FRENCH REFLEXIVE PRONOUNS		
PERSON	**SINGULAR**	**PLURAL**
1st Person	*me* (muh) me	*nous* (noo) us
2nd Person	*te* (tuh) you	*vous* (voo) you
3rd Person	*se* (suh) him, her	*se* (m) (say) them

Fortunately, reflexive pronouns are pretty easy to keep straight, because they always match the subject of the sentence. Whenever the object of the verb, or reflexive pronoun, (for example, *te* or "you") is the same as the subject (for example, *tu* or "you"), the action is being performed reflexively. When you use a reflexive verb, all you have to do is match the object pronoun with the subject and use it with the appropriate verb.

Normally, reflexive verbs are used in the singular. When used in the plural, the meaning usually changes, and it's called a reciprocal verb (discussed in the following section). It is probably best to think of French reflexive verbs as idiomatic expressions (see Chapter 2 for a definition of that term).

The following reflexive verbs describe actions that commonly occur around the house. These are known as pronomial verbs, because they take a pronoun before their conjugation in this construction. You may also encounter these verbs used nonreflexively (in which case, they have different meanings), but they tend to appear most often in reflexive constructions. When they do, they carry the following meanings.

TABLE 13-2

PRONOMIAL VERBS		
REFLEXIVE VERB	**PRONUNCIATION**	**ENGLISH**
s'appeler	sah-pah-lay	to be named; to be called
se réveiller	se ray-vay-yay	to wake up
se lever	se luh-vay	to get up
s'endormir	sahn-dohr-meer	to fall asleep
s'étirer	say-tee-ray	to stretch
se laver	se lah-vay	to wash (oneself)
se sécher	se say-shay	to dry (oneself)
se raser	se rahz-ay	to shave (oneself)
s'habiller	sahb-ee-ay	to get dressed
se coiffer	se kwaff-ay	to comb one's hair
se brosser	se brah-say	to brush
se maquiller	se ma-kee-ay	to put on makeup
se reposer	se ruh-po-say	to rest
se déshabiller	se day-sab-ee-ay	to undress (oneself)

In theory, all of these verbs can be used with other pronouns as the direct object, but then the verbs are not being used reflexively. Only when the direct object matches the subject is the verb being used in a reflexive construction.

English also tends to handle many of these verbs idiomatically. Just because a reflexive pronoun appears in French, it doesn't mean that a corresponding English word is required; "to wash up," "to wake up," and "to fall asleep" are all examples of English verbs that use a completely different construction from French. Often, the English expressions don't translate literally very well into French, either. Treat them all as idiomatic expressions that require a little bit of extra care in translation. Treat reflexive pronouns as a signpost that tells you that the action is reverting back to the subject, and then choose the most appropriate English equivalent based on that. Here are two examples:

- *Je m'appelle David.* (I call myself David; my name is David.)
- *Il s'habille dans sa chambre.* (He is getting dressed in his bedroom.)

Other verbs can also be used reflexively, although they are more often used nonreflexively and have different meanings that way.

TABLE 13-3

MEANINGS OF VERBS USED REFLEXIVELY		
REFLEXIVE VERB	PRONUNCIATION	ENGLISH
s'en aller	sahn ah-lay	to go away
s'amuser	sah-moo-zay	to have a good time
se débrouiller	se day-brwee-ay	to get by, to manage
se demander	se duh-mahn-day	to wonder
se dépêcher	se day-pay-shay	to hurry
s'ennuyer	sahn-wee-ay	to get bored
s'entendre	sahn-tahn-druh	to get along
s'habituer à	sah-bee-choo-ay ah	to get used to
se rendre compte de	se rhan-druh kompt de	to realize
se tromper	se trahm-pay	to be wrong

Inversion can be used to form questions from sentences using pronominal verbs, but the pronoun retains its position in front of the verb. As a result, the reflexive pronoun tends to appear as the subject, especially when the *nous* or *vous* form is used. In actuality, the subject is situated after the verb, due to the inversion: *Vous êtes-vous amusés au cinéma hier soir?* (Did you have fun at the movies last night?)

Reflexive Verbs Used Reciprocally

Sometimes, reflexive verbs can be used with a different direct object. When this happens, the action is said to occur reciprocally—it happens equally between the subject and object, as a group, for the benefit of each other. Because of the nature of reciprocal verbs, you encounter them only in the plural; it is not possible to have a singular construction occur because it requires more than one person.

When considering reciprocal verbs, the object of the sentence and how it is used is important. When the object is the same as the subject, the verb is being used reflexively; when the object and the subject are different, the meaning is reciprocal.

When a verb is used reciprocally, it carries the action of the verb to a greater group of people, but still allows you to maintain a distinction between the two groups. One is represented by the subject pronoun, and the other by the object pronoun. In French, there is a distinction.

Reciprocal verbs don't always translate into English very easily, however. There is no direct equivalent translation, and the appropriate choice can vary. For the most part, "each other" will suffice to complete the meaning.

- *Vous vous parlez.* (You are speaking to each other.)
- *Nous nous regardons.* (We are looking at each other.)
- *Ils nous regardent.* (They are looking at us.)

The expression *l'un l'autre* can be added to the sentence, placed immediately after the verb, to clarify the sentence when this meaning is intended. The *un* will agree in gender and number with the subject; *l'autre* is used to indicate the object. Literally, it means "the one the other." When used together with a reciprocal verb, it carries the meaning of "together" or "each other." The plural form *les uns les autres* may also be used immediately after the verb. To translate, choose an English phrase that best fits the meaning of the sentence, such as "one another" or "each other": *Est-ce qu'ils sont chez vous, avec vos enfants?* (Are they at your house, with your kids?) *Oui, ils s'amusent les uns les autres.* (Yes, they are amusing one another.)

Remember that if a past participle is used with the verb *avoir*, it must agree with the preceding object pronoun, not the subject. Therefore, if the pronoun indicates two females, the past participle must be used in the feminine plural to agree: *Est-ce que Michel et Richard étaient chez vous, avec Sara et Marie?* (Were Michael and Richard at your house, with Sara and Marie?) *Oui, ils se sont amusés les uns les autres.* (Yes, they were amusing each other.)

If an object pronoun is not used, the past participle when conjugated with *avoir* does not have to agree with anything. Remember that a past participle, when used with the verb *être* as an auxiliary verb, changes only to match the subject. When using object pronouns in sentences that are formed with *être* constructions, do not modify the past participle to match the object. It must match the subject of the sentence. Refer to Chapter 12 for more information on verbs conjugated with *être* or check Appendix 2.

Verbs That Are Always Pronomial

The following verbs must be used in either reflexive or reciprocal constructions, because the verbs are always pronomial: In other words, they do not have a nonreflexive meaning. With the following list, whenever you see them used, you know that it will be used as a reflexive or reciprocal verb, because the verb doesn't actually exist in any other form. In addition to using the pronoun in front of the verb, some also take the preposition *de* after the verb. If the word immediately following *de* begins with a vowel, *de* is contracted to *d'*.

TABLE 13-4	VERBS THAT ARE ALWAYS PRONOMIAL		
	REFLEXIVE VERB	PRONUNCIATION	ENGLISH
	s'écrier	say-cree-ay	to exclaim
	s'écrouler	say-croo-lay	to collapse
	s'efforcer de	seff-ohr-say de	to strive
	s'empresser de	sahm-press-ay de	to hasten
	s'enfuir	sahn-fweer	to flee
	s'envoler	sahn-vohl-ay	to fly away
	s'évanouir	say-vahn-wheer	to faint
	se méfier de	se may-fee-ay de	to distrust
	se moquer de	se mo-kay de	to make fun of
	se soucier de	se soo-see-ay de	to mind
	se souvenir de	se soo-vehn-eer de	to remember
	se suicider	se soo-ay-see-day	to kill oneself
	se taire	se tehr	to be silent

Forming the Future Tense

The future tense adds another dimension to your growing French vocabulary. By understanding this tense, you can talk about what is going to happen in the near future and the distant future and also compare a future action that will be completed before another action or event occurs at some later point in the future, such as "Will you have finished this chapter by noon tomorrow?"

English Future-Tense Constructions

The English constructions for future tenses are actually quite similar to the past-tense constructions (see Chapter 14); they just move in the opposite direction in time.

To refer to events that will occur in the future, English uses the word "will." (Remember that the word "will" can often be contracted when it is used after a word that ends in a vowel, so expressions like "he'll" actually mean "he will" and, therefore, indicate an event in the future tense.)

- I **will go** to the store.
- We**'ll do** it later.

SSENTIALS Remember that you can also use the verb "to go" with an infinitive to indicate the immediate future in both languages. In French, simply conjugate the verb *aller* (to go) in the present tense and follow it with a verb used in the infinitive.

There is another future tense in English that's used to indicate events that will be completed at some point in the future. In English, it is known as the future perfect because it is an event that will be completely finished, or perfected. Here are some examples:

- By six o'clock, I **will have gone** to the store.
- When the dessert has finished baking, we **will have finished** supper.

The future perfect is much like the pluperfect (see Chapter 12) in formation, but of course, the event being referred to will not have yet happened. Can you identify where the future perfect was used in the preceding sentence? "Will not have yet happened" is another example of the future perfect tense being used in English.

The Future Tense in French

In French you have three ways to form the future tense: *le futur proche*, *le futur simple*, and *le futur antérieur*.

Le Futur Proche

In English, we can use the verb "to go" to indicate something that is going to happen in the immediate future, such as "I am going to go to the movies." The verb "to go" appears in that sentence twice—once conjugated with the subject, and the other appearing as the infinitive. The verb *aller* can be used the same way in French: *Je vais aller au cinéma.* (I am going to go to the cinema.)

You can also use *aller* with virtually any other infinitive verb to indicate anything that will happen in the very near future. In French, this is known as the *futur proche* (near future) and is very simple, as follows:

- *Je vais acheter un billet.* (I am going to buy a ticket.)
- *Je vais vendre le livre.* (I am going to sell the book.)

Le Futur Simple

There are more formal ways of speaking of future events, and the *futur simple* is the most commonly used. In some ways, it is one of the more interesting tenses, because it follows a unique conjugation pattern. Like the others, it uses special verb endings, but instead of chopping off parts of the infinitive, it uses the infinitive itself.

To give you an idea of how the *futur simple* looks, here is the verb *regarder* conjugated in the *futur simple*.

TABLE 14-1

REGARDER CONJUGATED IN THE *FUTUR SIMPLE*		
PERSON	**SINGULAR**	**PLURAL**
1st Person	*je regarderai* (jhe re-gar-der-ay)	*nous regarderons* (noo re-gar-der-ohn)
2nd Person	*tu regarderas* (tchoo re-gar-der-a)	*vous regarderez* (voo re-gar-der-ay)
3rd Person	*il regardera* (eel re-gar-der-ah)	*ils regarderont* (eel re-gar-der-ohn)
	elle regardera (ell re-gar-der-ah)	*elles regarderont* (ell re-gar-der-ohn)

As you can see, the verb takes on a unique appearance with the presence of the "r." The "r" is distinctly pronounced in spoken French, so when you hear it, you know that someone is referring to something in the future tense. In English, instead of having a special verb form to indicate the future, we use the word "will" as an auxiliary word; when you see the construction in English, you'll probably want to use the *futur simple* in French.

To form the future tense with most verbs, simply add the following endings to the infinitive form.

TABLE 14-2

PERSON	*FUTUR SIMPLE* **VERB ENDINGS**	
	SINGULAR	PLURAL
1st Person	-*ai*	-*ons*
2nd Person	-*as*	-*ez*
3rd Person	-*a* (m)	-*ont* (m)
	-*a* (f)	-*ont* (f)

When conjugating verbs that end in -*re* in the future tense, simply drop the "e" from the ending, but keep the "r," as shown in **TABLE 14-3**.

TABLE 14-3

PERSON	*PRENDRE* **CONJUGATED IN THE** *FUTUR SIMPLE*	
	SINGULAR	PLURAL
1st Person	*je prendrai*	*nous prendrons*
	(jhe prahn-dray)	(noo prahn-drohn)
2nd Person	*tu prendras*	*vous prendrez*
	(tchoo prahn-dra)	(voo prahn-dray)
3rd Person	*il prendra*	*ils prendront*
	(eel prahn-dra)	(eel prahn-drohn)
	elle prendra	*elles prendront*
	(ell prahn-dra)	(ell prahn-drohn)

Take a look at the following examples:

- *Je prendrai un examen.* (I will take a test; I will be taking a test.)
- *Nous voyagerons.* (We will travel, we are going to travel.)

- *Nous ne regarderons pas le film.* (We will not see the film; we won't watch the film.)

When pronouncing verbs in the future tense, the emphasis shifts to the last syllable, so the pronunciation does not sound the same as the infinitive. Practice pronouncing verbs in the future tense until you can include the "r" sound distinctly without putting too much emphasis on it.

Naturally, there are exceptions with irregular formations that you will have to watch for—a number of verbs have an irregular stem when used in the future tense—but you will get used to them with practice, because they tend to be fairly commonly used. Not all irregular verbs have irregular future stems, so you'll need to memorize these individually.

TABLE 14-4

IRREGULAR STEMS IN THE *FUTUR SIMPLE*			
VERB	**FUTURE STEM**	**VERB**	**FUTURE STEM**
avoir	*aur–*	*pouvoir*	*pourr–*
être	*ser–*	*recevoir*	*recevr–*
aller	*ir–*	*savoir*	*saur–*
devoir	*devr–*	*valoir*	*vaudr–*
envoyer	*enverr–*	*venir*	*viendr–*
faire	*fer–*	*voir*	*verr–*
falloir	*faudr–*	*vouloir*	*voudr–*
pleuvoir	*pleuvr–*		

You can also consult the verb conjugation tables in Appendix 2 to find the future stems of verbs.

TABLE 14-5

	VOIR CONJUGATED IN THE *FUTUR SIMPLE*	
PERSON	**SINGULAR**	**PLURAL**
1st Person	*je verrai*	*nous verrons*
	(jhe vay-ray)	(noo vay-rohn)
2nd Person	*tu verras*	*vous verrez*
	(tchoo vay-ra)	(voo vay-ray)
3rd Person	*il verra*	*ils verront*
	(eel vay-ra)	(eel vay-rohn)
	elle verra	*elles verront*
	(ell vay-ra)	(ell vay-rohn)

Le Futur Antérieur

There is another tense you can use to refer to events in the future, known as the *futur antérieur*. It is similar to the *plus-que-parfait* (see Chapter 12), in that it compares the time relationship between two events; it just operates in the other direction. In English, it is known as the future perfect, because it indicates that one action will be completed before another action or event occurs at some later point in the future. Here are two examples:

- *Est-ce que vous serez partis à cinq heures demain?* (Will you have left by 5 o'clock tomorrow?)
- *Nous aurons étudié le livre quand nous écrirons l'examen.* (We will have studied the book when we take the test.)

Also like the *plus-que-parfait*, it is relatively easy to form, combining other tenses to refer to events in the future. You can conjugate any verb in the *futur antérieur* by using its past participle with its auxiliary verb conjugated in the *futur simple*. See **TABLE 14-6**.

TABLE 14-6

PERSON	SINGULAR	PLURAL
ALLER CONJUGATED IN THE FUTUR ANTÉRIEUR		
1st Person	*je serai allé(e)* (jhe sir-ay ah-lay)	*nous serons allé(e)s* (noo sir-ohn ah-lay)
2nd Person	*tu seras allé(e)* (tchoo sir-ah ah-lay)	*vous serez allé(e)s* (voo sir-ay ah-lay)
3rd Person	*il sera allé* (eel sir-ah ah-lay)	*ils seront allés* (eel sir-ohn ah-lay)
	elle sera allée (ell sir-ah ah-lay)	*elles seront allées* (ell sir-ohn ah-lay)

Because the future perfect is formed with the past participle (see Chapter 12), you won't have to worry about the irregular endings some verbs use in the future, because you'll only be conjugating *avoir* or *être* in the future. You will, however, have to make sure that the past participle agrees with the subject when the verb is conjugated with *être* as the auxiliary.

Verbs that take *être* as the auxiliary will use the past participle with *être*, conjugated in the *futur simple*. As with the *passé composé*, the past participle must agree in gender and number with the subject.

Note that when the *futur antérieur* is used, the *futur simple* is also used, because both events have yet to occur. In English, when using a similar construction, we don't usually use the future tense with both events; one usually slips into the present, while the event that is dependent upon it is cast into the future. Remember that in French, the *futur simple* is used to complement the *futur antérieur*.

CHAPTER 15
Forming the Conditional Tense

In English, you sometimes refer to events that haven't yet happened or that may not happen at all. These are known as conditional statements. They usually imply something that could happen, but whose outcome depends on some other event. We often construct these phrases in English using the words "would," "should," or "could."

Uses of the Conditional Tense

In some ways, the conditional tense is like an imaginary tense. It doesn't refer to concrete events in the past, present, or future. It refers to things that could happen or may happen, but there is no guarantee as to the actual outcome, as in "I would go to the store if it weren't raining." The conditional tense is used to refer to potential situations. The expression may contain an element of doubt or uncertainty about the statement being made. It is a rather abstract tense in both English and French, not referring to the here and now, but rather an uncertain state of events, such as in the following examples:

- *Nous voudrions aller au magasin.*
  (We would like to go to the store.)
- *Est-ce que vous iriez avec nous?*
  (Would you go with us?)
- *J'acheterais un billet.*
  (I would buy a ticket.)

There is nothing certain about the outcome of any of these events; each is a mere statement of intention. Conjugated in the present tense, the phrase would translate as "we want to go to the store." Inferred with the conditional, however, is an element of doubt, as the decision may be up to someone else, or it may depend on some other event.

SSENTIALS   When the conditional tense is used, there is always a sense of doubt as to its completion. The tense usually carries a sense of speculation about the event. Unlike the other tenses, an idea expressed in the conditional can't really be tied to a specific time period, because the event itself isn't even a sure thing. The outcome is never guaranteed, and sometimes isn't really even expected.

In Chapter 8, the word *si* used to respond affirmatively to a negative question. It can also be used as a conjunction that means "if" and is often used with the conditional tense to describe uncertain events. This is very similar to the English construction. We use "if" all the time when referring to things in the conditional:

- *Je parlerais à l'homme si je e connaissais.*
  (I would speak to the man **if** I knew him.)

For the most part, the English word "would" can be your trigger for when to use the conditional tense in French. Be careful, however, that you don't get it confused with the use of "would" in the sense of "used to," which actually takes the imperfect tense (see Chapter 12).

As you are learning the language, pay special attention to the conditional tense to make sure that you don't confuse it with the future. You will also have to remember how to balance each conditional tense, using the appropriate past tense to complement it. For more information on the future tense, see Chapter 14.

Using the Conditional Tense to Be Polite

With certain verbs, the conditional tense serves to cast the statement into a very polite tone. As a result, these verbs are often used in the conditional, especially when making requests. It is considered more formal and less demanding.

As a result, you will often encounter the verbs *aimer, pouvoir,* and *vouloir* used in the conditional tense. This is actually very similar to the English way of asking questions politely, so you shouldn't have too much difficulty with them. *Aimer* transforms into "would like," *pouvoir* into "could," and *vouloir* into "would like."

You can use these forms in any situation when you wish to be polite and courteous. When speaking with persons of authority, it is sometimes a good idea to use the conditional tense. When somebody commands respect, respond with the conditional tense.

When ordering a meal in a restaurant, the exchange with your waiter will almost always occur using the conditional tense. (See Chapter 17 for more on restaurants.)

TABLE 15-1	EXCHANGE WITH A WAITER	
WAITER	**YOU**	
Voudriez-vous quelque chose, madame? (Would you like something, Madam?)	*Oui. Je voudrais un filet mignon.* (Yes. I would like a filet mignon.)	
Et qu'est-ce que vous voudriez boire? (And what would you like to drink?)	*Du thé, s'il vous plaît.* (Some tea, please.)	
C'est tout? (That's everything?)	*Oui. Merci.* (Yes. Thank you.)	

The waiter is being very polite to you, using the conditional tense in addition to referring to you using the formal *vous* form. Responding in the conditional refers to your preference, instead of phrasing it as a specific request, as would happen using the present tense indicative conjugation. This level of respect is evident in English, too; it's very similar to the phrase "I'll have . . ." that often gets used when ordering. Remember to be polite to your waiter, thank him or her, and refer to him as *monsieur*, or to her as *madame* or *mademoiselle.*

Naturally, a restaurant isn't the only place you will want to be polite. Hotel employees, flight attendants, tour guides, customs officials, and all other human beings always appreciate people who are courteous, thoughtful, and considerate. Using the conditional tense conveys that sense, so get comfortable using it. People will appreciate you for it.

The Past Conditional Tense

The past conditional tense is used to refer to the same kinds of events as the conditional, but simply in the past. Don't let its construction fool you. Despite the fact that it looks complex with its auxiliary construction, it is a simple reference to past events in French. In English, this is often accomplished by saying "would have," for example: *Nous aurions voulu aller au magasin.* "We would have liked to go to the store."

Keep in mind that the past conditional tense is a past tense; don't fall into the trap of thinking it's in the future because the formation of the auxiliary verb reminds you of the future. Learn to recognize when avoir or être is being conjugated in the conditional; the distinct sounds of the conjugated verb endings should help (see the following section). Then let the past participle remind you that this is occurring in the conditional past and doesn't have anything to do with the future tense.

When the main clause is used in the past conditional, the subordinate clause must be conjugated using the *plus-que-parfait* (see Chapter 12). If used with any other tenses, the statements just wouldn't make sense: *J'aurais été riche si j'ai fait des études à l'université.* (I would have been rich if I attended university.)

Forming the Conditional Tense

In French, the conditional tense has its own verb form, so you will always be able to recognize it. You have to be careful, however, not to confuse it with the future tense. To form the conditional tense in French, you use the future stem of the verb, but you conjugate it with the *imparfait* verb endings.

TABLE 15-2

IMPARFAIT **VERB ENDINGS**		
PERSON	**SINGULAR**	**PLURAL**
1st Person	-*ais*	-*ions*
2nd Person	-*ais*	-*iez*
3rd Person	-*ait* (m)	-*aient* (m)
	-*ait* (f)	-*aient* (f)

As a result, the construction of the conditional tense is relatively straightforward. Just use the same stem of the verb you would use to create the future tense and tack on the imperfect ending. The conditional tense conjugation of the regular verbs is illustrated in the following sections.

-er Verbs

For -*er* verbs, simply use the infinitive form of the verb as the stem, as with *parler*.

TABLE 15-3	*CONDITIONNEL* **CONJUGATION OF** *PARLER*	
SINGULAR	**PLURAL**	
je parlerais (jhe pahrl-rhay)	*nous parlerions* (noo pahrl-rhee-ohn)	
tu parlerais (tchoo pahrl-rhay)	*vous parleriez* (voo pahrl-rhee-ay)	
il parlerait (eel pahrl-rhay)	*ils parleraient* (eel pahrl-rhay)	
elle parlerait (ell pahrl-rhay)	*elles parleraient* (ell pahrl-rhay)	

-ir Verbs

Verbs ending in *-ir*, like *finir*, also use the infinitive form as the conditional stem.

TABLE 15-4	*CONDITIONNEL* **CONJUGATION OF** *FINIR*	
SINGULAR	**PLURAL**	
je finirais (jhe feh-neer-ay)	*nous finirions* (noo feh-neer-ee-ohn)	
tu finirais (tchoo feh-neer-ay)	*vous finiriez* (voo feh-neer-ee-ay)	
il finirait (eel feh-neer-ay)	*ils finiraient* (eel feh-neer-ay)	
elle finirait (ell feh-neer-ay)	*elles finiraient* (ell feh-neer-ay)	

-re Verbs

To form the conditional stem of *-re* verbs, simply drop the "e" from the end, as with *prendre*.

TABLE 15-5	*CONDITIONNEL* **CONJUGATION OF** *PRENDRE*	
SINGULAR	**PLURAL**	
je prendrais (jhe prahn-dray)	*nous prendrions* (noo prahn-dree-ohn)	
tu prendrais (tchoo prahn-dray)	*vous prendriez* (voo prahn-dree-ay)	
il prendrait (eel prahn-dray)	*ils prendraient* (eel prahn-dray)	
elle prendrait (ell prahn-dray)	*elles prendraient* (ell prahn-dray)	

Like the *imparfait*, the unique pronunciation of the endings should help you to discern quite easily between the future and the conditional.

The only ones that are pronounced the same are the *je* forms, so pay close attention to them.

Verbs that have an irregular stem in the future tense also use that same irregular stem to form the conditional. The following list of verbs with irregular future stems is included for your convenience; for more information, consult Chapter 14, where the future tense is discussed in detail.

TABLE 15-6

IRREGULAR FUTURE STEMS		
VERB	FUTURE STEM	ENGLISH
avoir	*aur-*	to have, to hold
être	*ser-*	to be
aller	*ir-*	to go
devoir	*devr-*	to have to, to be obliged to
envoyer	*enverr-*	to send
faire	*fer-*	to make, to do
falloir	*faudr-*	to be necessary
pleuvoir	*pleuvr-*	to rain
pouvoir	*pourr-*	to be able to
recevoir	*recevr-*	to receive, to accept
savoir	*saur-*	to know
venir	*viendr-*	to come
voir	*verr-*	to see
vouloir	*voudr-*	to want

Conjugating Subordinate Clauses

When the main clause of the sentence is used in the conditional, the subordinate clause must be conjugated using the imperfect tense (see Chapter 12). This grammatical construction is a requirement to balancing off the sentence. From the beginning, get used to doing it this way, because it is the only way that is correct. When *si* is used with the conditional tense, *si* forms the subordinate clause. It is conjugated in the imperfect tense and is dependent upon the main clause, which is cast in the conditional: *Si j'avais une voiture, je conduirais à l'école.* (If I had a car, I would drive to school.)

The subordinate clause is easy to identify. In the preceding example, the phrase "if I had a car" cannot stand on its own; therefore, it is the subordinate clause. Its meaning is not complete unless it gets tacked on to the main clause. As you can see, the tense construction follows the English pattern very closely.

The subordinate clause will usually leave you hanging a bit, leaving you feeling unfulfilled; it doesn't tell you enough information. It doesn't make sense unless it's attached to the main clause and so must be cast in the imperfect tense. The part of the sentence that can stand on its own and still make sense, the main clause, is then conjugated in the conditional tense.

English constructions in the conditional are not nearly as precise, so simply use whatever makes the most sense when translating from French. When translating from English into French, it's even easier, as you can simply identify each clause and conjugate the rest of the sentence in the appropriate associated tense.

Forming the Past Conditional Tense

The similarities between the conditional and future tenses extend to the past, too. Like the construction of the future perfect, the past conditional tense uses the present conditional conjugation of the auxiliary verb, whether it is *avoir* or *être*. The appropriate past participle is then added, and any necessary agreements are made. For more information on the agreement of past participles, refer to Chapter 12.

Avoir

Remember that past participles used with *avoir* must agree in gender and number with any preceding diret object pronouns. Refer to Chapter 12 for more information.

TABLE 15-7

CONDITIONNEL CONJUGATION OF AVOIR	
SINGULAR	PLURAL
j'aurais (jho-rhay)	nous aurions (noo-zhohr-ee-ohn)
tu aurais (tchoo ohr-ay)	vous auriez (voo-zhohr-ee-ay)
il aurait (eel ohr-ay)	ils auraient (eel zohr-ay)
elle aurait (ell ohr-ay)	elles auraient (ell zohr-ay)

Take a look at the following examples:

- *J'aurais entendu.* (I would have heard.)
- *Tu aurais vu.* (You would have seen.)
- *Il aurait appris.* (He would have learned.)

Être

Remember that past participles used with *être* must agree with the preceding subject pronoun; object pronouns do not modify the past participle when used with *être* as the auxiliary verb.

TABLE 15-8

CONDITIONNEL CONJUGATION OF ÊTRE	
SINGULAR	PLURAL
je serais (jhe sehr-ay)	nous serions (noo sehr-ee-ohn)
tu serais (tchoo sehr-ay)	vous seriez (voo sehr-ee-ay)
il serait (eel sehr-ay)	ils seraient (eel sehr-ay)
elle serait (ell sehr-ay)	elles seraient (ell sehr-ay)

Here are some examples:

- *Tu serais venu.* (You would have come.)
- *Elle serait allée.* (She would have gone.)
- *Ils seraient nés.* (They would have already been born.)

The Verb *Devoir* in the Conditional Tense

The verb *devoir* takes on a unique meaning when used in the conditional tense. It is the equivalent of the English construction "should" or "ought to," as in "I should go to the store" or "I ought to go fishing." See the following examples:

- *Je devrais aller au magasin.* (I should go to the store.)
- *Nous devrions étudier à la bibliothèque.* (We should study at the library.)

In French, this is done using the verb *devoir* in the conditional tense. Normally, *devoir* means "to have to"; it can also be interpreted as "must do something." When placed in the conditional, however, it implies that there is some doubt as to whether the event will actually occur. It imports an obligation of an almost moral nature; quite often, there will be an unspoken "but," inferring that the event may, in fact, never take place at all. In some grammatical circles, using *devoir* in the conditional is known as the "tense of regret" for that very reason.

Devoir has an irregular future stem, so it uses *devr-* as the stem in the conditional. Remember not to confuse the conditional conjugation of *devoir* with the imperfect conjugation, because they each have completely different meaning. In the imperfect tense, *devoir* would mean "used to have to." It still implies the obligation. Only when the statement is cast in the conditional does the necessary doubt enter the picture to trigger the same response as a "should" construction does in English.

CHAPTER 16

Understanding the Subjunctive Mood

The subjunctive mood is used to convey statements of opinion or things that aren't based in complete fact. It carries a degree of subjectivity or personal desire. In French, the subjunctive mood is widely used in certain constructions, and you will encounter it often.

Understanding the French Subjunctive

English makes limited use of the subjunctive. For example, while "I wish it **was** raining" may be common in spoken English, "I wish it **were** raining" is the correct use of the English subjunctive. To help keep it straight in your head, think of the subjunctive as an emotive expression. It is quite often used with phrases like "wish," "hope," and "doubt," describing things that aren't certain facts or foregone conclusions. It expresses a person's beliefs, rather than stating things as out-and-out fact.

The subjunctive mood follows a certain construction in French, being used to refer to things that are not based in fact. Doubts, beliefs, suspicions, opinions, and desires are not, as a rule, rooted in fact. In French, these are usually conveyed using the subjunctive.

The mere presence of subjectivity or doubt in a sentence isn't the only prerequisite for the use of the subjunctive, however: For a sentence to be used in the subjunctive, it must have a main clause and a subordinate clause, and each must have a different subject. In the example, "He doubts that I'll go to France," the subordinate clause consists of "that I'll go to France." "I'll" is actually a contraction of "I will"; English tends to put these constructions into a future tense. In similar sentences in French, the subjunctive is used to conjugate the verb in the subordinate clause.

When the subjunctive is used in French, it will always be used with a relative pronoun, such as *qui* or *que* (see Chapter 9). For the most part, *que* will be the most common word you'll encounter being used with the subjunctive: *Il doute que nous voyagions.* (He doubts that we will travel.)

The subjunctive itself does not necessarily carry any specific meaning; it simply points out an element of subjectivity or doubt. You can't always make a direct translation of subjunctive sentences; they will sound stilted and artificial in English. Because the subjunctive isn't widely used in English, when translating from French, you will have to use phrases that fit within the meaning of the sentence: *Je veux qu'il achète un billet.* (I would like him to buy a ticket.)

In the preceding example, a literal translation would run along the lines of "I want that he should buy a ticket," which really doesn't make a whole lot of sense. Instead, look to the essence of the sentence. The main clause indicates that "I," as the subject, "want" something. The *que* is your signpost into the subjunctive. It can be translated as "that," but the word is often omitted entirely in English.

In the subordinate clause, the fact that the subjunctive is used tells you that the statement is not factual. It is based on the main clause, which is an expression of the desire of the subject. The subordinate clause would translate as "he buys a ticket" if the verb were being used in the indicative, but with the subjunctive, a slightly different translation is called for. It must be related back to the main clause. After you've achieved this result, you can translate the sentence pretty much however you like, provided that you maintain the central meaning.

If you find that you cannot remember a certain construction when you are in a French conversation, try using the indicative mood. Native French speakers will expect the subjunctive but will likely be able to extrapolate the meaning from your words.

In English, instead of making a separate subordinate clause, we usually build onto the main clause using object pronouns, infinitives, and other words to make up the sentence. So, in the preceding example, "I would like him to buy a ticket" sums up the core meaning of the French subjunctive sentence. Don't worry that you're not maintaining the subjunctive in English; we simply don't use it very often, and even when its usage is called for, it usually gets ignored. Instead, spend your efforts on learning when the subjunctive is called for in French.

The subjunctive mood is very much an advanced construction, and mastering it will put you well on the way to full fluency. Even if you're not comfortable using it, you should at least be able to recognize when other people are using it; when you hear it, know that a subjective statement is being made.

The subjunctive mood is used only when the main clause has a different subject from the subordinate clause. If the two clauses use the same subject, the subjunctive clause is grafted onto the main clause using infinitives, much like we tend to do in English.

Il veut que je finisse mes devoirs. (He wants me to finish my homework.)
Je veux finir mes devoirs. (I want to finish my homework.)

If the sentence does not have an element of doubt or subjectivity, the subjunctive is not used; the sentence is cast in the regular indicative mood, relating a fact. When this happens, the tense follows whatever you'd normally use in English: *Il sait que nous finirons.* (He knows that we will finish.)

If you introduce an element of doubt or subjectivity, the subjunctive gets used in the subordinate clause. When translating into English, you will probably have to use a different form, one that more closely mirrors the preceding example, despite the use of the subjunctive.

Forming the Subjunctive Mood

Fortunately, the subjunctive is rather unique in its formation, so you should usually be able to tell when it's being used. In order to translate from English to French, you have to familiarize yourself with the kinds of situations that call for the subjunctive mood, so you know when to use it. You can learn more about these in the "Specific Uses of the Subjunctive" section, later in this chapter. Mastering the subjunctive is not easy, because the subjunctive isn't emphasized in the English language. Because it doesn't really have a solid English equivalent, however, you may need to spend some extra time with it before you get the full gist.

To form the present subjunctive with regular verbs, you must first obtain the subjunctive stem. This is based on the present indicative conjugation of the verb in the third person plural (see Chapter 6). Simply drop the *-ent* ending, and you have your stem. Because of this construction, most irregular verbs end up following a regular formation pattern in the subjunctive. The following endings are then added to the end of the subjunctive stem.

TABLE 16-1

SUBJUNCTIVE VERB ENDINGS		
PERSON	SINGULAR	PLURAL
1st Person	*-e*	*-ions*
2nd Person	*-es*	*-iez*
3rd Person	*-e* (m)	*-ent* (m)
	-e (f)	*-ent* (f)

You'll note that the third person plural endings are actually the same. When the third person plural is used in the subjunctive, you'll have to know from the sentence construction that it is being used in the construction, because nothing about the verb actually tells you.

This section demonstrates the present-tense conjugation of the three kinds of regular verb endings, irregular verbs, and common verbs that become irregular. Pay particularly close attention to the *nous* and *vous* forms; these endings sound very much like the imperfect endings, but are, in fact, present subjunctive. You need to rely on the construction to know that these are being used in the subjunctive—you can't actually tell from the verb form itself.

-er Verbs

All *-er* verbs follow the pattern in **TABLE 16-2.**

TABLE 16-2	SUBJUNCTIVE CONJUGATION OF *PARLER*	
SINGULAR	**PLURAL**	
je parle (jhe pahrl)	*nous parlions* (noo pahrl-ee-ohn)	
tu parles (tchoo pahrl)	*vous parliez* (voo pahrl-ee-ay)	
il parle (eel pahrl)	*ils parlent* (eel pahrl)	
elle parle (ell pahrl)	*elles parlent* (ell parhl)	

-ir Verbs

All *-ir* verbs follow the pattern in **TABLE 16-3.**

TABLE 16-3	SUBJUNCTIVE CONJUGATION OF *FINIR*	
SINGULAR	**PLURAL**	
je finisse (jhe feh-neece)	*nous finissions* (noo feh-nee-see-ohn)	
tu finisses (tchoo feh-neece)	*vous finissiez* (voo feh-nee-see-ay)	
il finisse (eel feh-neece)	*ils finissent* (eel feh-neece)	
elle finisse (ell feh-neece)	*elles finissent* (ell feh-neece)	

-re Verbs

All *-re* verbs follow the pattern in **TABLE 16-4.**

TABLE 16-4	SUBJUNCTIVE CONJUGATION OF *RIRE*	
	SINGULAR	**PLURAL**
	je rie (jhe rhee)	*nous riions* (noo rhee-ee-ohn)
	tu ries (tchoo rhee)	*vous riiez* (voo rhee-ee-ay)
	il rie (eel rhee)	*ils rient* (eel rhee)
	elle rie (ell rhee)	*elles rient* (ell rhee)

Irregular Verbs in the Subjunctive

The following irregular verbs also have irregular formations in the subjunctive, following no real consistent pattern. Memorize these verbs so that they'll always be on the tip of your tongue.

TABLE 16-5	SUBJUNCTIVE CONJUGATION OF *ALLER*	
	SINGULAR	**PLURAL**
	j'aille (jh-eye)	*nous allions* (noo ah-lee-ohn)
	tu ailles (tchoo eye)	*vous alliez* (voo ah-lee-ay)
	il aille (eel eye)	*ils aillent* (eel lye)
	elle aille (ell eye)	*elles aillent* (ell lye)

TABLE 16-6	SUBJUNCTIVE CONJUGATION OF *AVOIR*	
	j'aie (jhay)	*nous ayons* (noo-zay-ohn)
	tu aies (tchoo ay)	*vous ayez* (voo-zay-ay)
	il aie (eel ay)	*ils aient* (eel-lay)
	elle aie (ell ay)	*elles aient* (ell-lay)

TABLE 16-7	SUBJUNCTIVE CONJUGATION OF *ÊTRE*	
	je sois (jhe swah)	*nous soyons* (noo swoy-ohn)
	tu sois (tchoo swah)	*vous soyez* (voo swoy-ay)
	il soit (eel swah)	*ils soient* (eel swah)
	elle soit (ell swah)	*elles soient* (ell swah)

TABLE 16-8	SUBJUNCTIVE CONJUGATION OF *FAIRE*	
SINGULAR		**PLURAL**
je fasse (jhe fass)		*nous fassions* (noo fass-ee-ohn)
tu fasses (tchoo fass)		*vous fassiez* (voo fass-ee-ay)
il fasse (eel fass)		*ils fassent* (eel fass)
elle fasse (ell fass)		*elles fassent* (ell fass)

TABLE 16-9	SUBJUNCTIVE CONJUGATION OF *POUV.OIR*	
je puisse (jhe pweece)		*nous puissions* (noo pwee-see-ohn)
tu puisses (tchoo pweece)		*vous puissiez* (voo pwee-see-ay)
il puisse (eel pweece)		*ils puissent* (eel pweece)
elle puisse (ell pweece)		*elles puissent* (ell pweece)

TABLE 16-10	SUBJUNCTIVE CONJUGATION OF *SAVOIR*	
je sache (jhe sash)		*nous sachions* (noo sash-ee-ohn)
tu saches (tchoo sash)		*vous sachiez* (voo sash-ee-ay)
il sache (eel sash)		*ils sachent* (eel sahsh)
elle sache (ell sash)		*elles sachent* (ell sahsh)

TABLE 16-11	SUBJUNCTIVE CONJUGATION OF *VOULOIR*	
je veuille (jhe vayy)		*nous voulions* (noo voo-lee-ohn)
tu veuilles (tchoo vayy)		*vous vouliez* (voo voo-lee-ay)
il veuille (eel vayy)		*ils veuillent* (eel vayy)
elle veuille (ell vayy)		*elles veuillent* (ell vayy)

Common Verbs That Become Irregular in the Subjunctive

The following tables contain a number of common verbs that have slightly irregular constructions in the subjunctive. The only difference is in the *nous* and *vous* forms, which change to assist in the pronunciation.

TABLE 16-12

SUBJUNCTIVE CONJUGATION OF *BOIRE*

SINGULAR	PLURAL
je boive (jhe bwahv)	nous buvions (noo boo-vee-ohn)
tu boives (tchoo bwahv)	vous buviez (voo boo-vee-ay)
il boive (eel bwahv)	ils boivent (eel bwahv)
elle boive (ell bwahv)	elles boivent (ell bwahv)

TABLE 16-13

SUBJUNCTIVE CONJUGATION OF *CROIRE*

je croie (jhe krwah)	nous croyions (noo kroy-ee-ohn)
tu croies (tchoo krwah)	vous croyiez (voo kroy-ee-ay)
il croie (eel krwah)	ils croient (eel krwah)
elle croie (ell krwah)	elles croient (ell krwah)

TABLE 16-14

SUBJUNCTIVE CONJUGATION OF *DEVOIR*

je doive (jhe dwahv)	nous devions (noo dev-ee-ohn)
tu doives (tchoo dwahv)	vous deviez (voo dev-ee-ay)
il doive (eel dwahv)	ils doivent (eel dwahv)
elle doive (ell dwahv)	elles doivent (ell dwahv)

TABLE 16-15

SUBJUNCTIVE CONJUGATION OF *PRENDRE*

je prenne (jhe prehnn)	nous prenions (noo pren-ee-ohn)
tu prennes (tchoo prehnn)	vous preniez (voo pren-ee-ay)
il prenne (eel prehnn)	ils prennent (eel prehnn)
elle prenne (ell prehnn)	elles prennent (ell prehnn)

TABLE 16-16

SUBJUNCTIVE CONJUGATION OF *TENIR*

je tienne (jhe tee-enn)	nous tenions (noo ten-ee-ohn)
tu tiennes (tchoo tee-enn)	vous teniez (voo ten-ee-ay)
il tienne (eel tee-enn)	ils tiennent (eel tee-enn)
elle tienne (ell tee-enn)	elles tiennent (ell tee-enn)

TABLE 16-17	SUBJUNCTIVE CONJUGATION OF *VENIR*	
SINGULAR	**PLURAL**	
je vienne (jhe vee-ehnn)	*nous venions* (noo vehn-ee-ohn)	
tu viennes (tchoo vee-ehnn)	*vous veniez* (voo vehn-ee-ay)	
il vienne (eel vee-ehnn)	*ils viennent* (eel vee-ehnn)	
elle vienne (ell vee-ehnn)	*elles viennent* (ell vee-ehnn)	

TABLE 16-18	SUBJUNCTIVE CONJUGATION OF *VOIR*	
je voie (jhe vwah)	*nous voyions* (noo voy-ee-ohn)	
tu voies (tchoo vwah)	*vous voyiez* (voo voy-ee-ay)	
il voie (eel vwah)	*ils voient* (eel vwah)	
elle voie (ell vwah)	*elles voient* (ell vwah)	

Practice reviewing these verb forms, and the constructions will come to you. Try reading the conjugation tables out loud. Rote memory often helps with these verbs.

Specific Uses of the Subjunctive

This section outlines a number of specific uses of the subjunctive mood, used with expressions of emotion, doubt, opinion, and desire. The subjunctive is expected in these situations, so study them carefully.

Expressions of Emotion Using the Subjunctive

Emotive statements are inherently subjective; they describe something that the subject of the main clause is feeling. The element of doubt or subjectivity is present, because an emotion isn't really considered fact. While other people may be feeling the same thing, the expression is saying something about the personal state of being of the subject, so the subjunctive is called for, whether the sentence is being used interrogatively, as a question; indicatively, as a statement of fact about the emotions of the speaker; or as a negative expression.

As you may recall from Chapter 6, many emotions are idiomatic expressions formed using *avoir*, such as *avoir peur de*, meaning "to be afraid of something." Other emotions are formed using the verb *être* followed by the appropriate adjective. Because it is an adjective, it must agree with the subject or subject pronoun, both in gender and number.

The French subjunctive usage doesn't necessarily lend itself easily to an English translation, so use whatever makes the most sense in English when translating.

Here are a number of expressions that can be used to convey emotion. When they are used with a subordinate clause that has a different subject from the main clause, the subjunctive is used.

- *être content* (to be pleased)
- *être désolé* (to be sorry)
- *être fâché* (to be angry)
- *être heureux* (to be happy)
- *être surpris* (to be surprised)

Remember that the subjunctive is not used when the two clauses both share the same subject. If there is no change in subject between the main and subordinate clauses, a different construction is used; instead of using the subjunctive in the subordinate clause, an infinitive is used after the preposition *de,* as follows:

- *Il est content de finir le livre.* (He is pleased to finish the book.)
- *Est-ce que tu es fâché de ne pas réussir à cet examen?* (Are you angry at not passing this test?)

This construction does not necessarily change the meaning any great deal; in English, we would still probably translate both types of sentences the same way. When the element of subjectivity is present with more than one subject, the subjunctive is the appropriate choice in French. When there is no change in subject, you know that it's still a subjunctive idea, but that the construction is not used in that case in French. In those cases, *que* and the subjunctive is not used; *de* and an infinitive is used, instead.

Expressions of Opinion Using the Subjunctive

Opinions are not, as a rule, subjective. They usually indicate the thoughts or beliefs of the subject of the main clause, which is a statement of fact, thus removing the element of subjectivity. But when opinions are used in the negative or in interrogative statements to ask a question, an element of doubt or subjectivity is then introduced; therefore, the subjunctive gets used in these constructions.

Remember that when a sentence is used interrogatively, the subjectivity of the statement is determined from the perspective of the subject of the main clause. This is why these expressions call for the subjunctive when used negatively or interrogatively; when you're asking these types of questions, you're introducing a subjective element, asking for another person's opinion. Watch for the following verbs, because whenever they are used in an interrogative or a negative construction, the subordinate clause uses the subjunctive mood: *croire* (to believe), *penser* (to think), and *espérer* (to hope). Note the following examples:

- *Je ne pense pas que tu ailles.* (I do not think that you are going.)
- *Est-ce que tu crois que le guichet soit ouvert?* (Do you believe that the ticket office is open?)
- *Nous n'espérons pas que vous deviez aller.* (We do not hope that you have to go.)

When constructions of thought or opinion are used affirmatively, these sentences may still use the word *que*. While *que* is necessary in most subjunctive constructions, its presence doesn't automatically tell you that the subjunctive is present or required.

If the sentence is being used affirmatively, there is no doubt; it is simply a statement of belief. While it is indeed a statement of subjective belief, the subjective belief itself is a fact, and is therefore conjugated in the indicative mood instead of the subjunctive: *Je crois que tu partiras demain.* (I believe that you will leave tomorrow.)

With expressions of opinion, then, the subjunctive is used in all of the following circumstances:

- When the subject of the main and subordinate clauses are different.
- There is an element of subjectivity present, as evidenced by doubt.

- When the sentence is being used in the interrogative or negative. (Affirmative statements are cast in the indicative, because they are actually statements of fact.)

Expressions of Doubt Using the Subjunctive

When either of the expressions *douter* (to doubt) or *être douteux* (to be doubtful) are used and the phrase is a subjective statement, the subjunctive is used in the subordinate clause, as follows:

- *Je doute que vous parliez à ma mère.*
  (I doubt that you will talk to my mother.)
- *Il est douteux que nous finissions.*
  (He is doubtful that we will finish.)

With expressions of doubt, the subjunctive is used in all of the following circumstances:

- When the subject of the main and subordinate clauses are different.
- When an element of subjectivity is present, as evidenced by the doubt.
- When the sentence is being used in the affirmative.

Otherwise, these statements are cast in the indicative mood. Refer to Chapter 6 for more information on regular verb construction.

Expressions of Desire Using the Subjunctive

Expressions of desire can also be termed as expressions of will. They illustrate the wants or desires of the subject of the main clause, so if the subordinate clause has a different subject, the subjunctive mood is used. The following verbs are commonly used in this construction: *désirer* (to desire), *préférer* (to prefer), *souhaiter* (to wish), and *vouloir* (to want).

You will have to take certain liberties when translating into English. Most often, it will be entirely appropriate to use an infinitive construction in English. Remember, however, that these statements call for the subjunctive in French, so when translating in that direction, the subjunctive mood must be used. See the following examples:

- *Il veut que tu ailles avec lui.* (He wants you to go with him.)
- *Je préfère que nous parlions avec lui.* (I prefer that we speak with him.)
- *Est-ce que vous voulez que je le fasse?* (Do you want me to do it?)

With expressions of desire, then, the subjunctive is used in all of the following circumstances:

- When the subject of the main and subordinate clauses are different.
- When an element of subjectivity is present, as evidenced by doubt.
- When the sentence indicates the personal desires of the subject of the main clause.

Exceptions to Using the Subjunctive

The subjunctive is never used when the main clause and the subordinate clause share the same subject. There must always be two different subjects for the subjunctive to be properly used. This is one of the most important points to remember about the subjunctive; as you practice it, you should practice using the infinitive constructions, too, so that you'll always be prepared.

With certain verbs that involve granting permission or issuing an order, the subjunctive is not used, even though it is a direct expression of the wants and desires of the subject of the main clause. The following verbs are the ones to watch out for: *conseiller* (to advise; to recommend), *demander* (to ask for), *dire* (to say; to tell), *permettre* (to permit; to allow). When these verbs are used, they appear with two prepositions. The preposition *à* is used to indicate the other person involved, as the direct object, while the preposition *de* is used to indicate the thing that the person is being asked to do, as in the following examples:

- *Je demande à Jean d'aller au magasin.* (I am asking John to go to the store.)
- *Il dit à moi de faire les achats.* or *Il me dit de faire les achats.* (He told me to do the shopping.)

This construction can seem a little backward to us, because we very seldom have the direct object used with a preposition in English.

Memorize this construction, and remember not to use the subjunctive mood in this case.

The Past Subjunctive

The past subjunctive is formed much like the simple past tense, the *passé composé* (see Chapter 12). Simply conjugate the auxiliary verb in the subjunctive and use the past participle, making sure that the past participle makes any necessary pronoun agreements.

The past subjunctive is used to indicate events that took place before the action described by the verb in the main sentence. Consider the following English examples:

- I thought that he looked familiar.
- He wanted you to go there.
- We hope that you had a good time.

In all of these examples, the action in the subordinate clause took place before the verb in the main clause, even though it isn't necessarily obvious in English. The phrase "he wanted you to go there" is another English alternative to the subjunctive; in French, the construction would appear more like "he wanted that you should have come here:" *Il voulait que vous y soyez allés.*

The past subjunctive, however, is used only when the event took place before the event described by the main clause. If the event in the subordinate clause took place later or actually did not take place at all, the subjunctive is not used. Remember, too, that the subjunctive is used only with two different subjects; if the subject of the subordinate clause is the same, use an infinitive instead.

CHAPTER 17

Traveling in French-Speaking Countries

Pack up your carry-on; it's time to travel with your French skills. Whether you're traveling in French-speaking regions of North America or in one of the French-speaking countries in Europe or Africa, you'll need to build your travel vocabulary. This chapter shows you how.

Modes of Transportation

The following vocabulary list includes a number of French words associated with travel and methods of transportation. A great way to practice these words is to name the types of vehicles you see on your drive to work. Quiz yourself on these words by making yourself say the French names whenever you see a car, bus, train, or anything else in these lists.

FACTS

When planning a trip to France, remember that you must have a passport, and a visitor's visa is required if you plan to stay for longer than ninety days. Your travel agent will be able to help you apply for any necessary visas, or you can contact a local French consulate yourself. If you require any permits, you must obtain them in advance, so leave enough time to obtain one before your planned departure date.

TABLE 17-1

TYPES OF TRANSPORTATION		
VOCABULARY	**PRONUNCIATION**	**ENGLISH**
la voiture	la vwah-choor	car
le taxi	le taks-ee	taxi
le transport	le trahns-pohr	transportation
le camion	le kah-mee-ohn	truck
un autobus	u-naut-oh-booce	bus
le bus	le bus	bus
le métro	le may-troh	subway
un avion	u-nah-vee-ohn	plane

TABLE 17-2

AT THE AIRPORT		
un aéroport	u-nay-rho-pohr	airport
la piste	la peest	runway
la tour de contrôle	la toohr de kon-trohl	control tower
la compagnie aérienne	la kohm-pay-nyee ay-rhee-enn	airline

VOCABULARY	PRONUNCIATION	ENGLISH
les informations (f)	lay-sihn-fohr-mass-yohn	information
un enregistrement	u-nahn-rehj-eest-mahn	baggage check-in
des bagages (m)	day bay-gahj	counter
les bagages à main (m)	lay bay-gahj ah mehn	handbags, carry-on luggage
un embarquement	u-nahm-bark-mahn	boarding
la salle d'embarquement	la sahll dahm-bark-mahn	departure lounge
la carte d'embarquement	la carte dahm-bark-mahn	boarding pass
la porte	la pohrt	gate
la livraison des bagages	le rhe-treh day bay-gahj	baggage claim area
le terminal	le tehr-mee-nahl	terminal
un ascenseur	u-nah-sahn-suhr	elevator
faire la queue	fehr la kooh	to wait in line

TABLE 17-3

	ON THE PLANE	
un avion supersonique	u-nah-vee-ohn soo-pehr-sohn-eek	supersonic plane
le jet	le jhet	jet
le jumbo-jet	le jhum-bo-jhet	jumbo jet
le charter	le shar-ter	charter flight
une aile	ooh-naye	wing
une hélice	ooh-nay-leece	propeller
un hublot	u-nooh-bloh	window
la ceinture	la sayn-choor	seat belt
une issue de secours	ooh-neece-you de sek-oohr	emergency exit
la sortie de secours	la sohr-tee de sek-oohr	emergency exit
la place	la plahss	seat
le vol	le vohl	flight
le vol direct	le vohl dee-rekt	direct flight

TABLE 17-3	ON THE PLANE (CONTINUED)	
VOCABULARY	PRONUNCIATION	ENGLISH
le vol interne	le vohl ihn-tehrn	domestic flight
le vol international	le vohl ihn-tehr-nass-ee-oh-nehl	international flight
une altitude	ooh-nahl-tee-tude	altitude
la vitesse	la vee-tess	speed
le départ	le day-pahr	departure
le décollage	le day-kohl-ahj	take-off
une arrivée	ooh-nahr-ee-vay	arrival
un atterrissage	u-nah-tehr-ee-sahj	landing
un atterissage forcé	u-nah-tehr-ee-sahj fohr-say	emergency landing
une escale	ooh-nehs-kahl	stopover
le retard	le reh-tarhd	delay
le pilote	le pee-loht	pilot
un hôte de l'air	u-note de lehr	steward, flight attendant
une hôtesse de l'air	ooh-noh-tess de lehr	stewardess, flight attendant
le steward	le stew-ahrd	steward
le passager	le pahss-ahj-ay	passenger
la passagère	la pahss-ahj-ehr	passenger
annulé	ahn-oo-lay	canceled
en retard	ahn reh-tahrd	delayed
fumeurs	fooh-muhr	smoking
non fumeurs	nohn fooh-muhr	nonsmoking

TABLE 17-4

TRAINS, BUSES, AND SUBWAYS		
VOCABULARY	PRONUNCIATION	ENGLISH
l'arrière (m)	lahr-ee-ehr	the back
l'avant (m)	lah-vahn	the front
la gare routière	la gehr rooh-tee-ehr	bus station
la gare d'autobus	la gahr doh-toh-booce	bus station
un abribus	u-nah-bree-booce	bus shelter
un arrêt d'autobus	u-nah-reht doh-toh booce	bus stop
le guichet	le gee-shay	ticket office
le distributeur de tickets	le dees-tree-buh-tuhr de tee-kay	ticket dispensing machine
la salle d'attente	la sahll dah-tahnt	waiting room
le métro	le may-tro	subway
la gare	le gahr	train/subway station,
le station de métro	le stah-syohn de may-troh	subway station
le train	le trehn	train
le quai	le kwy	platform
un billet aller-retour	le bee-ay allay reh-toor	round trip ticket
un billet simple	le bee-ay sahmp	one-way ticket
le prix	le pree	price

Travel Destinations

The following vocabulary list includes a number of French terms associated with traveling, including customs and travel destinations.

FACTS

The Louvre is perhaps one of the most famous museums in the world, housing such famous works as Leonardo Da Vinci's *Mona Lisa* and Vincent Van Gogh's *Portrait de l'Artiste.* The Louvre's collection of artistic works is vast; if it's on your list of attractions to visit in Paris, make sure you schedule enough time to see and appreciate all that the Louvre has to offer.

TABLE 17-5

	IN THE HOTEL	
VOCABULARY	PRONUNCIATION	ENGLISH
complet	khom-pleh	no vacancies
fermé	fehr-may	closed
confortable	cohn-fohr-tahb	comfortable
compris	cohm-pree	included
un hôtel	u-noh-tell	hotel
le prix par jour	le pree pahr jhoor	price per day
la note	la noht	bill
le pourboire	le poohr-bwahr	tip
le service	le sehr-veece	service
la réclamation	la ray-clah-mass-yohn	complaint
la réservation	la ray-zehr-vass-yohn	booking, reservation
le bar	le bahr	bar
le parking	le pahr-keeng	parking lot
un ascenseur	u-nahn-sahn-soohr	elevator
le directeur	le dee-rek-tuhr	manager
le réceptionniste	le ray-sep-see-yohn-eest	receptionist
la réceptionniste	la ray-sep-see-yohn-eest	receptionist
le guardien de nuit	le gahr-djehn de nwee	night guard, porter
la femme de chambre	le fahm de sham-bruh	maid, chambermaid
l'eau chaude (f)	lo showd	hot water
le cabinet de toilette	le kah-bee-neh de twah-lett	small bathroom
la chambre pour une personne	la sham-bruh poohr oohn pehr-sohnn	single room
la chambre pour deux personnes	la sham-bruh poohr doo pehr-sohnn	double room
la chambre à deux lits	la sham-bruh ah doo lee	twin room
le grand lit	le grahn lee	double bed

ESSENTIALS

The French Embassy in Washington, D.C. operates a Web site that provides information on news, culture, trade, and other items of interest to the traveler. You can find the Embassy of France at *www.info-france-usa.org*.

TABLE 17-6

TOUR DESTINATIONS		
VOCABULARY	PRONUNCIATION	ENGLISH
le restaurant	le rehs-toh-rahn	restaurant
le musée	le moo-zay	museum
la banque	la bahnk	bank
une église	ooh-nay-gleez	church
le cinéma	le sin-ay-mah	movie theater
le théâtre	le tay-atruh	theater
la poste	la pohst	post office
le parc	le parhk	park
un hôpital	u-noh-pee-tahl	hospital
le commissariat	le kohm-ee-sehr-ee-ah	police station

TABLE 17-7

CUSTOMS		
le passeport	le pahss-pohr	passport
une ambassade	ooh-nahm-bahss-ahd	embassy
la douane	la doo-when	customs
le visa	le vee-za	visa

TABLE 17-8

DIRECTIONS		
à gauche	ah gohsh	left
à droite	a drwahtt	right
tout droit	too drwah	straight, straight ahead
à côté de	ah ko-tay de	next to
en avant de	ah-nah-vahn de	in front of

TABLE 17-8

DIRECTIONS *(CONTINUED)*		
VOCABULARY	PRONUNCIATION	ENGLISH
en arrière de	ah-nehr-ee-ehr de	in back of
en haut	ahn oh	up
en bas	ahn ba	down
près	preh	near
près de	preh de	near to
loin	lwehn	far
loin de	lwehn de	far from

You'll usually find French people accommodating when giving directions and the like, but there are always some people who just aren't very nice. Always be polite, which should help, address your audience using the formal *vous,* and say "please" and "thank you." If you find someone who is just plain rude, thank the person and move on. Someone else will be more helpful.

TABLE 17-9

CITIES, COUNTRIES, CONTINENTS, AND NATIONALITIES		
Genève (f)	jhuh-nev	Geneva
Londres (f)	lon-druh	London
Paris (m)	pahr-ee	Paris
Moscou (m)	mos-koo	Moscow
les États-Unis (m)	lay-zeh-tahy-oohn-ee	United States
l'Allemagne (f)	lahl-mahn-yuh	Germany
l'Angleterre (f)	lon-gluh-tehr	England
le Canada	le cah-nah-dah	Canada
l'Irlande (f)	leer-lahn-duh	Ireland
la France	la frahns	France
l'Asie (f)	lah-zee	Asia
l'Amérique du Nord (f)	lah-mehr-eek doo nor	North America

VOCABULARY	PRONUNCIATION	ENGLISH
l'Amérique du Sud (f)	lah-mehr-eek doo suhd	South America
l'Europe (f)	leur-ohp	Europe
l'Australie (f)	los-trah-lee	Australia
l'Afrique (f)	lah-freek	Africa
une Française	oohn frahn-sey	a Frenchwoman
un Anglais	un ahn-glay	an Englishman
une Anglaise	oohn ahn-glay	an Englishwoman

To describe a person's nationality, French sometimes uses the name of a language. When used in this fashion, it is capitalized. If the same word, such as *français*, is used to indicate a language, the word is not capitalized.

Money

Because money is always an issue when traveling, the following vocabulary list includes some common French terms related to money and banking.

TABLE 17-10

MONEY		
VOCABULARY	PRONUNCIATION	ENGLISH
l'argent (m)	lahr-jhahn	money
l'argent de poche (m)	lahr-jhahn de posh	pocket money
de l'argent liquide (m)	de lahr-jhahn lee-keed	cash
la pièce	la pee-ess	coin
le billet de banque	le bee-ay de bahnk	bill, bank note
le porte-monnaie	le pohrt-mohn-ay	purse
le portefeuille	le pohrt-fway	wallet
le paiement	le pay-mahn	payment
la dépense	la day-pahns	expense
les économies (f)	lay-zay-kahn-oh-mee	savings
la banque	la bahnk	bank

TABLE 17-10

	MONEY *(CONTINUED)*	
VOCABULARY	PRONOUCIATION	ENGLISH
le bureau de change	le boo-rho de shahnhj	currency exchange outlet
le taux de change	le toh de shahnhj	exchange rate
le distributeur automatique des billets de banque	le dee-stree-boo-tuhr oh-toe-mah-teek day bee-ay de bahnk	cash machine
le compte d'épargne	le kohmpt day-pahrn	savings account
le compte sur livret	le kohmpt soor lee-vray	deposit account
le retrait	le reh-treh	withdrawal
le virement	le veer-mahn	transfer
la carte de crédit	la kahrt de kray-dee	credit card
la carte d'identité bancaire	la kahrt dee-dahn-tee-tay bahnk-ehr	bank card
le chéquier	le shay-kyay	check book
le carnet de chèques	le kahr-neh de shek	check book
le chèque	le shek	check
le chèque de voyage	le shek de vwoy-ahj	traveler's check
le franc	le frahnk	franc (monetary unit)
le franc français	le frahnk frahn-say	French franc
le franc belge	le frahnk belhj	Belgian franc
le franc suisse	le frahnk sweess	Swiss franc

ESSENTIALS

In Canada, natives of the province of Quebec use a unique term for the Canadian dollar. They call it *la piastre* or *les piastres.* Don't be surprised if you hear it from a shopkeeper as he or she is counting out your change.

In a Restaurant

The following vocabulary list includes a number of French words you may come across in a restaurant. Don't forget to peruse the beverage section, also in this chapter.

In movies and television, it is common to see a waiter referred to as *garçon* in French restaurants. In reality, this is disrespectful; it is the equivalent of referring to North American waiters as "boys" or "little ladies." In a restaurant, be polite to your server, use the conditional tense (see Chapter 15), leave a *pourboire*, and never call your server *garçon*, unless you're actually looking for rude service.

TABLE 17-11

BASIC RESTAURANT TERMS		
VOCABULARY	PRONUNCIATION	ENGLISH
le restaurant	le rhes-tohr-ahn	restaurant
le serveur	le sehr-veuhr	waiter
la serveuse	la sehr-veuze	waitress
le chef	le shef	cook
la chef	la shef	cook
l'addition (f)	lah-diss-yohn	check, bill
le menu	le meh-nu	set price meal
le pourboire	le poohr-bwahr	tip
commander	kho-mahn-day	to order
service compris	sehr-veece kahm-pree	tip included
service non compris	sehr-veece nohn kahm-pree	tip not included

TABLE 17-12

PLACING YOUR ORDER		
saignant	sehn-yahn	rare
pané	pah-nay	breaded
bleu	bleuh	rare
farci	fahr-see	stuffed
frit	free	fried

TABLE 17-12

PLACING YOUR ORDER *(CONTINUED)*		
VOCABULARY	PRONUNCIATION	ENGLISH
bouilli	boo-wee-ee	boiled
rôti	rho-tee	roasted
au gratin	oh grah-tehn	with melted cheese
à point	ah pwehn	medium rare
bien cuit	bee-ehn kwee	well done
la carte	la kahrt	menu
à la carte	ah la kahrt	side order
bon appétit	bohn nah-pay-tee	enjoy your meal
cuit	kwee	cooked
trop cuit	troh kwee	overdone
les hors d'œuvre (m)	lay zohr-duhv	appetizer
la soupe	la soop	soup
le potage	le poh-tahj	soup
le plat principal	le plah prihn-see-pahl	main course
la salade	la sahl-ahd	salad
le dessert	le deh-zehr	dessert

Beverages

The following list contains a number of French terms for things you can drink—memorize your favorites.

TABLE 17-13

HOT BEVERAGES		
VOCABULARY	PRONUNCIATION	ENGLISH
le café	le kha-fay	coffee
le café au lait	le kha-fay oh lay	coffee with milk
la camomille	la kha-mho-mee	chamomile tea
le chocolat chaud	le shok-oh-la show	hot chocolate
le thé	le tay	tea

TABLE 17-14

COLD BEVERAGES		
VOCABULARY	PRONUNCIATION	ENGLISH
l'eau (f)	low	water
l'eau minérale (f)	low mih-nay-rahl	mineral water
le lait	le lay	milk
le lait écrémé	le lay ay-kree-may	skim milk
le jus de fruit	le jhus de frwee	fruit juice
le jus de pomme	le jhus de pohm	apple juice
le jus d'orange	le jhus dohr-ahnj	orange juice
le boisson	la bwah-sohn	drink, beverage

TABLE 17-15

ALCOHOL AND SPIRITS		
l'alcool (m)	lahl-kuhl	alcohol
la bière	la bee-aihr	beer
le gin	le jhin	gin
le rhum	le rhoom	rum
le vin rouge	le vehn rhooj	red wine
le vin blanc	le vehn blahnk	white wine
la vodka	la vod-kah	vodka
le whisky	le wiss-kee	whiskey

QUESTIONS?

What's the difference between brandy and cognac?
The French pride themselves on both their brandy and cognac.
They are pretty much the same thing, but cognac is noted for its
higher quality. They are both made by distilling wine. Don't
mistake either of them for wine—they are both much stronger
and have a completely different taste.

Shopping Terms

The following vocabulary list contains a number of French verbs and expressions related to shopping.

TABLE 17-16

SHOPPING VOCABULARY		
VOCABULARY	**PRONUNCIATION**	**ENGLISH**
acheter	ahsh-eh-tay	to buy
choisir	shwa-zeer	to choose
coûter	koo-tay	to cost
dépenser	day-pahn-say	to spend
échanger	ay-shahn-jhay	to exchange
payer	pay-ay	to pay
vendre	vahn-druh	to sell
faire les courses	fehr lay koor	to do the shopping
faire du shopping	fehr du shah-ping	to go shopping
faire des achats	fehr day zay-shat	to go shopping
bon marché	boh mar-shay	cheap
cher / chère	shaihr, shaihrr	expensive
gratuit	grah-twee	free
en solde	ahn suld	reduced price
d'occasion	do-kah-zyohn	secondhand
la caisse	la kass	till, cash register
le client	le klee-ahn	customer
la cliente	la klee-ahnt	customer
le prix	le pree	price
le reçu	le reh-soo	receipt
le vendeur	le vahn-door	clerk, cashier
la vendeuse	la vahn-dooz	clerk, cashier
les provisions	lay pro-vee-zyohn	merchandise, shopping items
la taille	la tie	size
la pointure	la pwehn-choor	shoe size

Stores, Shops, and Markets

The following vocabulary list contains a number of French terms for different kinds of stores. If you get stuck when asking for a particular kind of store, you can always try asking for *le magasin de* whatever it is you're trying to find; if that doesn't work, try describing the kinds of things you buy there. As a last resort, you can always try the English word and hope that it conveys the message.

TABLE 17-17

SHOPPING VOCABULARY		
VOCABULARY	PRONUNCIATION	ENGLISH
une épicerie	ooh-nay-peece-rhee	grocery store
une agence de voyages	ooh-nay-jhans de vwoy-ahj	travel agency
la bijouterie	la bee-jhoo-tuh-ree	jewelry store
la blanchisserie	la blahn-shee-suhr-ee	laundry shop
la crémerie	la khray-mehr-ee	dairy
le lavomatic	le lah-vo-mah-tik	laundry shop
la boucherie	la boo-shehr-ee	butcher store
la boulangerie	la boo-lahn-jhehr-ee	bakery
la librairie	la lee-brehr-ee	bookstore
le grand magasin	le grahn may-gah-zehn	supermarket
le nettoyage à sec	le neh-twoy-ahj ah sek	dry cleaners
la teinturerie	la tayn-tuhr-ehr-ee	dry cleaning
la pharmacie	la fahr-mah-se	pharmacy
le disquaire	le dees-kehr	music shop
le marché	le mahr-shay	market
le fleuriste	le floohr-eest	florist
le coiffeur	le kwah-fuhr	hairdresser
la boutique	la boo-teek	small shop
la quincaillerie	la kain-kay-e-ree	hardware store
le magasin de vins et spiritueux	le may-gah-zehn de vehn ay spee-rhee-too-uh	liquor store
la pâtisserie	la pah-tiss-ehr-ee	cake shop
le marchand de fruits	le mahr-shahn de frwee	fruit merchant

TABLE 17-17

SHOPPING VOCABULARY (CONTINUED)		
VOCABULARY	PRONUNCIATION	ENGLISH
le marchand de légumes	le mahr-shahn de lay-guhme	vegetable merchant
le marchand de vin	le mahr-shahn de vehn	wine merchant

Movies

While traveling in French-speaking country, try to expose yourself to French media. You can see the French language in action, gaining experience with it in a real-life situation. And after you return from your trip, newspapers, television programs, movies, books, and Web sites are all great ways to retain your skills.

TABLE 17-18

MOVIE VOCABULARY		
VOCABULARY	PRONUNCIATION	ENGLISH
un acteur	uhn ak-teur	actor
une actrice	oohn ak-treece	actress
un billet	uhn bee-yay	ticket
une comédie	oohn cahm-ay-dee	comedy
une tragédie	oohn trah-jhay-dee	tragedy
acheter	ash-ett-ay	to buy
voir	vwahr	to see
un dessin animé	uhn dess-ehn ahn-ee-may	cartoon
un film	uhn feelm	film
un film en noir et blanc	uhn feelm ahn nwahr ay blahnk	black and white film
un film documentaire	uhn feelm dahk-yoo-mehn-tehr	documentary
un film historique	uhn feelm ee-stohr-eek	historical film
un film d'horreur	uhn feelm dhor-ehrr	horror film
un film de science-fiction	uhn feelm de see-ahns feek-see-ohn	science fiction film

VOCABULARY	PRONUNCIATION	ENGLISH
un western	uhn west-ehrn	Western
les sous-titres (m)	lay soo-teetr	subtitles
le metteur en scène	le met-ehr ahn senn	director
le théâtre	le tay-atr	theatre
le cinéma	le sinn-ay-mah	cinema
une vedette	oohn veh-dett	star
une vidéo	oohn vee-day-oh	video

Books, Newspapers, and Magazines

Spoken French is one thing to master, but it doesn't hurt to brush up on your written French, too. Signs, newspapers, books, and letters are all forms of written French you may encounter, so get used to reading it.

QUESTIONS?

How can I improve my French comprehension skills?
One great way to increase your French comprehension skills is to rent French movies with English subtitles. That way, you can listen to the words being spoken and still have the subtitles to fall back on when you don't understand. You can rewind the tape and listen again when you fear that there's something you've missed, and as an added challenge, you can even block the part of the screen that shows the subtitles, only consulting it when absolutely required.

Reading these materials can help you hone your French skills, too. Here is a list of words that are commonly used when referring to media that contain written French.

TABLE 17-19	MEDIA VOCABULARY		
VOCABULARY	**PRONUNCIATION**	**ENGLISH**	
un livre	uhn lee-vruh	book	
un roman	uhn ro-mahn	novel	
un écrivain	uhn ay-kree-vehn	author	
la librairie	la lee-brehr-ee	bookstore	

TABLE 17-19

MEDIA VOCABULARY *(CONTINUED)*		
VOCABULARY	PRONUNCIATION	ENGLISH
un journal	uhn jhoor-nahl	newspaper
un journaliste	uhn jhoor-nahl-eest	journalist
une journaliste	oohn jhoor-nahl-eest	journalist
un article	uhn ahr-teek	article
un magazine	uhn may-gah-zeen	magazine
une revue	oohn reh-vyoo	magazine
les petites annonces	lay peh-teet ahn-awnss	classified ads
une photo	oohn fo-tow	photograph
la photographie	la fo-tow-gra-fee	photography
la poésie	la po-ay-zee	poetry
un poème	uhn po-ehm	poem
une bande dessinée	oohn bahnd deh-see-nay	comic strip
écrire	ay-kreer	to write
lire	leer	to read

FACTS

If you decide to watch some French videos to help improve your French, consider looking into their written counterparts, too. Most movies are either based on a novel or have a novelization released shortly after the movie comes out, so you will probably be able to find it in written form. Because you already know the story, it will make it a little easier to understand.

TV, Radio, and the Internet

Depending on where you live, you may be able to access some French TV shows or radio broadcasts. Many television shows are available via satellite transmission, while others are broadcast on local special-interest stations, and many French radio stations are available via shortwave radio transmissions. Check your local listings for details. You can also find a good number of broadcasts on the Internet, in addition to other French resources available on the Web.

The Internet has made an impact on the entire world, bringing it much closer together. There is an incredible variety of French Web sites available, including sites that will help you with your pronunciation by providing you with sound clips to listen to. Don't forget about this wonderful free resource while you're learning the French language. For more French computer terms, see Chapter 18.

TABLE 17-20

MEDIA VOCABULARY		
VOCABULARY	PRONUNCIATION	ENGLISH
en direct	ahn dee-rekt	live
regarder	re-gahr-day	to watch
la télévision	la tay-lay-vee-zyohn	television
une chaîne	oohn shehn	channel
un documentaire	uhn dok-yoo-mehn-tehr	documentary
un épisode	uhn ay-pee-sod	episode
le petit écran	le peh-tee-tay-krahn	television
une publicité	oohn poo-blee-see-tay	commercial
allumer	ahl-oo-may	to turn on
diffuser	di-foo-zay	to broadcast
passer à la télé	passay ah la tay-lay	to appear on tv
l'hypertexte (m)	lee-pehr-text	hypertext
un domaine	uhn doe-mehn	domain
une adresse universelle (f)	oohn-drehs oo-nee-vehr-sell	Uniform Resource Locator; URL
une contribution	oohn kahn-treh-byoo-syohn	posting
un forum	uhn fohr-uhm	newsgroup
un signet	uhn sig-neh	bookmark

TABLE 17-20

MEDIA VOCABULARY *(CONTINUED)*		
VOCABULARY	**PRONUNCIATION**	**ENGLISH**
une liste de signets	oohn leest de sig-neh	bookmark file, bookmark list
la toile d'araignée mondiale (TAM)	la twahl dahr-ehn-yay mohn-dee-ahl	World Wide Web
la toile	la twahl	World Wide Web
un logiciel de navigation	uhn lo-jhee-see-ell de nah-vee-gass-yohn	Web browser
un navigateur	uhn nah-vee-gah-toor	Web browser
l'Internet (m)	leen-tehr-neht	Internet

CHAPTER 18

Studying and Working in French-Speaking Countries

If you get an opportunity to study or work in a French-speaking region, take it! The experience will immerse you into the French language, which is an ideal way to learn—and learn quickly! This chapter helps you master some of the French terminology that goes along with studying and working.

School Terms

The following vocabulary list includes some of the more common terms associated with going to school.

TABLE 18-1

SCHOOL TERMS		
VOCABULARY	**PRONUNCIATION**	**ENGLISH**
le livre	le lee-vruh	book
le dictionnaire	le deek-see-ohn-ehr	dictionary
le professeur	le proh-fess-eur	teacher
la bibliothèque	la bee-blee-oh-tek	library
le cahier	le kah-yay	notebook
une école	oohn ay-khol	school
un étudiant	uhn ay-too-dee-ahn	student
une étudiante	oohn ay-too-dee-ahnt	student
le stylo	le stee-loh	pen
le crayon	le kray-ohn	pencil
la gomme	la gohm	eraser
les devoirs (m)	lay de-vwah	homework
un examen	uhn ek-sah-mahn	test
la salle de classe	la sahl deh klahs	classroom
le classeur	le klahs-eur	binder
le papier	le pah-pyay	paper
le cours	le koohr	course

ESSENTIALS

In French, the word *professeur* is always masculine, even if the teacher is female. Other words, such as *étudiant* and *étudiante*, can change to reflect the sex of the person to whom the word refers. You can learn more about these kinds of words in Chapter 5.

Technology

Technology has become increasingly important in our lives, to the point where it has become difficult to avoid a computer, if you were so inclined.

TABLE 18-2

COMPUTER TERMS		
VOCABULARY	PRONUNCIATION	ENGLISH
un ordinateur	uhn ohr-dee-nah-teur	computer
la disquette	la dees-ket	floppy disk
le disque	le deesk	hard disk
le lecteur de disquettes	le lek-teur de dees-kets	disk drive
la messagerie électronique	la mes-a-jhehr-ee eh-lek-trohn-eek	e-mail
une erreur	oohn ehr-eur	error
une icône	oohn ee-kohn	icon
le fichier	le feesh-yay	file
le clavier	le klah-vyay	keyboard
la mémoire	la mehm-wah	memory
la souris	la soo-ree	mouse
le mot de passe	le moh de pahs	password
une imprimante	oohn eem-pree-mahnt	printer
un écran	uhn ay-krahn	screen
le logiciel	le loh-jhee-syel	software
le virus	le veer-ous	virus

The Working World

The following vocabulary lists contain a number of French words that are often used to describe various aspects of the working world. In order to make it easier for you to remember, the categories are broken out between verbs, adjectives, and nouns.

TABLE 18-3

VERBS COMMONLY ASSOCIATED WITH WORK		
VOCABULARY	PRONUNCIATION	ENGLISH
travailler	trah-vye-ay	to work
avoir l'intention de	ah-vwahr l'ahn-tahn-syohn de	to intend to
devenir	de vehn-eer	to become
s'intéresser à	sahn-tay-ress-ay ah	to be interested in
avoir de l'ambition	ah-vwahr de lahm-bee-syohn	to be ambitious
avoir de l'expérience	ah-vwahr de l'eks-peer-ee-ahnce	to have experience
manquer d'expérience	mahn-kay d'eks-peer-ee-ahnce	to lack experience
être sans emploi	eh-truh sahn-zemp-lwah	to be unemployed
chercher un emploi	shehr-shay oohn ahm-plwah	to look for work; to look for a job
refuser	reh-fooz-ay	to reject
accepter	ak-sept-ay	to accept
trouver un emploi	troo-vay ooh nahm-plwah	to find a job
trouver du travail	troo-vay doo trah-vye	to find work
réussir	ray-yoo-seer	to be successful
gagner	gahn-yay	to earn
gagner sa vie	gahn-yay sa vee	to earn a living
payer	pay-ay	to pay
prendre des vacances	prahn-druh day vah-kahnss	to take a vacation
prendre un jour de congé	prahn-druh oohn jhoor de kohn-jhay	to take a day off
licencier	lee-sahns-yay	to lay off
renvoyer	rahn-vwoy-ay	to dismiss
démissionner	day-meece-yohn-ay	to resign
quitter	kee-tay	to leave
prendre sa retraite	prahn-druh sa reh-treht	to retire

TABLE 18-4

ADJECTIVES COMMONLY ASSOCIATED WITH WORK		
VOCABULARY	PRONUNCIATION	ENGLISH
difficile	dif-ee-seel	difficult
facile	fass-eel	easy
intéressant	ihn-tay-ress-ahn	interesting
passionnant	pahss-ee-oh-nahn	exciting
ennuyeux	ahn-wee-oo	boring
dangereux	dahn-jhay-rhoo	dangerous
important	ahm-pohr-tahn	important
utile	ooh-teel	useful

TABLE 18-5

NOUNS ASSOCIATED WITH JOBS		
le contrat	le khon-trah	contract
le contrat de travail	le khon-trah de trah-vye	employment contract
la demande d'emploi	la deh-mahnd dem-plwah	job application
une annonce	ooh-nahn-ohnss	advertisement, announcement
une offre d'emploi	ooh-nah-fruh dem-plwah	job vacancy
la paye	lay pay	pay, wages
le salaire	le sahl-ehr	salary, wages
la semaine de quarante heures	la seh-mehn de kahr-ahnt euhr	forty-hour week
les impôts	la-zihm-po	tax
une augmentation	ooh-nahg-mehn-tass-yohn	pay raise
le voyage d'affaires	le vwoy-ahj daff-ehr	business trip

Professions and Jobs

The vocabulary in this section includes a number of French terms for different types of occupations. Many of them have an alternate masculine and feminine form, depending on the sex of the person the word is being used to represent. With some of the words, only the article changes, while others undergo more of a transformation.

TABLE 18-6

LIST OF PROFESSIONS		
VOCABULARY	PRONUNCIATION	ENGLISH
un agriculteur	uh-nay-gree-kuhl-choor	farmer
un artiste	uh-nahr-teest	artist
une artiste	ooh-nahr-teest	artist
un assistant social	uh-nahss-ees-tahn so-see-el	social worker
une assistante sociale	ooh-nahss-ees-tahn so-see-ell	social worker
un astronaute	uh-nah-stroh-naht	astronaut
une astronaute	ooh-nah-stroh-naht	astronaut
un avocat	uh-nah-vo-ka	lawyer
une avocate	ooh-nah-vo-kat	lawyer
le bijoutier	le bee-jhoo-tee-ay	jeweler
la bijoutière	la bee-jhoo-tee-ehr	jeweler
le boucher	le boo-shay	butcher
la bouchère	la boo-shehr	butcher
le douanier	le dwehn-ee-yay	customs officer
la douanière	la dwehn-ee-ehr	customs officer
le facteur	le fak-tuhr	letter carrier
la factrice	la fak-treece	letter carrier
le fleuriste	le fluhr-eest	florist
la fleuriste	la fluhr-eest	florist
le gendarme	le jhan-dahrm	police officer
un infirmier	uh-nahn-fehr-mee-ay	nurse
une infirmière	ooh-nahn-fehr-mee-ehr	nurse
un ingénieur	uh-nahn-jhay-nuhr	engineer
le journaliste	le jhoor-nahl-eest	journalist

VOCABULARY	PRONUNCIATION	ENGLISH
la journaliste	la jhoor-nahl-eest	journalist
le pasteur	le pahs-tuhr	minister
le prêtre	le preh-truh	priest
la religieuse	la rehl-ee-jhuz	nun
le secrétaire	le sek-ray-tehr	secretary
la secrétaire	la sek-ray-tehr	secretary
le traducteur	le trah-duk-tuhr	translator
la traductrice	la trah-duk-treece	translator

The following professions don't differentiate gender when it comes to the sex of the person the word is being used to represent. *Un mannequin,* for example, can be used to describe both male and female models, but there is no feminine form of the word. It is always used in the masculine. Review the following words and remember not to use them with another gender.

TABLE 18-7

PROFESSIONS THAT DO NOT DIFFERENTIATE GENDER		
VOCABULARY	PRONUNCIATION	ENGLISH
le mannequin	le mahn-ek-ehn	model
un écrivain	uh-nay-kree-vehn	writer
le docteur	le dok-tuhr	doctor
le médeicin	le may-dis-ehn	doctor
le savant	le sah-vahn	scholar, scientist

CHAPTER 19

Family, Friends, and You!

Even if your family and friends aren't remotely French and have no desire to speak the language, you can practice your French skills by thinking of (and referring to) to your family, friends, pets, body parts, and clothing by their French terms. Your loved ones—including, perhaps, Rover—may tire of your game, but you'll benefit by rapidly improving your vocabulary.

Family

The following vocabulary list includes French terms for common familial relationships. These words are all nouns, can appear as the subject or object of the sentence, and follow the same rules as the nouns in Chapter 5.

TABLE 19-1

YOUR FAMILY		
VOCABULARY	PRONUNCIATION	ENGLISH
le cousin	le koo-zehn	cousin
la cousine	la koo-zeen	cousin
la femme	la fehm	wife
la famille	la fah-mee	family
la fille	la fee	daughter
le fils	le feece	son
le frère	le frehr	brother
la grand-mère	la grahn-mehr	grandmother
le grand-père	le grahn-pehr	grandfather
les grand-parents (m)	les grahn-pahr-anh	grandparents
le mari	le mahr-ee	husband
la mère	la mehr	mother
la nièce	la nee-ess	niece
le neveu	le ne-vuh	nephew
un oncle	uh-nonk	uncle
les parents (m)	lay pahr-ahn	parents
le père	le pehr	father
la sœur	la soor	sister
la tante	la tahnt	aunt
la belle-mère	la bell-mehr	stepmother
le beau-père	le bo-pehr	stepfather
la demi-sœur	la d'mee-soohr	half-sister
le demi-frère	le d'mee-frehr	half-brother

Holidays and Occasions

The following vocabulary lists includes some special occasions and holidays that you probably spend celebrating with friends or family members. These expressions can stand on their own as simple expressions, or you can use them as part of other sentences.

TABLE 19-2	HOLIDAY GREETINGS		
VOCABULARY		**PRONUNCIATION**	**ENGLISH**
bon anniversaire		boh-nah-nee-vehr-sehr	happy birthday
bonne année		buhnn ah-nay	Happy New Year
félicitations		fay-lee-see-ta-syohn	congratulations
Joyeux Noël		jhwoy-oo no-ell	Merry Christmas
Joyeuses Pâques		jwoy-ooz pahck	Happy Easter
meilleurs vœux		may-euhr vuh	best wishes

Friends

The following vocabulary list includes some common French terms for friends.

TABLE 19-3	YOUR FRIENDS		
VOCABULARY		**PRONUNCIATION**	**ENGLISH**
un ami		uh-nah-mee	friend
une amie		oon-ah-mee	friend
le copain (m)		le ko-pahn	friend, pal,
la copine (f)		la ko-peen	mate, chum
le petit ami		le p-tee-tah-mee	boyfriend
la petite amie		la p-teet-ah-mee	girlfriend
le voisin		le vwah-zehn	neighbor
la voisine		lah vwah-zeen	neighbor

FACTS

There is a subtle difference in meaning between the terms *un ami* and *un copain* in French. In French, *un ami* is a very endearing term; it is used only for the closest of friends. In English, we sometimes assign a broad meaning to the term "friends," so the words are not really interchangeable. A person can go through life having many *copains*, but he or she will have a select few true *amis*.

Pets

To many people, pets can be like members of the family, so what better place to learn some words for different kinds of pets? The following list includes some common household pets. If you have a pet, be sure to memorize the word for him or her in French!

TABLE 19-4

PETS		
VOCABULARY	PRONUNCIATION	ENGLISH
un animal	uh-nah-nee-mal	pet
un chat	uhn sha	cat
un chien	uhn shee-ehn	dog
une souris	oohn soo-ree	mouse
un cheval	uhn she-vahl	horse
un poisson	uhn pwa-ssohn	fish
un hamster	uhn-ahm-ster	hamster
un oiseau	uh-nwa-zo	bird
un lapin	uhn lah-pehn	rabbit
un serpent	uhn sehr-pahn	snake
une tortue	oohn tohr-too	tortoise

Parts of the Body

The following vocabulary list contains some French terms for parts of the body. To help yourself remember these, touch each part of the body as you say the French word out loud.

TABLE 19-5	PARTS OF THE BODY		
VOCABULARY	**PRONUNCIATION**	**ENGLISH**	
les cheveux (m)	lay shuh-vuh	hair	
le corps	le kohr	body	
la tête	la tett	head	
le visage	le vee-sahj	face	
un œil	ooh-nway	eye	
les yeux (m)	lay yuh	eyes	
le nez	le nay	nose	
la joue	la jhoo	cheek	
la bouche	la boosh	mouth	
une oreille	ooh-nohr-ay	ear	
le cou	le koo	neck	
la poitrine	la pwah-treen	chest	
un estomac	uh-nay-sto-mak	stomach	
le bras	le brah	arm	
une épaule	ooh-nay-pahll	shoulder	
le coude	le kood	elbow	
le poignet	le pweh-nyay	wrist	
la main	la mehn	hand	
le doigt	le dwah	finger	
un ongle	uh-nahngl	fingernail	
le pouce	le pooce	thumb	
le dos	le doh	back	
la jambe	la jham	leg	
le genou	le jhen-oo	knee	
la cheville	la sheh-vee	ankle	
le pied	le pee-eh	foot	
un orteil	uh-nohr-tay	toe	

When referring to parts of the body in French, you don't use a possessive adjective like you do in English. While we say things like "my hand" or "my arm," in French, a reflexive verb is used instead (see Chapter 13):

- *Je me brosse les dents.* (I am brushing my teeth.)
- *Je me lave les mains.* (I am washing my hands.)
- *Je me coiffe les cheveux.* (I am doing my hair.)

If translated literally, these sentences say something like "I brush the teeth of myself," so you can't translate literally. This is just the way French handles actions that are performed on the self. When translating these phrases, use the English equivalent that makes the most sense.

Clothing

The following vocabulary list contains a number of French terms for clothing and other things you can buy in a shop, including men's and women's clothes. For your convenience, a separate section is broken out for each category.

TABLE 19-6

GENERAL CLOTHING ITEMS: *LES VÊTEMENTS*		
VOCABULARY	PRONUNCIATION	ENGLISH
le manteau	le mahn-toe	coat
le pardessus	le pahr-dess-oo	overcoat
un imperméable	uh-nahm-pehr-mee-ahblh	raincoat
la veste	la vest	jacket
le blouson	le bloo-zohn	jacket
le complet veston	le cohm-pleht veh-stohn	suit
le maillot	le my-oh	bathing suit
un uniforme	uh-noo-nee-fohrm	uniform
le pantalon	le pahn-tah-lohn	pants, trousers
le blue-jean	le bloo-jheen	blue jeans
le jean	le jheen	jeans
le pyjama	le pee-jha-mah	pajamas
la chemise	la shuh-meez	shirt
les chaussettes (f)	lay sha-sett	socks

TABLE 19-7

WOMEN'S CLOTHING: *LES VÊTEMENTS DE FEMME*		
VOCABULARY	PRONUNCIATION	ENGLISH
le bas	le bas	stocking
le bikini	le bee-kee-nee	bikini
la chemise de nuit	la shuh-meez de nwee	nightgown
le chemisier	le sheh-mee-see-ay	blouse
le collant	le koll-ahn	pantyhose, tights
la combinaison	la kohm-bee-nehz-ohn	slip
un ensemble	uh-nahn-sahmbl	woman's suit
la jupe	la jhoop	skirt
le jupon	le jhoo-pohn	half slip
la minijupe	la mee-nee-jhoop	miniskirt
la robe	la rhob	dress
la robe de chambre	la rhob de sham-bruh	robe, nightgown
le slip	le slihp	panties
le soutien-gorge	le soo-chehn-gohrj	brassiere
le tailleur	le tay-euhr	woman's suit

TABLE 19-8

MEN'S CLOTHING: *LES VÊTEMENTS D'HOMME*		
le caleçon	le kahl-ess-ahn	underwear
la ceinture	la sayn-choor	cummerbund, belt
la chemise	la sheh-meece	shirt
le costume	le koss-toom	suit
la cravate	la krah-vatt	tie
le maillot de corps	le my-oh de kohr	undershirt
le nœud papillon	le nweh pah-pee-ahn	bow tie
le smoking	le smo-keeng	tuxedo
le veston de sport	le veh-ston de spohr	sport jacket

TABLE 19-9

ACCESSORIES: *LES ACCESSOIRES*		
VOCABULARY	PRONUNCIATION	ENGLISH
une alliance (f)	ooh-nall-ee-ahns	wedding ring
la bague	la bhagg	ring
la bague de fiançailles	la bhagg de fee-ahn-sigh	engagement ring
le béret	le bay-ray	beret
la bijouterie	la bee-jhoo-tehr-ee	jewelry
la boucle d'oreille	la bouk dohr-ay	earring
le bouton de manchette	le boo-tohn de mahn-shett	cufflink
le bracelet	le brah-slay	bracelet
la broche	la brosh	brooch
le châle	le shahl	shawl
le chapeau	le shah-po	hat
les chaussures (f)	lay show-suhr	shoes
les chaussures à talons hauts (f)	lay show-suhr ah oh tahl-ahn	high-heeled shoes
le collier	le khal-yay	necklace
une épingle	ooh-nay-pahng	pin
le fixe-cravate	le feex krah-vatt	tie-clip
le foulard	le foo-lahr	scarf
les gants (m)	lay gahn	gloves
les lunettes (f)	lay looh-nehtt	glasses
les lunettes de soleil (f)	lay looh-nehtt de sohl-ay	sunglasses
la montre	la mohntruh	watch
le mouchoir	le moo-shwahr	handkerchief
les moufles (f)	lay moof	mittens
le pendentif	le pahn-dahn-teef	pendant
le parapluie	le pehr-ah-plwee	umbrella
le ruban	le rhoo-bahn	ribbon
le sac à dos	le sak ah doh	backpack
le sac à main	le sak ah mehn	purse, handbag

Colors

The following vocabulary list contains a number of French adjectives for colors. As adjectives, when they are used with a noun, they must agree in number and in gender. The masculine form of the adjective can also be used with an article to represent the color as a noun; for the most part, however, you will most often use these colors as adjectives to modify and describe nouns. See Chapter 10 for more on adjectives.

TABLE 19-10

COLORS		
MASCULINE	FEMININE	ENGLISH
noir (nwar)	*noire* (nwahr)	black
bleu (bleuh)	*bleue* (bleuh)	blue
marron (mahr-ahn)	*marron* (mahr-ahn)	brown
vert (vehr)	*verte* (vehrt)	green
gris (gree)	*grise* (greez)	grey
orange (ohr-ahnj)	*orange* (ohr-ahnj)	orange
rose (rhoze)	*rose* (rhoze)	pink
violet (vee-oh-lay)	*violette* (vee-oh-lett)	purple
rouge (rhooj)	*rouge* (rhooj)	red
blanc (blahnk)	*blanche* (blahnsh)	white
jaune (jhown)	*jaune* (jhown)	yellow

To form the plural for most of these adjectives, simply add an "s" to the end of the word, with the following exceptions:

- *Marron* and *orange* do not change in the plural; simply use the singular form of the word.
- The masculine plural form of grey still uses the word *gris*; because it already ends in an "s," so you don't add one.

Your House or Apartment

This chapter provides you with a number of French words commonly used to describe your daily routine and your home. To assist your memory, visualize each room and the things inside it and use the French words to describe them. You may also want to walk around the room and name things as you touch them.

Your Daily Routine

The following vocabulary list includes a number of French terms for activities you find yourself doing throughout the day. For convenience, the list is broken out into morning, afternoon, and evening routines.

TABLE 20-1

MORNING ROUTINE		
VOCABULARY	PRONUNCIATION	ENGLISH
le matin	le mah-tehn	morning
allumer la radio	ahl-oo-may la rha-djoh	to turn on the radio
bâiller	by-yay	to yawn
faire sa toilette	fehr sa twah-lett	to have a wash, to wash up
aller aux toilettes	ah-lay oh twah-lett	to go to the toilet
mettre ses verres de contact	me-truh say vehr de cohn-ta	to put in one's contact lenses
mettre son dentier	me-truh sohn dahn-chay	to put in one's false teeth
faire son lit	fehr son lee	to make the bed
prendre son petit-déjeuner	prahn-druh son p'tee day-jhoo-nay	to have breakfast
aller travailler	ah-lay trav-eye-ay	to go to work
verrouiller la porte	vehr-whee-ay la pohrt	to lock the door
tous les matins	too lay mah-tehn	every morning

TABLE 20-2

AFTERNOON ROUTINE		
l'après-midi (m)	la-preh mee-dee	afternoon
allumer la télévision	all-oo-may la tay-lay-vee-zyon	to turn on the television
arroser les plantes	ahr-oh-zay lay plahnte	to water the plants
éteindre la radio	ay-tahn-druh la rha-djoh	to turn off the radio

VOCABULARY	PRONUNCIATION	ENGLISH
rentrer à la maison	rhan-tray ah la may-zohn	to come home, to go home
rentrer de l'école	rhan-tray dah lay-kahl	to come back from school
rentrer du travail	rhan-tray doo trav-eye	to come back from work

TABLE 20-3

EVENING ROUTINE		
le soir	le swahr	evening
éteindre la télévision	ay-tahn-druh la tay-lay-vee-zyohn	to turn off the television
se reposer	se rhe-poe-zay	to have a rest
faire la sieste	fehr la see-est	to have a nap
se déshabiller	se day-sahb-ee-ay	to get undressed
fermer la porte	fehr-may la pohrt	to close the door
fermer les rideaux	ferh-may lay ree-doh	to close the curtains
mettre son réveil	met-ruh son ray-vay	to set the alarm clock

A Tour of Your Home

To continue to build your vocabulary, take a tour of your home, noting the following items.

TABLE 20-4

FURNITURE AND FIXTURES		
VOCABULARY	PRONUNCIATION	ENGLISH
la fenêtre	la fehn-etruh	window
la moquette	la mock-ett	carpet
les meubles	lay muhb	furniture
le mur	le muhr	wall
le plafond	le plah-fohnd	ceiling

TABLE 20-4

FURNITURE AND FIXTURES *(CONTINUED)*

VOCABULARY	PRONUNCIATION	ENGLISH
la porte	la pohrt	door
le rideau	le ree-do	curtain
le sol	le sohl	floor
le tapis	le tah-pee	rug
le divan	le dee-vahn	divan
le piano	le pee-ah-no	piano
la table basse	la tahb bahss	coffee table
le canapé	le kah-nah-pay	sofa
le fauteuil	le fo-tay	arm chair
le fauteuil à bascule	le fo-tay ah ba-skuhl	rocking chair
le bureau	le boo-rho	desk
la chaise	la shehz	chair
une imprimante	ooh-neem-pree-mahnt	printer
la lampe	la lahmp	lamp
un ordinateur	uh-nohr-dee-nah-tchoor	computer
le téléphone	le tay-lay-fohn	telephone
le buffet	le boo-fay	sideboard
la chaise	la shehz	chair
la table	la tahb	table
la pendule	la pehn-duhl	grandfather clock
une étagère	ooh-nay-tah-jhehr	shelf
une cheminée	oohn sheh-mee-nay	fireplace
la baignoire	la beh-nwahr	bath
le bain	le behn	bath
la douche	la doosh	shower
le lavabo	le lah-va-bo	washbasin
une armoire de toilette	ooh-nahr-mwahr de twah-lett	bathroom cabinet
la glace	la glahss	bathroom mirror

VOCABULARY	PRONUNCIATION	ENGLISH
le pèse-personne	le pehs pehr-sahn	bathroom scale
le savon	le sah-vohn	soap
la serviette de toilette	la sehr-vee-ett de twah-lett	towel
le drap de bain	le drah de behn	bath towel
une éponge	ooh-nay-pohnj	sponge
la brosse	la brohss	brush
le peigne	le payn	comb
la brosse à dents	la brohss ah dahn	toothbrush
la dentifrice	la dahn-tee-freece	toothpaste
le shampooing	le shahm-poo-ehng	shampoo
le bain moussant	le behn moo-sahn	bubble bath
les sels de bain (m)	lay sehl de behn	bath salts
le déodorant	le day-oh-dohr-ahn	deodorant
le papier hygiénique	le pah-pee-ay ee-jhay-ahn-eek	toilet paper
le sèche-cheveux	le sesh shuh-vuh	hair dryer
une affiche	ooh-naff-eesh	poster
une armoire	ooh-nar-mwahr	wardrobe, closet
la chaise	la shehz	chair
la commode	la cuh-mohdd	chest of drawers
la couverture	la koo-vehr-toohr	blanket
le couvre-lit	le koovr-lee	bedspread
le drap	le drah	sheet
un édredon	uh-nay-dreh-dohn	duvet
la lampe	la lahmp	lamp
le lit	le lee	bed
le matelas	le maht-la	mattress
la miroir	la mee-rwawr	mirror
un oreiller	uh-nohr-ay-ay	pillow
le réveil	le ray-vay	alarm clock
le vaisselier	le veh-sehl-yay	sideboard

Rooms in a House

In this vocabulary list, you'll learn words for parts of the house and various rooms.

TABLE 20-5

ROOMS		
VOCABULARY	PRONUNCIATION	ENGLISH
le balcon	le bahl-kohn	balcony
la buanderie	la bwahn-dree	laundry room
le bureau	le buh-ro	study
la cave	la kahv	cellar
la chambre	la shahm-bruh	bedroom
le couloir	le koo-lwahr	hall
la cuisine	la kwee-zeen	kitchen
un étage	uh-nay-tahj	floor, story
les escaliers (m)	lay-zes-kal-yay	stairs
le garage	le gah-rahj	garage
le grenier	le grehn-yay	attic
le jardin	le jhar-dehn	garden
la marche	la mahrsh	step
la porte	la pohrt	door
le sous-sol	le soo-sohl	basement
la salle à manger	la sahl a mahn-jhay	dining room
la salle de séjour	la sahl de say-jhoor	living room
le toit	le twah	roof
dedans	de-dahn	inside
dehors	d'hor	outside
en haut	ah-nohe	upstairs
en bas	ahn bah	downstairs

Want an easy and fun way to practice the French words for rooms of the house? Why not play the Parker Brothers game Clue in French? Not too many people have conservatories or ballrooms in the house, or even a library or study, for that matter, but it's still good practice. Simply use the rooms from the vocabulary list in Table 20-5 and rename the rooms to whatever you like. Following is a list of translations for the weapons, should you decide to play.

le couteau	le koo-toe	knife
le chandelier	le shahn-dell-yay	candlestick
le revolver	le rhe-vahl-vehr	revolver
la corde	la kohrd	rope
la clef à écrous	la klay ah ay-kroo	wrench
le conduit de plomb	le khan-dwee de plahm	lead pipe
le conseratoire	le kohn-sehr-va-twahr	conservatory
le petit salon	le p-tee sah-lonn	lounge
la salle de bal	la sahl de bahl	ballroom
la salle de billard	la sahl de bee-ahr	billiard room

Apartments

The following vocabulary list includes some French terms associated with renting an apartment.

TABLE 20-6

APARTMENT VOCABULARY		
VOCABULARY	**PRONUNCIATION**	**ENGLISH**
habiter	ah-bee-tay	to live
le loyer	le lwoy-ay	rent
louer	loo-ay	to rent
le locataire	le lo-kah-tehr	tenant
un appartement	uh-nah-pahrt-mahn	apartment
un immeuble	uh-nihm-oob	apartment building

TABLE 20-6

VOCABULARY	PRONUNCIATION	ENGLISH
le propriétaire	le pro-pree-ay-tehr	owner
la propriétaire	la pro-pree-ay-tehr	owner
le concierge	le kohn-see-ehrj	caretaker
la concierge	la kohn-see-ehrj	caretaker

APARTMENT VOCABULARY (CONTINUED)

Housework

The following vocabulary list includes a number of French terms associated with cleaning up and other actions that are performed around the house.

TABLE 20-7

VOCABULARY	PRONUNCIATION	ENGLISH
jeter	jhe-tay	to throw out
épousseter	ay-poo-suh-tay	to dust
laver	la-vay	to wash
rincer	rhahn-say	to rinse
essuyer	ess-wee-ay	to wipe, to dry
sécher	say-shay	to dry
faire les lits	fehr lay lee	to make the beds
repasser	rhe-pah-say	to iron
repriser	rhe-pree-zay	to darn
raccommoder	rah-kho-mudd-ay	to reconcile
s'occuper de	sock-oo-pay de	to look after
utiliser	oo-tihl-ee-zay	to use
aider	ay-day	to help
donner un coup de main	dohn-ay uhn koo de mehn	to give a hand
la ménagère	la may-nah-jhehr	housewife
la femme de ménage	la fehm de may-nahj	maid, cleaning lady
une aide ménagère	ooh-nehd may-nah-jhehr	help, home care
la bonne	la buhn	maid

HOUSEWORK

In the Kitchen and at the Market

This vocabulary list includes a number of French terms associated with the kitchen and cooking. Later in this chapter, you'll even get to follow a recipe for authentic French bread!

TABLE 20-8

KITCHEN AND MARKET TERMS		
VOCABULARY	PRONUNCIATION	ENGLISH
la chaise	la shehz	chair
la cuisine	la kwee-zeehn	kitchen
la table	la tahb	table
un évier	uh-nay-vee-ay	kitchen sink
un four à micro-ondes	uhn foohr ah mee-croh ohnd	microwave oven
le frigo	le free-go	fridge
le réfrigérateur	le rhray-fhree-jhay-rha-tuhr	refrigerator
le congélateur	le khon-jhay-lah-tuhr	freezer
la nourriture	la noo-rhee-choor	food
le lave-vaisselle	le lahv veh-sell	dishwasher
le four	le fuhr	oven
la cuisinière	la kwee-zee-nee-aihr	stove top
la cuisinière électrique	la kwee-zee-nee-aihr ay-lek-treek	electric stovetop
la cuisinière à gaz	la kwee-zee-nee-aihr ah gahz	gas stovetop
le gaz	le gahz	gas
l'électricité (f)	lek-tree-see-tay	electricity
le grille-pain	le gree pehn	toaster
la bouilloire électrique	la boo-ee-ahr ay-lek-treek	electric kettle
avoir faim	ah-vwahr fehm	to be hungry
manger	mahn-jhay	to eat
avoir soif	ah-vwahr swahf	to be thirsty
boire	bwahr	to drink
le repas	le reh-pah	meal
le petit-déjeuner	le p'tee day-jhoo-nay	breakfast
le déjeuner	le day-jhoo-nay	lunch

TABLE 20-8

VOCABULARY	PRONUNCIATION	ENGLISH
KITCHEN AND MARKET TERMS *(CONTINUED)*		
le dîner	le dee-nay	dinner
le goûter	le goo-tay	snack
le casse-croûte	le kass-kroot	snack
le pique-nique	le peek-neek	picnic
faire la cuisine	fehr la kwee-zeen	to cook
faire à manger	fehr ah mahn-jhay	to prepare a meal
faire la vaisselle	fehr lay vess-ell	to do the dishes
nettoyer	neh-twoy-ay	to clean
préparer	pray-pehr-ay	to prepare
couper	koo-pay	to cut
couper en tranches	koo-pay ahn trahnsh	to slice
râper	rha-pay	to grate
éplucher	ay-ploo-shay	to peel
bouillir	bwee-yay	to boil
frire	fhree-ray	to fry
griller	gree-yay	to grill; to toast
rôtir	rho-teer	to roast
mettre la table	meh-truh lah tab	to set the table
débarrasser	day-bahr-ass-ay	to clear the table

Your Grocery List

The following vocabulary lists contain a number of French words for food and grocery items. They are broken out into sections to make it easier for you to memorize.

TABLE 20-9

VOCABULARY	PRONUNCIATION	ENGLISH
VEGETABLES		
le légume	le lay-goom	vegetable
un pois	uhn pwah	pea

VOCABULARY	PRONUNCIATION	ENGLISH
la pomme de terre	la pohm de tehr	potato
les petits pois (m)	lay petee pwah	peas
un haricot	uh-naihr-ee-koh	bean
des frites (f)	day freet	French fries
le chou	le shoo	cabbage
le chou-fleur	le shoo-fluhr	cauliflower
les choux de Bruxelles (m)	lay shoo de bruh-say	brussels sprouts
la laitue	la leh-choo	lettuce
des épinards (m)	day-zay-pee-nahr	spinach
des brocolis (m)	day bro-koh-lee	broccoli
le maïs	le ma-ee	corn
la tomate	la to-mahtt	tomato
la concombre	la cohn-com-bruh	cucumber

TABLE 20-10

	FRUIT	
le fruit	le frwee	fruit, a piece of fruit
la pomme	la pohm	apple
la poire	la pwahr	pear
un abricot	uh-nab-ree-koh	apricot
la pêche	la pesh	peach
la prune	la pruhn	plum
la nectarine	la nehk-tah-reen	nectarine
le melon	le mehl-ohn	melon
un ananas	uh-nah-nah-nah	pineapple
la banane	la bah-nahn	banana
une orange	ooh-nohr-ahnj	orange
le pamplemousse	le pahmp-luh-mooce	grapefruit
le citron	le see-trohn	lemon
la fraise	la frez	strawberry
la framboise	la frahm-bwahz	raspberry
la cerise	la sehr-eece	cherry

TABLE 20-11

STAPLES		
VOCABULARY	PRONUNCIATION	ENGLISH
le pain	le pehn	bread
la baguette	la bah-gett	French bread
la tartine	la tahr-teen	bread and butter
la tartine au miel	la tahr-teen oh mee-ell	buttered bread with honey
le pain grillé	le pehn gree-ay	toast
le croissant	le krwah-sahn	croissant, crescent roll
le beurre	le beuhr	butter
la margarine	la mahr-jha-rheen	margarine
la confiture	la kohn-fee-choor	jam
le miel	le mee-ell	honey

TABLE 20-12

MEAT, POULTRY, SEAFOOD, AND EGGS		
la viande	la vee-ahnd	meat
le porc	le pohrk	pork
le jambon	le jham-bohn	ham
le veau	le vo	veal
le boeuf	le buhf	beef
un agneau	uh-nahn-yo	lamb
le mouton	le moo-tahn	mutton
le poulet	le poo-lay	chicken
la dinde	la dahnd	turkey
le canard	le kah-nahrd	duck
la volaille	la voh-layy	poultry
le biftek	le beef-tek	steak
les escargots (m)	lay-zes-kahr-go	snails
des cuisses de grenouille (f)	day kweece de grehn-wee	frogs' legs
la morue	la mohr-oo	cod
la sardine	la sahr-deen	sardine
la sole	la sohl	sole

VOCABULARY	PRONUNCIATION	ENGLISH
le thon	le ton	tuna fish
la truite	la trweet	trout
le saumon	le so-mohn	salmon
le sumon fumé	le so-mohn foo-may	smoked salmon
les fruits de mer (m)	lay frwee de mehr	seafood
le homard	le oh-mahr	lobster
la huître	la whee-truh	oyster
la crevette	la kreh-vett	prawn
la moule	la mool	mussel
un oeuf	uh-noof	egg
un œuf à la coque	uh-noof ah la cok	boiled egg
un œuf sur le plat	uh-noof suhr la pla	fried egg
des œufs au jambon (m)	day-zoof oh jham-bohn	ham and eggs
des œufs brouillés (m)	day-zoof brwee-ay	scrambled eggs
une omelette	ooh-nahm-lett	omelet

Food Vocabulary Memorization Tips

There are a number of ways you can increase your French food vocabulary. Try calling familiar foods by their French names. Write the French word on a label, and stick it to the package. When you're cooking, make a conscious effort to think about the names of the items in French. Working with them actively helps to entrench the words in your memory.

If you have friends who are learning the language, you can have great fun by having a French party. Have each friend bring a French dish and set up little signs with the French name on it next to each container. Have the guests quiz each other on the names of the food items.

Authentic French Bread—a Recipe

The following recipe shows you how to make French bread. If you like, you can make a traditional loaf or shape it into anything you like, including a French baguette. The recipe is included both in French and in English.

Pain Français

1 tasse d'eau tiède   2 tasses et demie de farine blanche
1 paquet de levure   1 cuiller à thé de sel

1. Dans un bol, mélanger l'eau, la levure, le sel, et une tasse de la farine. Couvrir, et laisser reposer une demi-heure.
2. Ensuite, commencer à rajouter de la farine et à mélanger le contenu du bol à la main jusqu'à ce que vous ayez une pâte consistante. Tourner sur une plaque farinée et pétrir afin d'obtenir une pâte lisse et elastique.
3. Remettre dans le bol beurré. Laisser lever pour environ une heure, jusqu'à ce que la pâte ait doublé.
4. Enfoncer la pâte avec un coup de poing. Laisser lever encore une heure.
5. Former en boule ou en baguette, laisser lever encore. Faire cuire dans un four à 375 dégrés, ayant mis un pot d'eau dans le four au moment du rechauffement. Selon sa forme, le temps de cuisson va varier.

French Bread

1 cup of warm water   2½ cups of white flour
1 package of yeast   1 teaspoon salt

1. In a bowl, mix the water, yeast, salt, and one cup of the flour. Cover and let rest for a half hour.
2. Next, begin adding flour and mixing by hand until you obtain a workable dough. Turn the dough out on a floured board and knead until you have a smooth, elastic dough.
3. Butter the bowl and return the dough to it. Allow to rise for about an hour until doubled in volume.
4. Punch down. Allow to rise for another hour.
5. Form the dough into a ball or a baguette and allow to rise again. Cook in a 375 degree oven in which you have placed a pan of water. Cooking time will vary according to the shape you have chosen.

French-to-English Dictionary

Legend	
a	adjective / adverb
conj	conjunction
fem	feminine
int	interrogative
irr	irregular verb
m	masculine
n	noun
past p.	past participle
pl.	plural
prep	preposition
pron	pronoun
se	reflexive
v	verb

à (prep) at, to, in, of, by

à bientôt see you soon

à côté de next to

à demain see you tomorrow

à droite right

à gauche left

à la carte side order

à la longue in the long run

à moitié half

à peu près nearly, about

à point medium rare

à propos by the way, at the right time

à quelle heure when, at what time

à toute à l'heure see you later

à vos souhaits bless you (after someone sneezes)

abribus (n m) bus shelter

abricot (n m) apricot

absolu (a) absolute

absolument (a) absolutely, arbitrarily

accent (n m) accent

accepter (v) to accept

accessoire (n m) accessory

accident (n m) accident

accomplir (v) to accomplish

accourir (v) to hasten

accueillir (v) to welcome

achat (n m) purchase

acheter (v) to buy

acteur (n m) actor

actif, active (a) active, busy, energetic

actrice (n f) actress

actuel, actuelle (a) present, current

addition (n f) check, bill

adieu farewell

admirateur, admiratrice (a) admirer

adresse universelle (n f) Uniform Resource Locator (URL)

aéroport (n m) airport

affiche (n f) poster

Afrique (n f) Africa

agacer (v) to irritate

agence de voyages (n f) travel agency

agir (v) to act

agneau (n m) lamb

agonir (v) to insult

agriculteur (n m) farmer

aide ménagère (n f) help, home care

aider (v) to help

aigu acute (accent)

aigu, aiguë (a) pointed, sharp, keen, acute

aile (n f) wing

aimer (v) to like, to love

aisément (a) easily, readily, freely, comfortably

alcool (n m) alcohol

Allemagne (n f) Germany

allemand (n m) German

aller (v irr) to go; *(past p.) allé*

aller aux toilettes to go to the toilet

aller travailler to go to work

alliance (n f) wedding ring

allumer la radio to turn on the radio

allumer la télévision to turn on the television

allumer (v) to turn on

alphabet (n m) alphabet

altitude (n f) altitude

ambassade (n f) embassy

ambigu, ambiguë (a) ambiguous

Amérique du Nord (n f) North America

Amérique du Sud (n f) South America

ami (n m) friend

amie (n f) friend

amitié (n f) friendship

amoureux, amoureuse (a) loving, enamored, in love

amusant, amusante, (a) amusing, entertaining

amuser (v se) to have a good time

ananas (n m) pineapple

ancien / ancienne before the noun former; after the noun old, ancient, antique

anglais (n m) English

Anglais (n m) an Englishman

Anglaise (n f) an Englishwoman

Angleterre (n f) England

animal (n m) animal

annonce (n f) advertisement, announcement

annoncer (v) to announce

annulé (a) canceled

antérieur, antérieure, (a) anterior, earlier, previous, former

août August

appartement (m) apartment

appeler (v) to call; *(se)* to be named; to be called

applaudir (v) to applaud

appuyer (v) to support

après (prep) after

après-midi (n m) afternoon

architecte (n m) (m only) architect

argent (n m) money

argent de poche (n m) pocket money

armoire (n f) wardrobe, closet

armoire de toilette (n f) bathroom cabinet

arrêt d'autobus (n m) bus stop

arrière (n m) the back

arrivée (n f) arrival

arriver (v) to arrive; *(past p.) arrivé*

arroser les plantes to water the plants

article (n m) article

artiste (n f) artist

artiste (n m) artist

ascenseur (n m) elevator

Asie (n f) Asia

assez (a) enough

assistance (n f) assistance

assistant social (n m) social worker

assistante sociale (n f) social worker

astronaute (n f) astronaut

attendre (v) to wait

atterissage forcé (n m) emergency landing

atterissage (n m) landing

au gratin with melted cheese

au revoir goodbye

ne . . . aucun no one, not one

augmentation (n f) pay raise

aujourd'hui today

aussi (conj) also, as, likewise, too, besides

Australie (n f) Australia

auto (n f) car

autobus (n m) bus

automne (n m) autumn

autre (a) other, another, different

avant (prep) before

avant (n m) the front

avant-bras (n m) forearm

avant-première (n f) dress rehearsal

avec (conj) with

aventure (n f) adventure

avion (n m) plane

avion supersonique (n m) supersonic plane

avocat (n m) lawyer

avocate (n f) lawyer

avoir (v) to have, to hold; (past p.) eu

avoir . . . ans to be an age

avoir besoin de to need

avoir chaud to be hot, to feel hot

avoir de l'ambition to be ambitious

avoir de l'expérience to have experience

avoir de la chance to have the opportunity

avoir envie de to feel like

avoir faim to be hungry

avoir froid to be cold, to feel cold

avoir honte de to be ashamed of

avoir l'air to seem

avoir l'intention de to intend to

avoir l'occasion de to have the opportunity

avoir lieu to take place

avoir mal to have an ache

avoir peur de to be afraid

avoir raison to be right

avoir soif to be thirsty

avoir sommeil to be sleepy

avoir tort to be wrong

avril April

bagages à main (m pl.) hand bags, carry-on luggage

bague de fiançailles (n f) engagement ring

bague (n f) ring

baguette (n f) French bread

baignoire (n f) bath

bail (n m) lease; (pl.) baux

bâiller (v) to yawn

bain (n m) bath

bain moussant (n m) bubble bath

balance (n f) balance

balayer (v) to sweep

balcon (n m) balcony

banane (n f) banana

bande dessinée (n f) comic strip

banque (n f) bank

bar (n m) bar

bas (n m pl.) stockings

bas, basse (a) low, inferior

bateau (n m) boat

bâtir (v) to construct, build

beau, belle (a) beautiful, fine, handsome, pretty

beaucoup much, many

beau-père (n m) stepfather

beauté (n f) beauty

bégayer (v) to stammer

bel see *beau*

belle-mère (n f) stepmother

béret (n m) beret

beurre (n m) butter

bibliothèque (n f) library

bidet (n m) bidet

bien (a) well, rightly, finely, much, very, entirely, completely

bien cuit well done

bien sûr of course

bière (n f) beer

biftek (n m) steak

bijou (n m) jewel

bijouterie (n f) jewelry store

bijoutier (n m) jeweler

bijoutière (n f) jeweler

bikini (n m) bikini

billet (n m) ticket

billet aller-retour (n m) round trip ticket

billet de banque (n m) bill, bank note

billet simple (n m) (m) one-way ticket

blanc, blanche (a) white, clean, blank

blanchisserie (n f) laundry shop

blé (n m) wheat

bleu (a) rare

bleu, bleue (a) blue

blouson (n m) jacket

blue-jean (n m) blue jeans

bœuf (n m) beef

boire (v) to drink; (past p.) bu

boire (n m) drink, beverage

boisson (n f) drink

bon / bonne before the noun: enjoyable; after the noun: good, kind, favorable

bon appétit enjoy your meal

bon marché cheap

bonjour hello, good morning, good afternoon

bonne (n f) maid

bonne chance! good luck!

bonne nuit good night, sleep well

bonsoir good evening

bouche (n f) mouth

boucher (n m) butcher

bouchère (n f) butcher

boucherie (n f) butcher store

boucle d'oreille (n f) earring

bouilli (a) boiled

bouillir (v) to boil

bouilloire électrique (n f) electric kettle

boulangerie (n f) bakery

boutique (n f) small shop

bouton de manchette (n m) cufflink

bracelet (n m) bracelet

bras (n m) arm

brave (a) before the noun: nice; after the noun: courageous

bravo well done

bref, brève (a) short, brief, concise

brièvement briefly, succinctly, in short

brillamment brilliantly, in a brilliant manner

broche (n f) brooch

brocolis (n m pl.) broccoli

brosse (n f) brush

brosse à dents (n f) toothbrush

brosser (v se) to brush

bruit (m) noise

buanderie (n f) laundry room

buffet (n m) sideboard

bureau (n m) study, office, desk

bureau de change (n m) currency exchange outlet

bus (n m) bus

cabinet de toilette (n m) small bathroom

cadeau (n m) gift

café (n m) coffee

café au lait (n m) coffee with milk

cahier (n m) notebook

caisse (n f) till, cash register

caleçon (n m) underwear

calme (a) tranquil, quiet, serene, calm

camion (n m) truck

camomille (n f) chamomile tea

Canada (n m) Canada

canadien, canadienne (a) Canadian

canal (n m) canal

canapé (n m) sofa

canard (n m) duck

carnaval (n m) carnival

carnet de chèques (n m) checkbook

carte (n f) menu

carte d'embarquement (n f) boarding pass

carte d'identité bancaire (n f) bank card

carte de crédit (n f) credit card

casse-croûte (n m) snack

cave (n f) cellar

ce, cet (m) this

cédille cedilla (accent)

ceinture (n f) cummerbund, belt, seat belt

célébrer (v) to celebrate

cerise (n f) cherry

certain, certaine (a) before the noun: unique; after the noun: guaranteed

ces (pron pl.) these

cette (f) this

chaîne (n f) a channel

chaise (n f) chair

châle (n m) shawl

chambre (n f) bedroom

chambre à deux lits (n f) twin room

chambre pour deux personnes (n f) double room

chambre pour une personne (n f) single room

chance (n f) chance

chandelier (n m) candlestick

changer (v) to change

chanson (n f) song

chapeau (n m) hat

chaque each, every

charger (v) to charge

charter (n m) charter flight

chaussettes (f pl.) socks

chat (n m) cat

chaud (a) hot

chaussures (f pl.) shoes

chaussures à talons hauts (f pl.) high-heeled shoes

chef (n f) cook

chef (n m) cook

cheminée (n f) fireplace

chemise (n f) shirt

chemise de nuit (n f) nightgown

chemisier (n m) blouse

chèque (n m) check

chèque de voyage (n m) traveler's check

chéquier (n m) checkbook

cher, chère (a) before the noun: dear; after the noun: dear, precious, expensive

chercher (v) to look

chercher un emploi to look for work; to look for a job

cheval (n m) horse

cheveux (n m) hair

cheville (n f) ankle

chez (prep) at the home of, at the office of

chien (n m) dog

chinois (n m) Chinese

chocolat chaud (n m) hot chocolate

choisir (v) to choose

choix (n m) choice

chou (n m) cabbage

chou-fleur (n m) cauliflower

choux de Bruxelles (m pl.) brussels sprouts

cinéma (n m) movie theater; cinema

cinquième fifth

circonflexe circumflex (accent)

cité (n f) city

citron (n m) lemon

classeur (n m) binder

clavier (n m) keyboard

clef à écrous (n f) wrench

client (n m) customer

cliente (n f) customer

coiffer (v se) to comb one's hair

coiffeur (n m) hairdresser

coin (n m) corner

collant (n m) pantyhose, tights

collier (n m) necklace

combien how much

combien de how many

combinaison (n f) slip

comédie (n f) comedy

commande (n f) command

commander (v) to order

commencer (v) to begin

comment how

commissariat (n m) police station

commode (n f) chest of drawers

compagnie aérienne (n f) airline

complet no vacancies

complet veston (n m) suit

complet, complète (a) complete, whole

comprendre (v) to understand; *(past p.)* compris

compris included

compte d'épargne (n m) savings account

compte sur livret (n m) deposit account

concierge (f) caretaker

concierge (m) caretaker

concombre (n f) cucumber

concret, concrète (a) concrete, solid

conduire (v) to drive. *(past p.)* conduit

conduit de plomb (n m) lead pipe

confiture (n f) jam

confortable (a) comfortable

congélateur (n m) freezer

conseiller (v) to advise, to recommend

conservateur, conservatrice (a) conservative, preserving

constamment (a) steadily, continually, constantly

content, contente (a) content, satisfied, pleased, glad

contigu, contiguë (a) adjoining, contiguous

contrat (n m) contract

contrat de travail (n m) employment contract

contribution (n f) posting

convenablement suitably, becomingly, decently

copain (n m) friend, pal, mate, chum

copine (n f) friend; (f) of *copain*

corail (n m) coral

corde (n f) rope

corps (n m) body

corriger (v) to correct

corrompre (v) to corrupt

costume (n m) suit

côté (n m) side

cou (n m) neck

coude (n m) elbow

couloir (n m) hall

couper (v) to cut

couper en tranches to slice

courir (v irr) to run

cours (n m) course

court, courte (a) short, brief, concise, limited

courtois, courtoise (a) courteous, polite

cousin (n m) cousin

cousine (n f) cousin

couteau (n m) knife

coûter (v) to cost

couverture (n f) blanket

couvre-lit (n m) bedspread

cravate (n f) tie

crayon (n m) pencil

créateur, créatrice (a) creative, inventive

crèmerie (n f) dairy

crevette (n f) prawn

croire (v) to believe

croissant (n m) croissant, crescent roll

cruel, cruelle (a) cruel, merciless

cuisine (n f) kitchen

cuisinière à gaz (n f) gas stovetop

cuisinière électrique (n f) electric stovetop

cuisinière (n f) stovetop

cuisses de grenouille (n f pl.) frogs' legs

cuit (a) cooked

culture (n f) culture

culturel, culturelle (a) cultural

d'occasion secondhand

dangereux, dangereuse (a) dangerous

dans (prep) in, during

de (prep) of, from

débarrasser (v) to clear the table

débrouiller (v se) to get by, to manage

décembre December

décollage (n m) take-off

découvrir (v) to discover; *(past p.)* découvert

dedans inside

défendre (v) to defend, to protect

dehors out, outside, out of doors

déjà (a) already, before, previously

déjeuner (n m) lunch

demain tomorrow

demande (n f) request

demande d'emploi (n f) job application

demander (v) to ask for. *(se)* to wonder

demi-frère (n m) half-brother

demi-sœur (n f) half-sister

démissionner (v) to resign

dentifrice (n f) toothpaste

dentiste (n f) dentist

déodorant (n m) deodorant

départ (n m) departure

dépêcher (v se) to hurry

dépense (n f) expense

dépenser (v) to spend

depuis since, for

dernier, dernière (a) last, latest

derrière (prep) behind, after

des some, any

descendre (v) to go down, to get off; *(past p.)* descendu

déshabiller (v se) to undress (oneself)

désirer (v) to want, to desire

dessert (n m) dessert

dessin animé (n m) cartoon

détail (n m) detail

détester (v) to hate

deuxième (a) second

devant (prep) in front, ahead

devenir (v irr) to become; *(past p.)* devenu

devoir (v irr) to have to; to owe; *(past p.)* dû

devoirs (n m) homework

dictionnaire (n m) dictionary

différence (n f) difference

différent, différente before the noun: diverse; after the noun: different, other

difficile (a) difficult

diffuser (v) to broadcast

dimanche Sunday

dinde (n f) turkey

dîner (n m) dinner

dire (v) to say, to tell; *(past p.)* dit

directeur (n m) manager

discret, discrète (a) discreet, cautious, shy

disquaire (n m) music shop

disque (n m) hard disk

disquette (n f) floppy disk

distributeur automatique des billets de banque (n m) cash machine

distributeur de tickets (n m) ticket dispensing machine

divan (n m) divan

dixième (a) tenth

docteur (n m) (m only) doctor

documentaire (n m) documentary

doigt (n m) finger

domaine (n m) domain

donc (conj) so, then, therefore

donner un coup de main (v) to give a hand

dormir (v irr) to sleep

dos (n m) back

douane (n f) customs

douanier (n m) customs officer

douanière (n f) customs officer

douche (n f) shower

douloureux, douloureuse (a) painful, hurting, sore

doux, douce (a) sweet, gentle, calm, fresh

drap (n m) sheet

drap de bain (n m) bath towel

drôle (a) before the noun: bizarre; after the noun: funny

eau (n f) water

eau chaude (n f) hot water

eau minérale (n f) mineral water

échanger (v) to exchange

école (n f) school

économies (f pl.) savings

écouter (v) to listen

écran (n m) screen

écrire (v) to write; *(se)* to exclaim; *(past p.)* écrit

écrivain (n m) (m only) writer, author

écrouler (v se) to collapse

édredon (n m) duvet

effacer (v) to erase

efforcer de (v se) to strive

effrayer (v) to frighten

église (n f) church

égyptien, égyptienne (a) Egyptian

électricité (n f) electricity

elle (pron) she

elles (pron) they

émail (n m) enamel

embarquement (n m) boarding

embrayer (v) to couple

employé (n m) employee

employer (v) to employ

empresser de (v se) to hasten

en (prep) in, on, to, as, like, by

en aller (v se) to go away

en arrière de in back of

en attendant in the meantime

en avant de in front of

en bas down, downstairs

en direct live

en haut up, upstairs

en même temps at the same time

en retard delayed

en solde reduced price

enchanté (m) pleased to meet you

enchantée (f) pleased to meet you

enchanteur, enchanteresse (a) enchanting

encore again

endormir (v se) to fall asleep

enfant (n m) child

enfin at last, finally, after all, lastly, in short

enfuir (v se) to flee

ennuyer (v) to bore. *(se)* to get bored

ennuyeux, ennuyeuse (a) boring, tedious, dull, tiresome

enrayer (v) to check

enregistrement des bagages (n m) baggage check-in counter

ensemble (a) together, at the same time

ensemble (n m) woman's suit

ensuite next

entendre (v) to hear. *(se)* to get along

entrer (v) to enter, to come in; *(past p.)* entré

enveloppe (n f) envelope

envoler (v se) to fly away

envoyer (v) to send

épais, épaisse (a) thick, dense

épandre (v) to scatter, to strew

épaule (n f) shoulder

épicé (a) spicy

épicer (v) to spice

épicerie (n f) grocery store

épinards (n m pl.) spinach

épingle (n f) pin

épisode (n m) episode

éplucher (v) to peel

éponge (n f) sponge

épousseter (v) to dust

erreur (n f) error

escale (n f) stopover

escalier (n m) stairs

escargots (m pl.) snails

espagnol (n m) Spanish

espérer (v) to expect, to hope, to wish

espoir (n m) hope

essayer (v) to try

essence (n f) gasoline

essentiel, essentielle (a) essential

essuyer (v) to wipe, to dry

est (n m) east

est-ce que (int) is it that

estomac (n m) stomach

et (conj) and

étage (n m) floor, story

étagère (n f) shelf

États-Unis (n m) United States

été (n m) summer

éteindre (v) to turn off

éteindre la radio to turn off the radio

éteindre la télévision to turn off the television

étirer (v se) to stretch

étranger, étrangère (a) foreign, unknown, strange

être (v irr) to be; *(past p.)* été

être à to belong to someone

être content to be pleased

être désolé to be sorry

être fâché to be angry

être heureux to be happy

être sans emploi to be unemployed

être surpris to be surprised

étude (n f) study

étudiant (n m) student

étudiante (n f) student

étudier (v) to study

Europe (n f) Europe

européen, européenne (a) European

évanouir (v se) to faint

éventail (m) fan

évidemment (a) evidently

évier (n m) kitchen sink

évocateur, évocatrice (a) evocative

examen (n m) test

excellence (n m) excellence

excusez-moi excuse me

extérieur, extérieure (a) exterior, external

facile (a) easy

façon (n m) manner

facteur (n m) letter carrier

facture (n f) invoice, bill

faillir (v) to fail

faim hungry

faire (v) to do, to make. *(past p.)* fait

faire à manger to prepare a meal

faire attention à to pay attention to someone

faire des achats to go shopping

faire du shopping to go shopping

faire la cuisine to cook

faire la queue to wait in line

faire la sieste to have a nap

faire la vaisselle to do the dishes

faire les courses to do the shopping

faire les lits to make the beds

faire sa toilette to have a wash, to wash up

faire son lit to make the bed

falloir (v) to be necessary

famille (n f) family

farci (a) stuffed

farine (n f) flour

fauteuil (n m) armchair

fauteuil à bascule (n m) rocking chair

faux, fausse (a) false, wrong, untrue, fake, forged

favori, favorite (a) favorite

femme (n f) wife

femme de chambre (n f) maid, chambermaid

femme de ménage (n f) maid, cleaning woman

femme facteur (n f) letter carrier

fendre (v) to split, to crack, to cut open

fenêtre (n f) window

fermé, fermée (a) closed

fermer (v) to close

fermer la porte to close the door

fermer les rideaux to close the curtains

festival (n m) festival

feu (n m) fire

février February

fichier (n m) file

fille (n f) daughter

film d'horreur (n m) horror film

film de science-fiction (n m) science fiction film

film documentaire (n m) documentary

film en noir et blanc (n m) black and white film

film historique (n m) historical film

film (n m) film

fils (n m) son

finir (v) to finish

fixe-cravate (n m) tie-clip

flatteur, flatteuse (a) flattering, complimentary

fleurir (v) to blossom, to bloom

fleuriste (n f) florist

fleuriste (n m) florist

fol (a) see fou

fondre (v) to melt, to dissolve

forêt (n f) forest

forum (n m) newsgroup

fou, folle (a) mad, demented, wild, foolish

foulard (n m) scarf

four à micro-ondes (n m) microwave oven

four (n m) oven

fournir (v) to furnish

frais (n f pl.) expenses

frais, fraîche cool, fresh, new, youthful

fraise (n f) strawberry

framboise (n f) raspberry

franc (n m) franc (monetary unit)

franc belge (n m) Belgian franc

franc français (n m) French franc

franc suisse (n m) Swiss franc

Français (n m) a Frenchman

français, française (a) French

Française (n f) a Frenchwoman

France (n f) France

fréquemment (a) frequently

frère (n m) brother

frigo (n m) fridge

frire (v) to fry

frit, frite (a) fried

frites (f pl.) French fries

froid, froide (a) cold

fruit (n m) fruit, a piece of fruit

fruits de mer (n m) seafood

fumeur smoker

gagner (v) to earn

gagner sa vie to earn a living

gants (m pl.) gloves

garage (n m) garage

garantir (v) to guarantee

garçon (n m) boy

gardien de nuit (n m) night guard, porter

gare (v) station, train station, subway station

gare d'autobus (n f) bus station

gare routière (n f) bus station

gâteau (n m) cake

gaz (n m) gas

gendarme (n m) police officer

Genève (f) Geneva

genou (n m) knee

gens (n m pl.) people

gentil, gentille (a) noble, gentle, pretty, nice, kind

gentiment (a) prettily, gracefully

gin (n m) gin

glace (n f) bathroom mirror

gomme (n f) eraser

goûter (n m) snack

grammaire (n f) grammar

grand, grande (a) large, big; before the noun: great; after the noun: tall

grand lit (n m) double bed

grand magasin (n m) supermarket

grand-mère (n f) grandmother

grand-parents (n m) grandparents

grand-père (n m) grandfather

gras, grasse (a) fat, greasy, rich

gratuit free

grave (a) accent (grave)

grec, grecque (a) Greek, Grecian

grenier (n m) attic

grille-pain (n m) toaster

griller (v) to grill, to toast

gris, grise (a) gray

gros, grosse (a) big, large, bulky

guichet (n m) ticket office

habiller (v se) to get dressed

habiter (v) to live

habitude (n f) habit

habituel, habituelle (a) habitual

habituer à (v se) to get used to

hamster (a) hamster

haricot (n m) bean

haut, haute (a) high, tall, upper, haughty

hélice (n f) propeller

heure (n f) hour

heureux, heureuse (a) happy, blissful

hibou (n m) owl

hier (a) yesterday

hiver (n m) winter

homard (n m) lobster

hôpital (n m) hospital

hors d'œuvre (m pl.) appetizer

hôte de l'air (n m) steward, flight attendant

hôtel (n m) hotel

hôtesse de l'air (n f) stewardess, flight attendant

hublot (n m) window

huitième (a) eighth

huître (n f) oyster

hypertexte (n m) hypertext

ici (a) here, in this place, now, this time

icône (n f) icon

il (pron m) he

il y (a) there is, there are

ils (pron m pl.) they

immeuble (n m) apartment building

imperméable (n m) rain coat

important, importante (a) important

inférieur, inférieure (a) inferior, lower

infirmier (n m) nurse

infirmière (n f) nurse

informations (f pl.) information

ingénieur (n m) engineer

inquiet, inquiète (a) anxious, restless

insérer (v) to insert

intelligent, intelligente (a) intelligent, smart

intéressant (a) interesting

intéresser à (v se) to be interested in

intérieur, intérieure (a) interior, inner, internal

Internet (n m) Internet

interrompre (v) to interrupt

Irlande (n f) Ireland

israélien, israélienne (a) Israeli

issue de secours (n f) emergency exit

italien, italienne (a) Italian

jaloux, jalouse (a) jealous, envious

jamais ever; with *ne,* never

jambe (n f) leg

jambon (n m) ham

janvier (n m) January

japonais (a) Japanese

jardin (n m) garden

jaune (a) yellow

je (pron) I

jean (n m) jeans

jet (n m) jet

jeter (v) to throw, to throw out

jeu (n m) game

jeudi (n m) Thursday

joli, jolie (a) pretty, pleasing, neat, fine, nice

joue (n f) cheek

journal (n m) newspaper

journaliste (n f) journalist

journaliste (n m) journalist

juillet (n m) July

juin (n m) June

jupe (n f) skirt

jupon (n m) half slip

jus d'orange (n m) orange juice

jus de fruit (n m) fruit juice

jus de pomme (n m) apple juice

là (pron) there

lait (n m) milk

lait écrémé (n m) skim milk

laitue (n f) lettuce

lampe (n f) lamp

lapin (n m) rabbit

laquelle (pron) which, that

large (a) broad, wide, large, extensive

las, lasse (a) tired, weary, bored

lavabo (n m) washbasin

laver (v) to wash. *(se)* to wash (oneself)

lave-vaisselle (n m) dishwasher

lavomatic (n m) laundry shop

leçon (n f) lesson

lecteur de disquettes (n m) disk drive

légume (n m) vegetable

lequel (pron) which, that

lesquelles (pron) which, that

lesquels (pron) which, that

lettre (n f) letter

leur (pron) their

lever (v se) to get up

liberté (n f) liberty

librairie (n f) bookstore

licencier (v) to lay off

limonade (n f) lemonade

lire (v) to read; *(past p.)* lu

liste de signets (n f) bookmark file, bookmark list

lit (n m) bed

livre (n f) pound

livre (n m) book

locataire (m) tenant

logiciel (n m) software

logiciel de navigation (n m) Web browser

loin (a) far, distant, at a distance

loin de far from

Londres London

long, longue (a) long, slow, tedious, drawn out

longtemps (a) long, a long while

louer (v) to rent

loyer (n m) rent

lundi Monday

lunettes (f pl.) glasses

lunettes de soleil (f pl.) sunglasses

madame, mesdames (pl.) Mrs.

mademoiselle, mesdemoiselles (pl.) Miss

magasin (n m) shop

magasin de vins et spiritueux (n m) liquor store

magazine (n m) magazine

magicien (n m) magician

mai (n m) May

maillot de corps (n m) undershirt

maillot (n m) bathing suit

main (n f) hand

maintetant now, at this moment, at present

mais (conj) but

maïs (n m) corn

maison (n f) house

majeur, majeure (a) major, main, chief, greater

mal (a) wrong, badly

malheureux, malheureuse (a) unhappy, unfortunate, unlucky

malin, maligne (a) malicious, mischievous, malignant

manche (n f) sleeve

manche (n m) handle

manger (v) to eat

mannequin (n m) model

manquer d'expérience to lack experience

manteau (n m) coat

maquiller (v se) to put on makeup

marchand de fruits (n m) fruit merchant

marchand de légumes (n m) vegetable merchant

marchand de vin (n m) wine merchant

marche (n f) step

marché (n m) market

mardi Tuesday

margarine (n f) margarine

mari (n m) husband

marron, marron (a) brown

mars (n m) March

matelas (n m) mattress

mathématiques (pl.) mathematics

matin (n m) morning

mauvais, mauvaise (a) bad, ill, mischievous, evil, naughty

me (pron) me

médecin (n m) (m only) doctor

méfier de (v se) to distrust

meilleur, meilleure (a) better, preferable, correctly, more comfortably

mélanger (v) to mix

melon (n m) melon

même (a) before the noun: same; after the noun: exact

mémoire (n f) memory

ménagère (n f) housewife

menteur, menteuse (a) lying, false, deceitful

menu (n m) set-price meal

merci thank you

merci beaucoup thank you very much

mercredi Wednesday

mère (n f) mother

messagerie électronique (n f) e-mail

métro (n m) subway

mettre (v) to put, to place. *(past p.)* mis

metteur en scène (n m) director

mettre la table to set the table

mettre ses verres de contact to put in one's contact lenses

mettre son dentier to put in one's false teeth

mettre son réveil to set the alarm clock

meuble (n m) furniture

miel (n m) honey

mineur, mineure (a) lesser, minor

minijupe (n f) miniskirt

miroir (n m) mirror

mode (n f) fashion, manner, way, custom

mode (n m) mode

moderne, moderne (a) modern, up to date

moins (a) less, fewer

moitié (n f) half

mol (a) **see** *mou*

monsieur, messieurs (pl.) Mr.

monter (v) to climb; *(past p.)* monté

montre (n f) watch

moquer de (v se) to make fun of

moquette (n f) carpet

morceler (v) to break up, to parcel

mordre (v) to bite, to gnaw

morue (n f) cod

Moscou Moscow

mot de passe (n m) password

mou, molle (a) soft, limp, flabby, weak

mouchoir (n m) handkerchief

moufles (f pl.) mittens

moule (n f) mussel

mourir (v) to die;
  (past p.) mort

moutarde (n f) mustard

mouton (n m) mutton

moyen, moyenne (a) middle

muet (a) silent

mur (n m) wall

musée (n m) museum

musicien (n m) musician

nager (v) to swim

naissance (n f) birth

naître (v) to be born;
  (past p.) né

nationalité (n f) nationality

naturel, naturelle (a) natural

naturellement (a) naturally

navigateur (n m) Web browser

ne . . . aucunement not at all,
  not in the least

ne . . . guère not much, not
  very, only a little

ne . . . jamais never

ne . . . nul no one, nobody, not
  one

ne . . . nulle part nowhere

ne . . . nullement not at all, by
  no means

ne . . . pas not

ne . . . pas . . . non plus no
  longer

ne . . . pas du tout not at all

ne . . . pas encore not yet

ne . . . pas un not one, not
  even one

ne . . . personne no one, nobody.

ne . . . plus no longer

ne . . . point no, not at all, none

ne . . . que only

ne . . . rien nothing, not
  anything

ne . . . toujours pas not yet

nettoyage à sec (n m) dry
  cleaning

nettoyer (v) to clean

neuf, neuve (a) new, brand-new

neuvième (a) ninth

neveu (n m) nephew

nez (n m) nose

ni (conj) neither, nor

nièce (n f) niece

nœud papillon (n m) bow tie

noir, noire (a) black

nombreux, nombreuse (a)
  numerous, harmonious

non no

non fumeurs non smoking

nord (n m) north (le nord)

note (n f) bill

nourriture (n f) food

nous (pron) we, us

nouveau, nouvel (a) before the
  noun: additional; after the
  noun: new, recent, novel

novembre (n m) November

noyer (v) to drown

obéir à (v) to obey

objet (n m) object

obtenir (v irr) to obtain

occuper de (v se) to look after

octobre (n m) October

œil (n m) eye

œuf (n m) egg

œuf à la coque (n m) boiled egg

œuf sur le plat (n m) fried egg

œufs au jambon (n m pl.) ham
  and eggs

œufs brouillés (n m pl.)
  scrambled eggs

offre d'emploi (n f) job vacancy

offrir (v irr) to offer;
  (past p.) offert

oiseau (n m) bird

omelette (n f) omelet

oncle (n m) uncle

ongle (n m) fingernail

optimisme (n m) optimism

orange (n f) orange

ordinateur (n m) computer

oreille (n f) ear

oreiller (n m) pillow

orteil (n m) toe

ou (conj) or

où (prep) when, in which,
  where, at which, from which

ouest (n m) west

oui yes

ouvrir (v irr) to open;
  (past p.) ouvert

paiement (n m) payment

pain (n m) bread

pain grillé (n m) toast

pamplemousse (n m) grapefruit

pané (a) breaded

pantalon (n m) pants, trousers

papier (n m) paper

papier hygiénique (n m) toilet
  paper

par hasard by accident, by
  chance

parade (n f) parade

parapluie (n m) umbrella

parc (n m) park

pardessus (n m) overcoat

pardon? pardon me?

pareil, pareille (a) similar, equal

parent (n m) parent

Paris (n m) Paris

parisien, parisienne (a) Parisian

parking (n m) parking lot

parler (v) to speak

parler à to speak to someone

partir (v irr) to leave;
  (past p.) parti

parvenir (v) to attain, to
  succeed; *(past p.)* parvenu

passager (n m) passenger

passagère (n f) passenger

passeport (n m) passport

passer à la télé to appear
  on TV

passionnant (a) exciting

pasteur (n m) minister

patiemment (a) patiently

pâtisserie (n f) cake shop

pauvre (a) before the noun:
  unfortunate; after the noun:
  penniless

pavé (n m) pavement

paye (n f) pay, wages

payer (v) to pay

pêche (n f) peach

pêcheur, pécheresse (a) sinning

peigne (n m) comb

pendant during, while

pendentif (n m) pendant

pendre (v) to hang, to hang
  up, to suspend

pendule (n f) grandfather clock

penser (v) to think

penser à to think about
  someone

perdre (v) to lose, to waste

père (n m) father

permettre (v) to permit, to
  allow

personne (n f) person

pèse-personne (n m) bathroom
  scale

pessimisme (n m) pessimism

petit (a) little, small, short,
  very young

petit ami (n m) boyfriend

petit écran (n m) television

petit peu little, not much, few,
  not very, not many

petit-déjeuner (n m) breakfast

petite amie (n f) girlfriend

petites annonces (n f) classified ads

petits pois (m pl.) peas

peu (a) few, little, not much

peut-être perhaps, maybe, could be

pharmacie (n f) pharmacy

pharmacien (n m) pharmacist

photo (n f) photograph

photographie (n f) photography

piano (n m) piano

pièce (n f) coin

pied (n m) foot

pilote (n m) pilot

pique-nique (n m) picnic

piste (n f) runway

pitié (n f) pity

place (n f) seat

placer (v) to place, to put

plafond (n m) ceiling

plaire (v) to please; *(past p.)* plu

plaire à to please someone

plat principal (n m) main course

pleuvoir (v) to rain; *(past p.)* plu

poème (n m) a poem

poésie (n f) poetry

poignet (n m) wrist

pointure (n f) shoe size

poire (n f) pear

pois (n m) pea

poisson (n m) fish

poitrine (n f) chest

pomme (n f) apple

pomme de terre (n f) potato

pondre (v) to lay (as in eggs)

porc (n m) pork

porte (n f) door, gate

portefeuille (n m) wallet

porte-monnaie (n m) purse

porter (v) to wear, to carry

portugais (n m) Portuguese

poste (n f) mail, post office, postal service

poste (n m) post

postérieur, postérieure (a) posterior, later, behind

potage (n m) soup

pouce (n m) thumb

poulet (n m) chicken

pour (prep) for

pourboire (n m) tip

pourquoi (int) why

pouvoir (v irr) to be able; *(past p.)* pu

préférer (v) to prefer

premier, première (a) first

prendre (v) to take; *(past p.)* pris

prendre des vacances to take a vacation

prendre sa retraite to retire

prendre son petit déjeuner to have breakfast

prendre un jour de congé to take a day off

préparer (v) to prepare

près de near to

près (prep) near, by

présenter à to give something to someone

prêtre (n m) priest

printemps (n m) spring

prison (n f) prison

prix (n m) prize, price

prix par jour (n m) price per day

probablement (a) probably

prochain, prochaine (a) before the noun: following; after the noun: next

professeur (n m) professor, teacher

projeter (v) to project

promenade (n f) walk

prononcer (v) to pronounce

propre (a) before the noun: own; after the noun: clean

propriétaire (n f) owner

propriétaire (n m) owner

provisions (f pl.) merchandise, shopping items

prune (n f) plum

public, publique (a) public

publicité (n f) a commercial

puis (conj) then

pyjama (n m) pajamas

quai (n m) (m) platform

quand (int) when

quatrième (a) fourth

que (pron) that, which, what. *ne* only

quel (pron m) what, which

quelle (pron f) what, which

quelles (f pl.) what, which

quelque part somewhere

quelquefois sometimes

quels (m pl.) what, which

qui (pron) who or whom

quitter (v) to leave

quoi (pron) what

quotidien, quotidienne (a) daily

raccommoder (v) to reconcile

radio (n f) radio

rafraîchir (v) to refresh

raison (n f) reason

râper (v) to grate

rappeler (v) to remind

raser (v se) to shave (oneself)

rasoir (n m) razor

rayer (v) to delete, to scratch, to erase

réceptionniste (n f) receptionist

réceptionniste (n m) receptionist

recevoir (v irr) to receive, to get; *(past p.)* reçu

réclamation (n f) complaint

reçu (n m) receipt

redescendre (v) to come down again; *(past p.)* redescendu

réel, réelle (a) real, actual, genuine

réfrigérateur (n m) refrigerator

refuser (v) to reject

regarder (v) to watch

regretter (v) to regret, to grieve

rejeter (v) to reject, to throw again

religieuse (n f) nun

remonter (v) to go up again; *(past p.)* remonté

remplacer (v) to replace

renaître (v) to be born again. *(past p.)* rené

rendre (v) to return, to restore, to give back, to repay

rendre compte de (v se) to realize

rentrer (v) to return, to come back

rentrer à la maison to come home, to go home

rentrer de l'école to come back from school

rentrer du travail to come back from work

renvoyer (v) to return, to dismiss

repartir (v) to go out again; *(past p.)* reparti

repas (n m) meal

repasser (v) to iron

replet, replète (a) obese, stout

répondre (v) to answer, to reply

reposer (v se) to have a rest, to take a nap

repriser (v) to darn

réservation (n f) booking, reservation

ressembler à (v) to look like, to resemble

ressortir (v) to come out again; *(past p.)* ressorti

restaurant (n m) restaurant

rester (v) to remain, to stay

retard (n m) delay

retomber (v) to fall again; *(past p.)* retombé

retourner (v) to return, to go back

retrait (n m) withdrawal

réussir (v) to be successful

réveil (n m) alarm clock

réveiller (v se) to wake up

revenir (v irr) to come back

revolver (n m) revolver

revue (n f) magazine

rhum (n m) rum

riche (a) rich, wealthy, valuable

rideau (n m) curtain

rincer (v) to rinse

robe (n f) dress

robe de chambre (n f) robe, nightgown

roman (n m) novel

rompre (v) to break, to snap, to break off

rose, rose (a) pink

rôtie (a) roasted

rôtir (v) to roast

rouge, rouge (a) red

roux, rousse (a) reddish, red-haired

ruban (n m) ribbon

russe (n m) Russian

sac à dos (n m) backpack

sac à main (n m) purse, hand bag

saignant (a) rare

saison (n f) season

salade (n f) salad

salaire (n m) salary, wages

sale (a) before the noun: bad; after the noun: dirty

salle à manger (n f) dining room

salle d'attente (n f) waiting room

salle d'embarquement (n f) departure lounge

salle de bain (n f) bathroom

salle de classe (n f) classroom

salle de séjour (n f) living room

salut! Hi! Bye!

samedi Saturday

sans (a) without

sans (conj) without

sans doute doubtless

santé bless you (after someone sneezes)

sarcasme (n m) sarcasm

sardine (n f) sardine

saumon (n m) salmon

savant (n m) (m only) scholar, scientist

savoir (v irr) to know; *(past p.)* su

savon (n m) soap

science (n f) science

se (pron) him, her, they

sec, sèche (a) dry, arid, plain

sèche-cheveux (n m) hair dryer

sécher (v) to dry. *(se)* to dry (oneself)

secrétaire (n f) secretary

secrétaire (n m) secretary

seizième (a) sixth

sels de bain (n m) bath salts

semaine de quarante heures (n f) forty-hour week

sentence (n f) verdict

septembre (n m) September

septième (a) seventh

serpent (n m) snake

serveur (n m) waiter

serveuse (n f) waitress

service (n m) service

service compris (n m) tip included

service non compris (n m) tip not included

serviette de toilette (n f) towel

servir (v irr) to serve

ses (pron) his, hers

seul (a) before the noun: only; after the noun: single

shampooing (n m) shampoo

si (conj) so, so much, yes, but yes, if

signe (n m) sign

signet (n m) bookmark

silence (n m) silence

s'il vous plaît please

slip (n m) panties

smoking (n m) tuxedo

sœur (n f) sister

soif (a) thirsty

soir (n m) evening

sol (n m) floor

sole (n f) sole

solitude (n f) solitude

songer (v) to dream, to imagine

sortie de secours (n f) emergency exit

sortir (v irr) to go out; *(past p.)* sorti

soucier de (v se) to mind

souffrir (v) to suffer; *(past p.)* souffert

souhaiter (v) to wish

soupe (n f) soup

soupirail (n m) ventilator

sourire (n m) smile

sourire (v) to smile; *(past p.)* souri

souris (n f) mouse

sous-sol (n m) basement

sous-titres (n m) subtitles

soutien-gorge (n m) brassiere

souvenir de (v se) to remember

souvent (a) often, frequently

station de métro (n m) subway station

steward (n m) steward

stylo (n m) pen

sud (n m) south

suicider (v se) to kill oneself

suivre (v) to follow; *(past p.)* suivi

sujet (n m) subject

supérieur, supérieure (a) superior, upper, higher

sur (prep) on, at, in, about

surprise (n f) surprise

table (n f) table

table basse (n f) coffee table

tailleur (n m) woman's suit

taire (v se) to be silent

tant pis never mind

tante (n f) aunt

tapis (n m) rug

tapis de bain (n m) bath mat

tard (a) late

tartine (n f) bread and butter

tartine au miel (n f) buttered bread with honey

taxi (n m) taxi

te (pron) you

teinturerie (n f) dry cleaners

tel, telle (a) such

téléphone (n m) telephone

téléphoner à (v) to telephone

télévision (n f) television

tendre (v) to stretch, to strain

tenir (v irr) to have, to hold; *(past p.)* tenu

tenir à to be attached to someone, to be related to someone

terminal (n m) terminal

tête (n f) head

thé (n m) tea

théâtre (n m) theatre

thon (n m) tuna fish

toile d'araignée mondiale [TAM] (n f) World Wide Web

toilette (n f) toilet

toit (n m) roof

tomate (n f) tomato

tomber (v) to fall. *(past p.)* tombé

tondre (v) to shear, to clip, to crop, to cut

tordre (v) to twist, to wring, to contort

tortue (n f) tortoise

tôt (a) soon, quickly, early

toujours (a) always, ever, forever

tour de contrôle (n f) control tower

tourisme (n m) tourism

tous les matins every morning

tout (a) all, whole, every

tout de suite immediately

tout droit straight, straight ahead

toux (n f) cough

traditionnel, traditionnelle (a) traditional

traducteur (n m) translator

traductrice (n f) translator

tragédie (n f) tragedy

train (n m) train

tranquille, tranquille (a) quiet, calm, tranquil, peaceful

transport (n m) transportation

travail (n f) work

travailler (v) to work

tréma (n m) umlaut (accent)

très (a) very, most, very much

troisième third

tromper (v se) to be wrong

trompeur, trompeuse (a) deceitful, false, misleading

trop (a) too, too much, too many

trop cuit (a) over done

trouver (v) to find

trouver du travail to find work

trouver un emploi to find a job

truite (n f) trout

tu (pron) you

uniforme (n m) uniform

universel, universelle (a) universal

usuel, usuelle (a) usual

utile (a) useful, beneficial

utiliser (v) to use

vacance (n f) vacancy

vacances (n f pl.) vacation

vaisselier (n m) sideboard

valise (n f) suitcase

valoir (v) to be worth

vase (n f) mud, slime

vase (n m) vase

veau (n m) veal

vedette (n f) star

vendeur (n m) clerk, cashier

vendeuse (n f) clerk, cashier

vendre (v) to sell

vendredi Friday

venir (v irr) to come; *(past p.)* venu

verrouiller la porte (v) to lock the door

vers (prep) toward, around

vert, verte (a) green

veste (n f) jacket

veston de sport (n m) sport jacket

viande (n f) meat

vidéo (n f) video

vieil (a) **see** vieux

vieux, vieille (a) old, ancient, aged, advanced in years

vif, vive (a) alive, live, living

ville (n f) city

vin (n m) wine

vin blanc (n m) white wine

vin rouge (n m) red wine

violet, violette (a) purple

virement (n m) transfer

virus (n m) virus

visa (n m) visa

visage (n m) face

vite (a) quick, quickly, fast, rapidly

vitesse (n f) speed

vitrail (n m) stained-glass window

vocabulaire (n m) vocabulary

vodka (n f) vodka

voilà there is, there are

voile (n f) sail

voile (n m) veil

voir (v) to see (irr); *(past p.)* vu

voisin (n m) neighbor

voisine (n f) neighbor

voiture (n f) car

vol (n m) flight

vol direct (n m) direct flight

vol international (n m) international flight

vol interne (n m) domestic flight

volaille (n f) poultry

voleur, voleuse (a) thief, robber, person who steals

vouloir (v irr) to want, to wish, to will; *(past p.)* voulu

vous (pron) you

voyage d'affaires (n m) business trip

voyager (v) to travel

vrai, vraie (a) true, real, right

vraiment (a) truly, in truth, indeed, really

western (n m) Western

whisky (n m) whiskey

y (pron) there, it

yeux (n m pl) eyes

Verb Conjugation Tables

"used to"
"was" ____ ing.

-er Verbs

Past continued
continuing

PARLER (TO SPEAK); PAST PARTICIPLE, PARLÉ

SUBJECT	PRESENT	PAST IMPERFECT	FUTURE	CONDITIONAL	SUBJUNCTIVE
je	parl^e	parl^{ais}	parler^{ai}	parler^{ais}	parl^e
tu	parl^{es}	parl^{ais}	parler^{as}	parler^{ais}	parl^{es}
il	parl^e	parl^{ait}	parler^a	parler^{ait}	parl^e
nous	parl^{ons}	parl^{ions}	parler^{ons}	parler^{ions}	parl^{ions}
vous	parl^{ez}	parl^{iez}	parler^{ez}	parler^{iez}	parl^{iez}
ils	parl^{ent}	parl^{aient}	parler^{ont}	parler^{aient}	parl^{ent}

-ir Verbs

FINIR (TO FINISH); PAST PARTICIPLE, FINI

SUBJECT	PRESENT	IMPERFECT	FUTURE	CONDITIONAL	SUBJUNCTIVE
je	fin^{is}	finiss^{ais}	finir^{ai}	finir^{ais}	finiss^e
tu	fin^{is}	finiss^{ais}	finir^{as}	finir^{ais}	finiss^{es}
il	fin^{it}	finiss^{ait}	finir^a	finir^{ait}	finiss^e
nous	fin^{issons}	finiss^{ions}	finir^{ons}	finir^{ions}	finiss^{ions}
vous	fin^{issez}	finiss^{iez}	finir^{ez}	finir^{iez}	finiss^{iez}
ils	fin^{issent}	finiss^{aient}	finir^{ont}	finir^{aient}	finiss^{ent}

-re Verbs

ATTENDRE (TO WAIT FOR); PAST PARTICIPLE, ATTENDU

SUBJECT	PRESENT	IMPERFECT	FUTURE	CONDITIONAL	SUBJUNCTIVE
j'	attend^s	attend^{ais}	attendr^{ai}	attendr^{ais}	attend^e
tu	attend^s	attend^{ais}	attendr^{as}	attendr^{ais}	attend^{es}
il	attend	attend^{ait}	attendr^a	attendr^{ait}	attend^e
nous	attend^{ons}	attend^{ions}	attendr^{ons}	attendr^{ions}	attend^{ions}
vous	attend^{ez}	attend^{iez}	attendr^{ez}	attendr^{iez}	attend^{iez}
ils	attend^{ent}	attend^{aient}	attendr^{ont}	attendr^{aient}	attend^{ent}

ais
ais
ait
ions
iez
aient

Irregular Verbs

ALLER (TO GO); PAST PARTICIPLE, ALLÉ

SUBJECT	PRESENT	IMPERFECT	FUTURE	CONDITIONAL	SUBJUNCTIVE
je	vais	allais	irai	irais	aille
tu	vas	allais	iras	irais	ailles
il	va	allait	ira	irait	aille
nous	allons	allions	irons	irions	allions
vous	allez	alliez	irez	iriez	alliez
ils	vont	allaient	iront	iraient	aillent

AVOIR (TO HAVE); PAST PARTICIPLE, EU

SUBJECT	PRESENT	IMPERFECT	FUTURE	CONDITIONAL	SUBJUNCTIVE
j'	ai	avais	aurai	aurais	aie
tu	as	avais	auras	aurais	aies
il	a	avait	aura	aurait	ait
nous	avons	avions	aurons	aurions	ayons
vous	avez	aviez	aurez	auriez	ayez
ils	ont	avaient	auront	auraient	aient

DEVOIR (TO HAVE TO); PAST PARTICIPLE, DÛ

SUBJECT	PRESENT	IMPERFECT	FUTURE	CONDITIONAL	SUBJUNCTIVE
je	dois	devais	devrai	devrais	doive
tu	dois	devais	devras	devrais	doives
il	doit	devait	devra	devrait	doive
nous	devons	devions	devrons	devrions	devions
vous	devez	deviez	devrez	devriez	deviez
ils	doivent	devaient	devront	devraient	doivent

DIRE (TO SAY, TELL); PAST PARTICIPLE, DIT

SUBJECT	PRESENT	IMPERFECT	FUTURE	CONDITIONAL	SUBJUNCTIVE
je	dis	disais	dirai	dirais	dise
tu	dis	disais	diras	dirais	dises
il	dit	disait	dira	dirait	dise
nous	disons	disions	dirons	dirions	disions
vous	dites	disiez	direz	diriez	disiez
ils	disent	disaient	diront	diraient	disent

ÉTRE (TO BE); PAST PARTICIPLE, ÉTÉ

SUBJECT	PRESENT	IMPERFECT	FUTURE	CONDITIONAL	SUBJUNCTIVE
je	suis	étais	serai	serais	sois
tu	es	étais	seras	serais	sois
il	est	était	sera	serait	soit
nous	sommes	étions	serons	serions	soyons
vous	êtes	étiez	serez	seriez	soyez
ils	sont	étaient	seront	seraient	soient

FAIRE (TO MAKE, DO); PAST PARTICIPLE, FAIT

SUBJECT	PRESENT	IMPERFECT	FUTURE	CONDITIONAL	SUBJUNCTIVE
je	fais	faisais	ferai	ferais	fasse
tu	fais	faisais	feras	ferais	fasses
il	fait	faisait	fera	ferait	fasse
nous	faisons	faisions	ferons	ferions	fassions
vous	faites	faisiez	ferez	feriez	fassiez
ils	font	faisaient	feront	feraient	fassent

METTRE (TO PUT); PAST PARTICIPLE, MIS

SUBJECT	PRESENT	IMPERFECT	FUTURE	CONDITIONAL	SUBJUNCTIVE
je	mets	mettais	mettrai	mettrais	mette
tu	mets	mettais	mettras	mettrais	mettes
il	met	mettait	mettra	mettrait	mette
nous	mettons	mettions	mettrons	mettrions	mettions
vous	mettez	mettiez	mettrez	mettriez	mettiez
ils	mettent	mettaient	mettront	mettraient	mettent

POUVOIR (TO BE ABLE TO, CAN); PAST PARTICIPLE, PU

SUBJECT	PRESENT	IMPERFECT	FUTURE	CONDITIONAL	SUBJUNCTIVE
je	peux	pouvais	pourrai	pourrais	puisse
tu	peux	pouvais	pourras	pourrais	puisses
il	peut	pouvait	pourra	pourrait	puisse
nous	pouvons	pouvions	pourrons	pourrions	puissions
vous	pouvez	pouviez	pourrez	pourriez	puissiez
ils	peuvent	pouvaient	pourront	pourraient	puissent

RECEVOIR (TO RECEIVE); PAST PARTICIPLE, REÇU

SUBJECT	PRESENT	IMPERFECT	FUTURE	CONDITIONAL	SUBJUNCTIVE
je	reçois	recevais	recevrai	recevrais	reçoive
tu	reçois	recevais	recevras	recevrais	reçoives
il	reçoit	recevait	recevra	recevrait	reçoive
nous	recevons	recevions	recevrons	recevrions	recevions
vous	recevez	receviez	recevrez	recevriez	receviez
ils	reçoivent	recevaient	recevront	recevraient	reçoivent

SAVOIR (TO KNOW); PAST PARTICIPLE, SU

SUBJECT	PRESENT	IMPERFECT	FUTURE	CONDITIONAL	SUBJUNCTIVE
je	sais	savais	saurai	saurais	sache
tu	sais	savais	sauras	saurais	saches
il	sait	savait	saura	saurait	sache
nous	savons	savions	saurons	saurions	sachions
vous	savez	saviez	saurez	sauriez	sachiez
ils	savent	savaient	sauront	sauraient	sachent

VOULOIR (TO WANT); PAST PARTICIPLE, VOULU

SUBJECT	PRESENT	IMPERFECT	FUTURE	CONDITIONAL	SUBJUNCTIVE
je	veux	voulais	voudrai	voudrais	veuille
tu	veux	voulais	voudras	voudrais	veuilles
il	veut	voulait	voudra	voudrait	veuille
nous	voulons	voulions	voudrons	voudrions	voulions
vous	voulez	vouliez	voudrez	voudriez	vouliez
ils	veulent	voulaient	voudront	voudraient	veuillent

Voir   To see   to believe   Boire (to drink)

Il voyait   elle croyait   Elle bu (she has drunk)

Index

We Have EVERYTHING!

Everything® **After College Book**
$12.95, 1-55850-847-3

Everything® **American History Book**
$12.95, 1-58062-531-2

Everything® **Angels Book**
$12.95, 1-58062-398-0

Everything® **Anti-Aging Book**
$12.95, 1-58062-565-7

Everything® **Astrology Book**
$12.95, 1-58062-062-0

Everything® **Baby Names Book**
$12.95, 1-55850-655-1

Everything® **Baby Shower Book**
$12.95, 1-58062-305-0

Everything® **Baby's First Food Book**
$12.95, 1-58062-512-6

Everything® **Baby's First Year Book**
$12.95, 1-58062-581-9

Everything® **Barbeque Cookbook**
$12.95, 1-58062-316-6

Everything® **Bartender's Book**
$9.95, 1-55850-536-9

Everything® **Bedtime Story Book**
$12.95, 1-58062-147-3

Everything® **Bicycle Book**
$12.00, 1-55850-706-X

Everything® **Breastfeeding Book**
$12.95, 1-58062-582-7

Everything® **Build Your Own Home Page**
$12.95, 1-58062-339-5

Everything® **Business Planning Book**
$12.95, 1-58062-491-X

Everything® **Candlemaking Book**
$12.95, 1-58062-623-8

Everything® **Casino Gambling Book**
$12.95, 1-55850-762-0

Everything® **Cat Book**
$12.95, 1-55850-710-8

Everything® **Chocolate Cookbook**
$12.95, 1-58062-405-7

Everything® **Christmas Book**
$15.00, 1-55850-697-7

Everything® **Civil War Book**
$12.95, 1-58062-366-2

Everything® **Classical Mythology Book**
$12.95, 1-58062-653-X

Everything® **Collectibles Book**
$12.95, 1-58062-645-9

Everything® **College Survival Book**
$12.95, 1-55850-720-5

Everything® **Computer Book**
$12.95, 1-58062-401-4

Everything® **Cookbook**
$14.95, 1-58062-400-6

Everything® **Cover Letter Book**
$12.95, 1-58062-312-3

Everything® **Creative Writing Book**
$12.95, 1-58062-647-5

Everything® **Crossword and Puzzle Book**
$12.95, 1-55850-764-7

Everything® **Dating Book**
$12.95, 1-58062-185-6

Everything® **Dessert Book**
$12.95, 1-55850-717-5

Everything® **Digital Photography Book**
$12.95, 1-58062-574-6

Everything® **Dog Book**
$12.95, 1-58062-144-9

Everything® **Dreams Book**
$12.95, 1-55850-806-6

Everything® **Etiquette Book**
$12.95, 1-55850-807-4

Everything® **Fairy Tales Book**
$12.95, 1-58062-546-0

Everything® **Family Tree Book**
$12.95, 1-55850-763-9

Everything® **Feng Shui Book**
$12.95, 1-58062-587-8

Everything® **Fly-Fishing Book**
$12.95, 1-58062-148-1

Everything® **Games Book**
$12.95, 1-55850-643-8

Everything® **Get-A-Job Book**
$12.95, 1-58062-223-2

Everything® **Get Out of Debt Book**
$12.95, 1-58062-588-6

Everything® **Get Published Book**
$12.95, 1-58062-315-8

Everything® **Get Ready for Baby Book**
$12.95, 1-55850-844-9

Everything® **Get Rich Book**
$12.95, 1-58062-670-X

Everything® **Ghost Book**
$12.95, 1-58062-533-9

Everything® **Golf Book**
$12.95, 1-55850-814-7

Everything® **Grammar and Style Book**
$12.95, 1-58062-573-8

Everything® **Guide to Las Vegas**
$12.95, 1-58062-438-3

Everything® **Guide to New England**
$12.95, 1-58062-589-4

Everything® **Guide to New York City**
$12.95, 1-58062-314-X

Everything® **Guide to Walt Disney World®,
Universal Studios®, and
Greater Orlando, 2nd Edition**
$12.95, 1-58062-404-9

Everything® **Guide to Washington D.C.**
$12.95, 1-58062-313-1

Everything® **Guitar Book**
$12.95, 1-58062-555-X

Everything® **Herbal Remedies Book**
$12.95, 1-58062-331-X

**Available wherever books are sold!
To order, call 800-872-5627, or visit everything.com**
Adams Media Corporation, 57 Littlefield Street, Avon, MA 02322. U.S.A.

Everything® **Home-Based Business Book**
$12.95, 1-58062-364-6

Everything® **Homebuying Book**
$12.95, 1-58062-074-4

Everything® **Homeselling Book**
$12.95, 1-58062-304-2

Everything® **Horse Book**
$12.95, 1-58062-564-9

Everything® **Hot Careers Book**
$12.95, 1-58062-486-3

Everything® **Internet Book**
$12.95, 1-58062-073-6

Everything® **Investing Book**
$12.95, 1-58062-149-X

Everything® **Jewish Wedding Book**
$12.95, 1-55850-801-5

Everything® **Job Interview Book**
$12.95, 1-58062-493-6

Everything® **Lawn Care Book**
$12.95, 1-58062-487-1

Everything® **Leadership Book**
$12.95, 1-58062-513-4

Everything® **Learning French Book**
$12.95, 1-58062-649-1

Everything® **Learning Spanish Book**
$12.95, 1-58062-575-4

Everything® **Low-Fat High-Flavor Cookbook**
$12.95, 1-55850-802-3

Everything® **Magic Book**
$12.95, 1-58062-418-9

Everything® **Managing People Book**
$12.95, 1-58062-577-0

Everything® **Microsoft® Word 2000 Book**
$12.95, 1-58062-306-9

Everything® **Money Book**
$12.95, 1-58062-145-7

Everything® **Mother Goose Book**
$12.95, 1-58062-490-1

Everything® **Motorcycle Book**
$12.95, 1-58062-554-1

Everything® **Mutual Funds Book**
$12.95, 1-58062-419-7

Everything® **One-Pot Cookbook**
$12.95, 1-58062-186-4

Everything® **Online Business Book**
$12.95, 1-58062-320-4

Everything® **Online Genealogy Book**
$12.95, 1-58062-402-2

Everything® **Online Investing Book**
$12.95, 1-58062-338-7

Everything® **Online Job Search Book**
$12.95, 1-58062-365-4

Everything® **Organize Your Home Book**
$12.95, 1-58062-617-3

Everything® **Pasta Book**
$12.95, 1-55850-719-1

Everything® **Philosophy Book**
$12.95, 1-58062-644-0

Everything® **Playing Piano and Keyboards Book**
$12.95, 1-58062-651-3

Everything® **Pregnancy Book**
$12.95, 1-58062-146-5

Everything® **Pregnancy Organizer**
$15.00, 1-58062-336-0

Everything® **Project Management Book**
$12.95, 1-58062-583-5

Everything® **Puppy Book**
$12.95, 1-58062-576-2

Everything® **Quick Meals Cookbook**
$12.95, 1-58062-488-X

Everything® **Resume Book**
$12.95, 1-58062-311-5

Everything® **Romance Book**
$12.95, 1-58062-566-5

Everything® **Running Book**
$12.95, 1-58062-618-1

Everything® **Sailing Book, 2nd Edition**
$12.95, 1-58062-671-8

Everything® **Saints Book**
$12.95, 1-58062-534-7

Everything® **Selling Book**
$12.95, 1-58062-319-0

Everything® **Shakespeare Book**
$12.95, 1-58062-591-6

Everything® **Spells and Charms Book**
$12.95, 1-58062-532-0

Everything® **Start Your Own Business Book**
$12.95, 1-58062-650-5

Everything® **Stress Management Book**
$12.95, 1-58062-578-9

Everything® **Study Book**
$12.95, 1-55850-615-2

Everything® **T'ai Chi and QiGong Book**
$12.95, 1-58062-646-7

Everything® **Tall Tales, Legends, and Outrageous Lies Book**
$12.95, 1-58062-514-2

Everything® **Tarot Book**
$12.95, 1-58062-191-0

Everything® **Time Management Book**
$12.95, 1-58062-492-8

Everything® **Toasts Book**
$12.95, 1-58062-189-9

Everything® **Toddler Book**
$12.95, 1-58062-592-4

Everything® **Total Fitness Book**
$12.95, 1-58062-318-2

Everything® **Trivia Book**
$12.95, 1-58062-143-0

Everything® **Tropical Fish Book**
$12.95, 1-58062-343-3

Everything® **Vegetarian Cookbook**
$12.95, 1-58062-640-8

Everything® **Vitamins, Minerals, and Nutritional Supplements Book**
$12.95, 1-58062-496-0

Everything® **Wedding Book, 2nd Edition**
$12.95, 1-58062-190-2

Everything® **Wedding Checklist**
$7.95, 1-58062-456-1

Everything® **Wedding Etiquette Book**
$7.95, 1-58062-454-5

Everything® **Wedding Organizer**
$15.00, 1-55850-828-7

Everything® **Wedding Shower Book**
$7.95, 1-58062-188-0

Everything® **Wedding Vows Book**
$7.95, 1-58062-455-3

Everything® **Weight Training Book**
$12.95, 1-58062-593-2

Everything® **Wine Book**
$12.95, 1-55850-808-2

Everything® **World War II Book**
$12.95, 1-58062-572-X

Everything® **World's Religions Book**
$12.95, 1-58062-648-3

Everything® **Yoga Book**
$12.95, 1-58062-594-0

Visit us at everything.com